Greatness in Waiting

Greatness in Waiting

An Illustrated History of the Early New York Yankees, 1903–1919

RAY ISTORICO

Foreword by MARTY APPEL

McFarland & Company, Inc., Publishers
Jefferson, North Carolina, and London

The present work is a reprint of the illustrated case bound edition of Greatness in Waiting: An Illustrated History of the Early New York Yankees, 1903–1919, *first published in 2008 by McFarland.*

LIBRARY OF CONGRESS CATALOGUING-IN-PUBLICATION DATA

Istorico, Ray.
Greatness in waiting : an illustrated history of the early New York Yankees, 1903–1919 / Ray Istorico ; foreword by Marty Appel.
p.   cm.
Includes bibliographical references and index.

ISBN 978-0-7864-7513-1
softcover : acid free paper ∞

1. New York Yankees (Baseball team)—History—20th century.
2. Baseball—New York (State)—New York—History—20th century.
I. Title.
GV875.N4I78   2013   796.357'64097471—dc22   2007040357

BRITISH LIBRARY CATALOGUING DATA ARE AVAILABLE

© 2008 Ray Istorico. All rights reserved

No part of this book may be reproduced or transmitted in any form or by any means, electronic or mechanical, including photocopying or recording, or by any information storage and retrieval system, without permission in writing from the publisher.

On the cover: The Yankees on Opening Day,
April 14, 1908, at Hilltop Park (Library of Congress)

Manufactured in the United States of America

*McFarland & Company, Inc., Publishers
Box 611, Jefferson, North Carolina 28640
www.mcfarlandpub.com*

ACKNOWLEDGMENTS

Special thanks to my father for fostering and supporting an interest in baseball. (He was born in 1921—the year in which the Yankees won their first pennant.)

My sincere appreciation to the following individuals and organizations for invaluable help in providing many of the images produced herein and for photo identification or editing assistance: The library staff, especially W.C. Burdick, of the National Baseball Hall of Fame; the Chicago Historical Society, especially Bryan McDaniel; the Library of Congress; Mark Rucker (Transcendental Graphics & The Rucker Archive); John Leidy; Victoria A. Giller, Edward Meyer and Viviana Ray (Ripley Entertainment Inc.); Mary Brace (www.brace photo.com); David Rudd (Cycleback.com); Matt Fulling; Steve L. Steinberg; Marc Okkonen; Chet Hoff (for his time and remembrances); Ren Speer; Tom Simon (for helping me contact John Leidy); Michael Aubrecht; Greg Bloom; Cesar Lopez (www.cubanball.com); David Skinner; Barry Sloate; Wayne Wilson (vice president, education services, LA84 Foundation); Sara Kaden, Arthur Epstein (the Godfather); Isabel Istorico; Stewart Turner; Tim Ebright; Dr. Lisa Sanders; Nicole Kinnunen, University of Michigan Photo Services; SABR (The Society for American Baseball Research).

Thanks to Mike Bosak, retired New York Police Department sergeant and police historian, for allowing the use of information from his copyrighted research on Bill Devery, to Rick Stattler for allowing the use of information from his copyrighted research on Arthur Irwin, and to Al Figone, emeritus professor, for allowing use of his research on the Pacific Coast League game fixing scandal. Thanks to Greg "Moonlight" Martin, president, and Chris "Grit" Morgan of Vintage Baseball Factory for their photograph.

Many thanks to Marty Appel for information on Yankee office locations, reviewing the finally completed book, and providing the foreword. Last but not least is certainly the apt description of his excellent contribution.

A special credit to Sean Foreman (www.Baseball-Reference.com).

If every picture tells a story I hope readers will enjoy the ones recounted in this book.

The Yankees were at that time what we used to call a joy club. Lots of joy and lots of losing. Nobody thought we could win and most of the time we didn't. But it didn't seem to bother the boys too much. They would just start singing songs in the infield right in the middle of the game.
—Roger Peckinpaugh, shortstop

Winning is habit. Unfortunately, so is losing.
—Vince Lombardi

Sports do not build character. They reveal it.
—Heywood Hale Broun, author/sports commentator

Table of Contents

Acknowledgments — v
Foreword by Marty Appel — 1
Preface — 3
Introduction—Who Are the Highlanders? — 5

1. The Best Team Money Could Buy? 1903 — 9
2. The Old Fox — 15
3. The First Bomber — 16
4. Happy Jack/Mistake Pitch, 1904 — 18
5. Back to Earth, 1905 — 29
6. An Enigma at First Base — 31
7. Dave Fultz, a Man for All Seasons — 36
8. Almost There, 1906-1907 — 39
9. Goodbye Griff (Two Versions), 1908 — 52
10. Apocalypse — 58
11. With a Little Help, 1909 — 60
12. The Emery Ball, 1910 — 69
13. "Drawing Flies," 1911 — 82
14. Harry in the House (of Horrors), 1912 — 92
15. "A Bunion and an Onion," 1913 — 103
16. No Chance, 1914 — 117
17. The New Breed, 1915 — 123
18. Big Bill — 126
19. Origin of the "NY" Logo — 130
20. Frankly Speaking — 132
21. Wild Bill, 1915 — 135

22. Mr. Ed (Sweeney)	145
23. The Unluckiest Pitcher in the League	148
24. Meanwhile, in Boston	151
25. Mystery Man, Arthur Irwin	153
26. The Entertainer	156
27. Transitions, 1916–1917	161
28. Miller Time, 1918	180
29. The Vermont Schoolmaster	184
30. The Original "Murderer's Row," 1918–1919	189
31. Undercurrents	206
32. The Ping of the Bat	214
33. Before They Were Famous	216
34. Where Have You Gone, Frank Gilhooley?	221
35. New Beginnings	223
Appendix 1: Honor Roll	225
Appendix 2: The Ones That Got Away	226
Bibliography	227
Index	229

Foreword
by Marty Appel

In 1973, when the original Yankee Stadium was being prepared for partial demolition as part of a $100 million refurbishing, I was a member of the team's public relations department.

And I had my eye on a quaint yet sturdy piece of the team's heritage.

In the Yankee clubhouse, about ten feet from the locker that Joe DiMaggio and then Mickey Mantle had used, stood an ancient black Mosler safe, about three feet high. You would open the front door and find individual drawers, each about 2 inches by 4 inches. Painted onto each drawer in white was the name of a 1903 New York Highlander—Chesbro, Ganzel, Elberfeld, Conroy, Keeler, Fultz, Tannehill, Griffith, Williams, etc. The paint was fading, but the safe was as strong and reliable as ever. And it was where the '73 Yankees—Murcer, Munson, Stottlemyre, White, Nettles, Lyle, Clarke, Michael—would place their wallets and keys and watches before suiting up for a game.

I knew those Highlander names, and I knew that this safe represented the current team's only link to its origin. There was nothing else; no files, no contracts, no signage, no equipment. I said several times to Pete Sheehy, our famous clubhouse man, "Pete, make sure nothing happens to this safe when they tear this place down!"

I had delved into these Highlander names a few years earlier when we decided to add a page called "Top 20 Yankees All Time" to our press guide. Bob Fishel, Bill Guilfoile, and I (the PR team), took it upon ourselves to research these lists in the major hitting and pitching categories. This was the year the first Macmillan *Baseball Encyclopedia* was published, which proved a fine research tool, although we needed to dig deeper to find Yankee totals when a player had been traded during a season and his stats were combined. It was not an easy project in those pre-computer days, and we logged our findings on legal pads in pencil before typing them out.

To my surprise, players from the pre–Yankee Stadium years found their way onto the charts. Among pitchers, for example, there was Ray Caldwell—twelfth in games pitched, eighth in innings, tenth in strikeouts. There was Jack Chesbro, eleventh in games, seventh in innings, eighth in wins, seventh in strikeouts, thirteenth in shutouts, third in complete games. Here was a surprise—Ford was first in ERA—not Whitey, but Russ! 2.54! Other names among the pitchers to appear on the charts were Al Orth, Jack Quinn, and Jack Warhop. Among the hitters, Willie Keeler was ninth in batting average, Hal Chase was nineteenth in hits, eighteenth in average and first in stolen bases! (Maybe first in games thrown, too?) Chase is still third as this is written, with Derek Jeter climbing fast.

So these players were real, they counted, they had stats and at one time, of course, they dominated the top 20, eventually replaced by the more glamorous teams of the '20s and beyond.

But what a ragtag franchise this had been! In its own way, it was a fun ball club, futile in attempts to win the pennant no matter how badly Ban Johnson wanted them to succeed. They almost defied efforts to stack the deck in their favor. Ultimately, they handed over to Murderer's Row a run of no pennants in 18 years, no world championships in 20. Another way to put it—they spotted the rest of the American League two decades' lead and still wound up with 26 world championships in the 20th century, by far the most in baseball.

Hilltop Park must have been something. How much would we pay today to see a lost film of a full game there? To see Willie Keeler hittin' 'em where they ain't, to see Happy Jack Chesbro loading one up, perhaps recalling the one that got away and cost them the '04 flag. To see Big Bill Devery sitting next to the Highlander bench, second-guessing Clark Griffith.

If humble beginnings were necessary to make the Yankees the world's most famous sports franchise, you could surely find those up at the Hilltop.

"Official" records indicate that 3,451,495 fans made their way to Hilltop Park between 1903 and 1912, less than the team draws today for a full season, or about 5,000 fans a game. What hearty souls they were, trekking to no man's land in upper Manhattan to see the team take their lumps days after day. Could they possibly imagine what lay ahead for this club?

Ray Istorico has done modern Yankee fans a great favor by bringing this forgotten era back to life for us all. This team was at times pathetic, at times hopeful, but always colorful and fun.

Oh, yes—the clubhouse safe?

Gone. It never made it to Shea Stadium during the refurbishing and never reappeared when we returned to the new stadium in 1976. I don't think we're going to see it suddenly appear in the new, new Yankee Stadium in 2009 either. I have no idea what happened to it, but I'm sad whenever I think of it. Like the lost memories of the Highlanders, no one who saw them play is around any more, and the safe—perhaps like Charles Foster Kane's "Rosebud" sled in *Citizen Kane*—is gone up in smoke forever.

Marty Appel was part of the Yankees public relations team, including its director, from 1968 to 1977, and television producer until 1992. He has written extensively on baseball history and serves as editor-at-large of Memories and Dreams, *the Baseball Hall of Fame magazine.*

Preface

The New York Yankees had a troubled birth, a rough coming of age period, and endured 20 seasons (most varying from mediocre to futile) before winning their first World Series title. The stops along the way in the growing pains of the early Yankees outlined in this book will prove an interesting journey. It was my intention to shed light on the unknowns as well as the stars and offer biographical details that might not be available in other works, which concentrated on the statistics and performance of the team as opposed to the players and people behind those statistics. All of the players pictured in this book arrived before the glory, before any pennants or World Series victories. Of the players pictured within these pages only Wally Pipp, Bob Shawkey, Urban Shocker, Aaron Ward and Carl Mays would win at least one World Series championship as a member of the Yankees. However, every player highlighted within helped write the earliest chapters of the most successful and powerful sport franchise in existence.

Introduction: Who Are the Highlanders?

"Who are the Highlanders?" was a comment from my eldest nephew. The Highlanders were the New York Yankees, the Highlanders name being utilized for the team upon its entrance into the American League in 1903, eventually being dropped in favor of a less cumbersome—and more effective—name. ("Let's go Highlanders!" would be an odd cheer if heard in Yankee Stadium today.)

The New York Yankee franchise in its earliest incarnation, on the island of Manhattan, was a far cry from the current Bronx Bombers, the baseball Goliath that eventually evolved in the Bronx, the team with which recent fans are most familiar. An overview of the origin of the Yankee franchise—and an explanation of the origin of the Highlanders name—is provided on the following pages.

The very existence of an American League franchise in New York City was due in part to the vision of one man—American League founder and president Ban Johnson—and the obnoxious behavior (some might also say treachery) of John McGraw. McGraw would later gain fame managing the New York Giants, but in 1901 and 1902, he was player/manager of the American League's Baltimore Orioles franchise. Ban Johnson intended to transfer the Baltimore franchise to New York City—in hopes of setting the younger American League on par with the older, well-established National League—and supposedly promised McGraw the managerial reins would remain in his hands when the shift occurred. McGraw's contentious behavior often overshadowed his baseball talent. Umpires were angered by his tantrums, and Johnson constantly fined McGraw, eventually suspending him indefinitely in 1902, coming to the decision to dismiss McGraw prior to transferring the team to New York.

Enraged, McGraw, along with New York Giants owner Andrew Freedman, devised a plan to sabotage the Baltimore team. Freedman bought controlling interest in the Baltimore team and released some of the team's star players—like Roger Bresnahan and Joe McGinnity—signing them to contracts with the Giants. John McGraw negotiated the release of his contract in return for stock in the Orioles that was transferred to Freedman, with McGraw himself also jumping ship to the Giants on July 8, 1902, becoming manager of the team. By late July 1902, Baltimore could not field a team. With players provided by Johnson they finished the season, winding up in last place. The Baltimore franchise then ceased to exist, not to return until 1954.

On March 12, 1903, a vote by American League representatives allowed the transfer of

Hilltop Park, the first home field of the Yankees (Library of Congress, Prints & Photographs Division, LC-USZ62-117224).

the Baltimore franchise to New York City.* The New York franchise was bankrolled for $18,000 by former New York City chief of police police/real estate mogul/mayoral candidate Big Bill Devery and Frank Farrell, an owner of gambling houses, saloons and racehorses. Devery was well connected to Tammany Hall, a powerful and corrupt organization that wielded great political power in New York for many years. The funds that supported their purchase of the team came from various—or dubious—sources. Devery made much of his cash from political payoffs, and Farrell's gambling dens were a major source of other income (gambling was illegal in New York City at this time). The two men's backgrounds were suspect enough that Ban Johnson saw fit to have Joe Gordon, a former coal-mining executive, installed as team president, serving as a "front man" for the two owners.

At the press conference welcoming the New York franchise, Gordon was the only one introduced to the public. Clark Griffith, a pitcher who won 20 games in six consecutive seasons (1894 to 1899) for Chicago of the National League and had recently found success as player/manager with the Chicago White Sox, was transferred from Chicago to manage the Yankees. Ban Johnson respected Griffith's success in Chicago and decided to reward him by placing him in charge of the new club. Future Hall-of-Famer Griffith served a triple role as starting pitcher, team captain, and manager in the field. That field, a nondescript tract leased from the New York Institute for the Blind, was between 165th and 168th streets and Broadway and Fort Washington avenues in the Washington Heights section of Manhattan. It was certainly not prime real estate.

According to *The Sporting News* of March 21, 1903: "There is not a level spot on the whole property. From Broadway, looking west, the ground starts in a low swamp filled with water, and runs up into a ridge of rocks.... The rocks will be blasted out and the swamp filled in.... The grandstand will be at the Southwest corner of the grounds."

Finding a parcel of land so far uptown was necessary because Andrew Freedman sold the New York Giants after the 1902 season. The man who now controlled the team—John T. Brush—operated on the same devious levels as Freedman and had Tammany Hall connections of his own. Brush drew the battle lines with his new American League rivals by indicating any land available to Farrell and Devery upon which they planned to build would soon have a street running through it or a building constructed upon it.

The new Yankee owners were no strangers to political intrigue themselves. Their strategy for circumventing Brush and his cronies was finding a spot that Brush never thought would be considered suitable for building a ballpark. Construction on the stadium, known as Hilltop Park, was completed in little more than a month, in time for the start of the 1903 season. It sat about 16,000 fans but considerably more (20,000 plus) often jammed into the field when the rules on standing room only were bent. There was also a special ticket allowance for fans wishing to bring their own chairs to sit between foul lines and the stands.

The ballpark's dimensions were immense, especially for the time in which it was constructed. Left field, facing north to 168th Street, was 365 feet away from home plate while center field was 542 feet away. Right field, across from Broadway, was originally 400 feet from home plate. New York's American League club was christened the "Highlanders." Newspapers found the name nearly impossible to fit into one-column headlines and most people thought the name was awkward. So what was the origin of the name? A crack British

---

This action was part of a larger "peace agreement" between the National and American leagues which took place at the St. Nicholas Hotel in Cincinnati. Ban Johnson was one of the AL representatives. The parties agreed to two eight-team leagues and that the AL would have a franchise in New York but would not establish a team in Pittsburgh. The AL also adopted the foul strike rule, which had existed in the NL.

military regiment, the Gordon Highlanders, existed at this time, and the team played near the "highest natural point" in Manhattan. These were certainly factors behind the name.

When and where the team officially became known as the "Yankees" has been under much dispute. Previously, 1913 had been reported as the point of the name change, with sports writer Jim Price credited with naming the team the "Yankees." However, a headline of June 21, 1904, in the *Boston Herald* refers to the acquisition of outfielder Patsy Dougherty by New York: "Dougherty as a Yankee" while a team postcard issued in 1911 reads "New York Highlanders." All things considered, New York's American League team was referred to as the "Yankees" long before an official name change came about.

1

THE BEST TEAM MONEY COULD BUY? 1903

The same epithet thrown at Yankee teams of recent vintage was also applied to their very first roster of players. Best team money could buy? Not quite. However, the team assembled from the remnants of the Baltimore franchise, fortified by the addition of National League imports, gave the newborn Yankees a formidable collection of pitching talent and experience (though the lineup itself would not be up to the slugging standard of future Yankee teams). "Manhattan Will Have Greatest Team in Years" said the *Boston Daily* newspaper on October 26, 1902. That the New York team would be competitive was not a surprise. The fledgling American League (originally the Western League, of minor league status, and renamed the American League on October 11, 1899) had too much riding on the venture into New York. The status—and to some extent economic strength and survival—of AL president Ban Johnson's league virtually depended on establishing a successful franchise in the Big Apple.* The president or commissioner of any sport league actively working to pursue transactions meant to strengthen any one team in particular would be unheard of today. To say that times were different back in the off-season of 1902-1903 is an understatement. Johnson did not need to look far in his search for talented players to stock the first Yankee team. The Pittsburgh Pirates had just racked up 103 wins and won the National League championship in 1902. They were "raided," specifically from the standpoint of starting pitchers Jack Chesbro and Jesse Tannehill, due to expiring contracts and Johnson's quest for talent to supply the Yankees. Looking at newspaper reports of the time, it is obvious that "Pittsburgh" had lost an "h."† "Pittsburg Team Torn to Pieces" ran a sports page headline: "Pitchers Chesbro and Tannehill, catchers O'Conner and Harry Smith, infielder [Wid] Conroy and outfielder 'Lefty' Davis have all left Pittsburg for the American League ranks, and [they] are booked for berths in the Gotham nine." Smith never appeared on the Yankees but the 28-year-old Chesbro was the real prize. He went 28-6 with a 2.17 ERA for the Pirates in 1902. Tannehill, at age 27, posted a 20-6 record with a 1.95 ERA.

---

*The supposed origins of New York City's nickname, "The Big Apple," are numerous, ranging from John J. Fitzgerald, a horse-racing writer for the *New York Morning Telegraph*, to jazz musicians—however, the nickname was in use as early as 1909 and an exact determination of its origin is difficult to access.
†Pittsburgh was incorporated as a city in 1816. The "h" was omitted by a printer's error but a previous charter, which burned in a fire at a courthouse, included it. In 1890, the United States Board on Geographic Names ruled that the final "h" should be dropped from the names of cities and towns ending in "burgh." A protest from citizens who preferred the historic spelling changed that. In 1911, the United States Board on Geographic Names reversed its decision. The "h" was then restored to Pittsburgh.

With player-manager Clark Griffith also taking the mound for the Yankees in 1903, AL president Ban Johnson was assured of the Yankees having a strong pitching staff. All of this was accomplished at the expense of the rival National League while no American League club was weakened in the process.

Working to assemble talent for the 1903 Yankee batting order to complement the pitching became an equal concern. From the defunct Baltimore franchise came second baseman Jimmy Williams. He batted .313 for Baltimore in 1902, with 8 home runs and 83 RBI. Williams was knocking in runs at a pace that far eclipsed other second basemen. Other than Cleveland's future Hall of Famer Nap Lajoie, Williams posted numbers in this deadball era of baseball that could only be dreamed of by the majority of AL and NL second basemen. He contributed a .267 batting average and 82 RBI to the Yankees in 1903. Providing additional spark to the lineup was National League veteran William (Wee Willie) Keeler, an outfielder who typically batted close to .400 (including a mark of .424 for the National League's Baltimore Orioles in 1897). In 11 seasons prior to signing with the Yankees, Keeler never batted below .300. Ban Johnson dropped the 31 year-old batting star into the Yankees' lap. According to *The New York Times* on December 10, 1902: "I signed Keeler myself," said Mr. Johnson, "and I found him an easy man to do business with." Keeler signed his name to a $10,000 contract and patrolled right field for the Yankees in 1903 while batting .313. Joining Keeler and left-fielder Alphonzo "Lefty" Davis in the outfield was Dave Fultz, formerly of the Philadelphia Athletics. Fultz, the only right-handed hitter in the 1903 Yankee outfield, had an impressive resume: He was a graduate of Brown University, where he starred on the football field, and earned a law degree from Columbia. He had led the AL in 1902 with 109 runs for Philadelphia and shared Yankee center field duties in 1903 with Herm McFarland. At 33, McFarland was another remaining player from the Orioles roster of 1902. McFarland batted .322 for the Orioles that year but slumped to .243 with the Yankees in 1903. John Ganzel, a man who would hold much significance for the Yankees, was picked up from the NL's Giants to play first base. The accumulated salary total for all this talent was about $200,000—$190,000 less than the minimum major-league baseball salary for one player in the 2008 season. The New York team made its way to Atlanta for spring training.

The *Atlanta Constitution* reported on March 19, 1903: "All fandom was set in a whirl by the arrival of the team, and for several hours in the afternoon the big New Yorkers were the center of attraction in the lobby of the Aragon (Hotel), where the fans congregated in numbers." The Yankees had a two-a-day workout schedule in early spring training—from 10 A.M. to 12 P.M. and 2 P.M. to 4 P.M. Soon they began exhibition games at Piedmont Park against the minor league Atlanta Crackers (a Single-A team at the time, then later a AA and AAA team that existed from 1901 until 1965).

The newborn Yankees first took the field on Wednesday, April 22, at American League Park in Washington, losing to the Senators 3–1. Jack Chesbro was the starting pitcher and Dave Fultz had the first base-hit in Yankee history that day—a hit and run single that drove in Willie Keeler in the first inning to score their only run. More accolades for the assembled Yankee team came from the *Washington Post*: "Where is there a pitching staff to beat or even equal it? ... Keeler, Fultz, and Davis, with McFarland as substitute, will care for the outer pastures. What an outfield!"

The first home game at Hilltop Park came on April 30, 1903, as the Yankees defeated the Washington Senators 6–2. Fans paid 50 cents for seats in a single deck-covered wooden grandstand that ran from first base to third base. Seats in the bleachers cost 25 cents. Box

The origins of a sports legend—group photograph of the 1903 Yankees. Back row, left to right: Ernie Courtney, infielder, Herman Long, shortstop, Doc Adkins, pitcher, John Ganzel, first baseman, Monte Beville, catcher, Dave Fultz, outfielder, Jimmy Williams, second baseman, Jack Chesbro, pitcher, Lefty Davis, outfielder. Front row, seated: Herm McFarland, outfielder, Jack O'Conner, catcher, Clark Griffith, manager and starting pitcher, Willie Keeler, outfielder, Wid Conroy, third baseman, Jesse Tannehill, pitcher. *Chicago Daily News* negatives collection, SDN-001404 (courtesy the Chicago Historical Society).

seats were priced at one dollar! All things considered not a bad price for seeing the "Greatest Team in Years." Unfortunately, for Yankee owners Frank Farrell and Bill Devery, manager Clark Griffith, AL President Johnson, as well as New York fans, this collection of talent never took form as a consistent winning machine in 1903. By June 4 they posted a won lost record of 15-22 and had lost 6 games in a row. On June 7, the *Washington Post* made note of the Yankees'/Highlanders' struggles: "The Gordon Highlanders have failed to make good and the New York papers are knocking the team to death. Worse than that, the people are staying away from the games. Clark Griffith is a better pitcher than manager." Griffith, on his way to a 14-11 record in 1903, might not have argued with that assessment.

The reason for the Yankees' disappointing showing in 1903 was not difficult to decipher: A. Excellent pitching from Jack Chesbro: 21-15 with a 2.77 ERA (300 hits in 324.7 innings pitched) B. A .500 record from Jesse Tannehill: 15-15 with a 3.27 ERA (258 hits in 239.7 innings pitched) C. An offense not scoring enough runs to maintain any type of winning streak. Williams and Ganzel, at 82 and 71 RBI respectively, would lead the club in 1903. The next highest RBI total was 45—achieved by third baseman Wid Conroy, outfielder Herm McFarland and shortstop Norman "Kid" Elberfeld (who was not even on the team until being acquired from the Detroit Tigers on June 10, 1903—the first trade in Yankee history). Elberfeld appeared in 90 games, taking over as starting shortstop, replacing veteran Herman Long, who was traded to the Tigers along with infielder Ernie Courtney for Elberfeld. By September 9, 1903, the crowds were still staying away, even as the Yankees swept the Philadelphia Athletics in a double-header at Hilltop Park to gain third place, the highest spot in the standings they would reach all year. The attendance figure for that day in the Yankees' 16,000 plus capacity home field: 2,604. The fact was the New York City subway (planned as the IRT—Interborough Rapid Transit) was not fully completed in 1903. Many fans were not willing to take the long trip (50 plus minutes from mid-town Manhattan) via train to see a team not living up to preseason expectations. In a pointed letter to Giants Owner/President John T. Brush printed in the *Chicago Daily Tribune*, Yankee team president Joe Gordon noted that added transportation convenience would mean better attendance at Hilltop Park and a fan base rallying in support of the Yankees: "While conceding your club has drawn more spectators than ours, I attribute this fact wholly to better transit facilities at the Polo

Carl Horner's composite photograph of the first Yankee team. This image was produced during the 1903 season, as Norman "Kid" Elberfeld, acquired in June, appears in the lower left corner (National Baseball Hall of Fame Library, Cooperstown, N.Y.).

Grounds. This condition, however, is merely temporary, and next season the underground rapid transit system will convey our patrons from the post office to our gate in twenty minutes." The subway trip did become easier in the future though it took a while longer than Gordon predicted. By 1906, a stop was added at 167th street—minutes away from the entrance to Hilltop Park.

1903—Aftermath

The box score of the September 9 double-header win against Philadelphia reveals manager Clark Griffith shook up the lineup from the beginning of the season in hopes of generating more offense, dropping Davis and McFarland down in the order.

Conroy 3B	Elberfeld SS	McFarland RF
Fultz CF	Williams 2B	Beville C
Ganzel 1B	Davis LF	Pitcher

Griffith also gave the veteran Willie Keeler the entire day off using Herm McFarland in right field both games. The lineup changes worked for the 4–0 and 6–3 double-header wins against the Athletics (with Griffith and Chesbro picking up the wins) but then came 3 losses in a row on September 10, 11 and 12 against the Athletics and Boston Red Sox. The starters in those 3 games were Harry Howell (9-6, 3.53 ERA), Jesse Tannehill (15-15, 3.27 ERA) and John Deering (4-3, 3.75 ERA).

In the deadball era, with scoring at a premium earned run averages are an especially revealing statistic. The American League average ERA in 1903 was 3.11. The respective scores: 5–2, 7–4, and 10–1 reveal how Yankee

Yankee left-hander Jesse Tannehill in 1903. The Yankees later became known for featuring left-handed pitching aces like Lefty Gomez, Whitey Ford, Ron Guidry and Andy Pettitte. Tannehill could have started that tradition as the Yankees began life relying on the right-left combination of Jack Chesbro and Tannehill. However, only Chesbro remained in New York and thrived, while Tannehill was jettisoned to the rival Boston Red Sox—a mistake on the part of the Yankees as his career unfolded. Tannehill's career won-loss record is 197-116, with a 2.79 ERA (*Chicago Daily News* negatives collection, SDN-001397, courtesy Chicago Historical Society).

starting pitchers other than Chesbro and Griffith struggled and how an inconsistent offensive attack meant the first-year Yankees would fall short of glowing off-season predictions. The 1903 Yankees won 72 games, finishing their inaugural year in 4th place. The season was a disappointment but the future of the franchise looked bright.

Changes to the Yankee roster were in store heading into 1904. The baseball winter meetings were held in Chicago and the New York club wasted no time in making a move to improve the team. On December 20, 1903, pitcher Jesse Tannehill was traded to the Boston Red Sox for pitcher Tom Hughes. The Yankees jumped at the chance to acquire a potential young star. Hughes, at age 24, went 20-7 with a 2.57 ERA for the 1903 World Series champion Red Sox while the veteran Tannehill posted a 15-15 mark. However, Tannehill, who turned 29 in the upcoming season, had the more imposing major-league resume, pitching for the consecutive National League champion Pirates in 1901 and 1902 and winning 20 games 4 times. In a five-year period from 1898 to 1902 Tannehill won at least 18 games each year and his earned run averages were consistently lower than the league average. However, Yankee manager Griffith referred to Tannehill as a "trouble maker." The Red Sox were anxious to acquire the left-handed Tannehill to add to an all right-handed staff led by future Hall-of-Famer Cy Young.

Yankee spring training was held in Atlanta again in 1904. On December 25, 1903, the *Atlanta Constitution* offered the following comments on Tannehill and Hughes: "The work of Tannehill last year was not equal to that done by him when with the Pittsburg team and Hughes is rated as an erratic pitcher, so the exchange is considered an even one."

The *Washington Post* of February 28, 1904, took a different view, saying that Tom Hughes was apparently well suited—maybe too well suited—for the bright lights and big city of New York: "The New York Americans may not be slated for the championship after all.... A change from the quiet of Boston to the glitter of Broadway will do Hughes no good. He likes the glitter too well." But the second year Yankees were ready to battle for the AL championship in 1904. The long-standing rivalry with the Boston Red Sox was about to begin.

2

THE OLD FOX

Clark Griffith, the first manager of the Yankees, is pictured in the year 1903, during which he won 14 games and lost 11, compiling an earned run average of 2.70. One of those wins was the first shutout in Yankee history, a 1–0 victory over the Chicago White Sox, his former team, on June 6, 1903. Griffith was a pivotal figure in securing and solidifying the existence of the American League in New York during the Yankees' earliest seasons. As a pitcher he won 237 games and was nicknamed "The Old Fox" for his crafty pitching techniques (such as concealing the ball in the plane of his body upon delivery as well as cutting, spitting upon and/or doctoring the baseball). "Griff," as he was often referred to by teammates, also utilized the screwball and claims to have invented that particular pitch. He later managed the Cincinnati Reds for three years and took the same role with the Washington Senators from 1912 to 1920. He was owner-president of the Senators for 35 years, from 1920 to 1955, presiding over three pennant-winning teams, and was elected to the Hall of Fame in 1946.

Clark Griffith (National Baseball Hall of Fame Library, Cooperstown, N.Y.).

3

THE FIRST BOMBER

John Henry Ganzel, of Kalamazoo, Michigan, holds a unique place in the span of Yankee history. Ganzel hit the first home run in team history. It happened on May 11, 1903, at Bennett Field in Detroit, during an 8–2 victory against the Tigers. Later in the contest the second home run in team history was hit by third baseman Wid Conroy. Conroy was noted for his running ability and led the Yankees in stolen bases in 1903, 1904 and 1907.

Ganzel was a first baseman who entered major league baseball in 1898, playing 15 games for the Pittsburgh Pirates. He compiled a .277 average for the Yankees over the 1903 season, with 71 runs batted in despite hitting only two more home runs that year. Ganzel also led AL first basemen in fielding and total chances per game. He dropped to .260 in 1904, with 48 RBI and 6 home runs. The Yankees were scouting a replacement in a Pacific Coast League phenomenon named Hal Chase. Ganzel's desire to purchase and play for a minor league team, and the spectre of competition for his own first base job with the Yankees, led to events with intrigue similar to the salary disputes of today's athletes.

Upon receiving his contract notice for 1905, Ganzel complained to a friend that it was for the same salary he was paid in 1904. Considering Ganzel's numbers in 1904 he was lucky not to receive a salary cut (which happened to second baseman Jimmy Williams after his .263 average and 2 home runs and 74 RBI in 1904—a decrease by only 4 points in batting average, 1 home run and 8 RBI from 1903). Ganzel refused to sign the contract. Appearing in the *New York Times* on January 19, 1905, was the comment: "Ganzel says that he will surely decline to

John Ganzel, who slugged the first home run in Yankee history, pictured in 1903 (*Chicago Daily News* negatives collection, SDN-001418, courtesy Chicago Historical Society).

go to New York unless it is as a last resort." The Yankees had other things on their mind. According to a report in an early 1905 issue of the periodical the *Sporting Life*: "If pitcher (Doc) Newton's reports about Chase's ability to cover first base are true, the Yankees will not need Ganzel this season." Ganzel was sold to the Detroit Tigers prior to the 1905 season but never reported to the Tigers. He purchased the Grand Rapids team of the Western League, intending to be a player-manager for them. Ganzel was unable to play first base for Grand Rapids since Yankee manager Clark Griffith refused to formally grant him a release. Ganzel was being held by the "reserve clause" in his original Yankee contract—due to the fact he had signed a 3-year deal with them but played only in 1903 and 1904.

While Ganzel could not be active on the field at first base for Grand Rapids in 1905, he did run the team's business operations that year. Griffith held a grudge and it lasted a long time. In February 1906, Ganzel paid Yankee management $3,000 for his unconditional release. He later reappeared with the Cincinnati Reds in 1907 and 1908, acting as team captain as well as playing first base. Ganzel was one of five brothers to participate in organized baseball (his brother Charlie played in the National League for 13 years). He was also part of a huge family—fifty-two persons in all at the time of his parents' 50th wedding anniversary. They were noted for their good health and long life spans. Ganzel passed away at the age of 84 on January 14, 1959, in Orlando, Florida.

4

Happy Jack/ Mistake Pitch, 1904

The Yankees headed into their sophomore season announcing an increase in capital for the team, assets having doubled from $100,000 in 1903 to $200,000 for 1904. The increased capital led to some roster changes for 1904. Jack O'Conner, who shared catching duties with Monte Beville in 1903, was sent to the St. Louis Browns at the end of the season for "Honest John" Anderson. Beville batted .194 in 1903 while O'Conner managed only a .203 average but was a better defensive receiver than Beville. O'Conner, who resided in St. Louis, apparently had reported "unfit for duty" as the Yankees made their final road trip of the 1903 season and was promptly suspended by Griffith. AL president Ban Johnson supposedly stepped in again in the Yankees' favor. According to the *Chicago Daily Tribune*: "The deal has been closed by Manager Clark Griffith ... and Manager (Jimmy) McAleer of the Browns, Ban Johnson is probably the man; however, who engineered the deal."

It appeared to be a great deal for the Yankees. O'Conner was 34 and his career was winding down. Anderson, a native of Norway and four years younger than O'Conner, had played first base in 1903, batting .284 with 78 RBI. His 1904 batting numbers for New York would be similar—.278 with 82 RBI. The switch hitting Anderson shared centerfield duties with Dave Fultz. Meanwhile, O'Conner played in only 14 games for St. Louis in 1904. Veteran catcher Jim "Deacon" McGuire was purchased from the Detroit Tigers and would share time behind the plate for New York in 1904 with rookie catcher John "Red" Kleinow. McGuire appeared in 97 games in 1904 while Kleinow caught 62 games. Their batting averages this season, .208 for McGuire and .206 for Kleinow, indicate the Yankee catching corps was not counted on for offensive help. Later Yankee catchers like Bill Dickey, Yogi Berra, Elston Howard, Thurman Munson and Jorge Posada combined defensive skills with excellent hitting ability but in baseball's early years a .200 average was tolerated as long as the catcher handled the pitching staff in a capable fashion.

Right-handed pitcher Jack Powell, also nicknamed "Red," was another new addition, coming to the Yankees in a trade with the St. Louis Browns in which the Yankees sent pitcher Harry Howell and cash to the Browns. Powell, who utilized a no-windup/sidearm delivery and constantly threw off-speed pitches, just missed being a teammate of the recently traded Jack O'Conner, who was Powell's brother-in-law. Powell continued to reside in St. Louis since it was there that he and O'Conner owned and ran a bar. Powell posted a 15-19 record with a 2.91 ERA in 1903, his record suffering from poor run support by the Browns—who scored 3.6 runs per game that year—finishing second to last in that category out of the

Hall-of-Famer Jack Chesbro, winner of 41 games in 1904, an American League record (National Baseball Hall of Fame Library, Cooperstown, N.Y.).

eight American League teams. Powell won 20 games three times prior to being traded to the Yankees and was being counted on heavily to fortify the Yankee starting staff led by ace Jack Chesbro.

Pitching, and expectations of a successful season, were on the mind of shortstop "Kid" Elberfeld when the Yankees again reported to Atlanta for 1904 spring training. As reported in the *Atlanta Constitution* on March 11, 1904: "[Elberfeld] has been engaged in the occupation of a farmer for the last few months and looks well and strong. He has a little farm of about twenty acres a few miles outside of Chattanooga and is preparing for that time when his effectiveness as a ball player will become a thing of the past. 'I am glad to get back to work again ... and I am in good condition.'" Elberfeld went on to predict good things for the Yankees in 1904: "I think that we have a good chance to finish high up in the league this year. The pitching staff is a hummer. Powell, Hughes, Griffith and Chesbro will be hard to beat." Elberfeld's opinion was shared by the *Los Angeles Times*, though they were not completely sold on New York's chances for winning the AL pennant: "The New York Highlanders look like a bunch that will be hard to beat, but Clark Griffith could not get all there was in his men out of them last year. No great change will be noticed in the faces; most of them will be familiar to fans who followed the American League last season...."

As for the rival Red Sox, called the Boston Pilgrims from 1903 to 1906, they entered 1904 trying to defend their World Series championship of 1903, which they won over the Pittsburgh Pirates. The 1903 "Fall Classic" was baseball's first AL vs. NL World Series. Thus the Red Sox hold the title of first team ever to be crowned World Series champions. Every member of a strong starting lineup was returning to the Boston club for 1904. Third baseman/player manager Jimmy Collins, a future Hall-of-Famer, and shortstop Fred Parent were key players in the infield. Parent, at .304, and outfielder Patsy Dougherty, at .331, led the Red Sox in hitting in 1903. Outfielder Buck Freeman, a five time .300 batter, hit .287 with 13 home runs (a huge total at the time) and knocked in 104 runs in 1903. The Boston pitching staff was formidable. It was led by future Hall-of-Famer Denton True "Cy" Young and "Big Bill" Dineen. (Actually, Young was bigger—Dineen stood 6'1" and weighed 190 lbs. while Young was 6'2" weighing 210 lbs.) Young also posted bigger winning numbers than Dineen, and won 511 games over a 22-year career. But Dineen would easily fit as the number one starting pitcher on any number of major league teams at the time. Dineen won 21 games in both 1902 and 1903 with earned run averages of 2.93 and 2.26 respectively. Yankee co-owner Frank Farrell, however, agreed with "Kid" Elberfeld, thinking the Yankees pitching staff of Chesbro, Hughes, Powell and Griffith might be superior to the Red Sox.

While the competition between New York and Boston would not be as heated as in later years—or as hate-filled between players of each team as in the 1970s—the intensity of the rivalry began in 1904.

One devoted Boston fan, Michael T. McGreevy, known as "Nuf Ced" McGreevy, founded a group of Red Sox fans called the "Royal Rooters." McGreevy was the owner of a Boston saloon called "Third Base." The word "fan" being short for "fanatical" certainly applied to McGreevy and his friends as he went on to lead the "Royal Rooters" for nearly thirty years. The "Royal Rooters" often traveled to New York for Red Sox road games, and made their presence known at Hilltop Park by boisterous cheering. Photos also exist of the group walking through the streets of Washington Heights on their way to Hilltop Park carrying the signs that read: "Boston Rooters."

The Red Sox and McGreevy's group of Boston fans had little to cheer about on Thursday, April 14th, 1904. The Yankees kicked off the season by beating the Red Sox 8–2 on Opening Day at Hilltop Park. "Kicked off" seems an apt term, since the weather was more similar to football season. The *Chicago Daily Tribune* reported: "In spite of a snow storm in the morning and genuine football weather in the afternoon, the American League season was opened on the Washington Heights diamond today in a blaze of glory. Nearly 16,000 persons passed the turnstiles and saw the New York Americans take the measure of the world's champions by a score of 8 to 2. With the subway still unable to carry the throng to the park ... this outpouring of enthusiastic fans far exceeded the expectations of club officials...." The game lasted one hour and thirty-five minutes. It featured a home run by Yankee starting pitcher Chesbro and two for Boston—by right fielder Freeman and shortstop Fred Parent. The next day, April 15th, was indicative of the back and forth battle that would ensue for the 1904 pennant, eventually consuming both fans and players alike. The Red Sox rebounded and won 4–1. The game also proved that New York fans were willing to brave cold conditions for the season opener but had other interests as the weekend approached. The attendance was 3,183. That figure is significant as it reflects the paid admission numbers sought out by a sportswriter, as opposed to the reportedly exaggerated totals given out by press agents the American League had posted at Hilltop Park. As the Yankees tried to wage a successful

The Enemy: Red Sox ace Cy Young. Boston went through a somewhat trying period with their team name from 1901 to 1907, first being known as the Americans (1901), then the Somersets (1902), the Pilgrims (1903 to 1906), and, finally, the Red Sox (beginning in 1907). Young appears here in a Boston uniform from 1902. Since "Somersets" probably did not fit, the stylized "B" and "A"—appearing only during 1902—might have been utilized to differentiate from the National League's Boston Braves. The Braves and the Red Sox wore a remarkably similar uniform in 1901, with "Boston" written across the chest. The socks of the Boston uniform would not actually be red until the 1908 season (Library of Congress, Prints & Photographs Division, LC-USZ62-47454).

battle against the Red Sox they still fought a losing battle in trying to win the allegiance of fans from the National League's Giants, who played their well-attended games at the Polo Grounds, which also sat 16,000 plus persons.

The actual attendance figures at Hilltop Park became an issue in 1904 as a report circulated indicating inflated numbers being handed out at Hilltop Park, making fan interest for the Yankees seem greater than what really existed. *Pittsburgh Dispatch* reporter C.B. Power's investigative work was cited in the *Washington Post*: "American League club owners and press agents in New York continue to send out glowing accounts of the attendance at the American League games in Gotham ... Pittsburg and New York played at the Polo Grounds ... to over 5,300 paid admissions, while at the American League park the crowd did not number 1,500. Still, the American League press agent gave out the attendance at over 6,000. There is absolutely little or no American League sentiment in New York at the present time, the people of the metropolis being strong supporters of the National. The average baseball fan of Gotham looks upon the American League as a minor organization, and he will not hesitate to tell you so if you give him half the chance." New York Giants manager John McGraw must have been pleased by this report.

The Boston fans were more devoted than Yankee fans during the early season games as the Red Sox marched to a 14-4 record by early May. At Huntington Avenue Baseball Grounds (home field of the Red Sox from 1901 to 1911) 11,102 fans packed the 11,500 capacity stadium on May 7th only to see the Yankees win 6–3. Jack Chesbro took the mound for the Yankees against "Big Bill" Dineen, a matchup that would prove vital to each team's pennant chances by season's end. It was the second game of a three game series (notable was the fact that no game was played on Sunday, as it was illegal to do so at the time).

The AL season standings on the morning of Monday, May 9, 1904, are below:

	Won	*Lost*		*Won*	*Lost*
Boston	14	4	Cleveland	8	8
Chicago	12	9	St. Louis	9	10
New York	9	7	Detroit	8	10
Philadelphia	9	7	Washington	1	15

Despite the Yankees' third place standing behind both the Red Sox and White Sox, New York manager Clark Griffith was optimistic: "It doesn't take many defeats to pull the leaders down to the bunch ... and there is no reason why our boys will not remain in the race, although we have not quite hit our regular gait yet." Griffith's optimism proved correct and the Yankees soon made up ground in a closely fought race to the pennant.

On June 11th the Yanks defeated the White Sox in Chicago by a score of 6–3 and pulled into second place, 4 games out of first place. The *Chicago Daily News* noted on June 12th: "Billy Keeler opened the game with a smash toward left, but Tannehill robbed him of the hit by a spectacular stab with his mitt, jumping in the air and holding the ball...." Keeler, who batted .343 this year, might have been wondering what he'd have to do for the newspapers to spell his name correctly. Tannehill referred to Lee Tannehill, the brother of former Yankee Jesse Tannehill. Jesse was in the midst of posting a 22-11 record for the Red Sox, with a 2.04 ERA.

Tom Hughes, the man Tannehill was traded for, struggled for the Yankees in 1904, winning 7 games and losing 11. By Thursday, June 16th, the Yankees had fallen back to 3rd place, while defeating the Browns at Sportsman's Park in St. Louis by a score of 10–3. On that day the Yankees' won lost record stood at 27-20. The Red Sox were 32-17, despite

Jack Chesbro at work (Transcendental Graphics/ruckerarchive.com).

losing two in a row to the White Sox. The Yankees were gaining ground but still lacked consistency.

Outfielder Dave Fultz was seeing limited playing time due to leg injuries sustained during his college football days at Brown. Fultz also coached for his alma mater the previous season and might have exacerbated the problems taking part in drills. In stepped AL president Ban Johnson (seemingly on cue when the New York team had problems). Unknown Yankee rookie infielder Bob Unglaub was sent to the Red Sox for left-fielder Patsy Dougherty. The trade sent shockwaves through Boston while New York fans were elated. Dougherty batted .342 for Boston in his rookie season of 1902, and avoided any "sophomore jinx" in 1903 by batting .331, and smashing two home runs in Game 2 of the 1903 World Series. While Boston fans were outraged over the trade Boston management was telling a whole different story: "The trade of Dougherty for Unglaub was made to help the Boston club and for no other reason. In [Bill] O'Neil I believe we have a great outfielder, and in Unglaub an infielder of ability whom we need. The trade was made only after consultation with manager James Collins and on his advice. We are doing all we can to win another pennant for Boston, and I believe that the fans of Boston will see Collins' judgement vindicated." Those were the words of Red Sox owner John Taylor in the June 19th edition of the *Boston Daily Globe*. Red Sox manager Jimmy Collins was also going overboard repeating the same story: "Mr. Taylor made the trade of Dougherty for Unglaub with my sanction, and I think the deal will prove to be in the best interest of the Boston club. I have always done the best I could for Boston, and I have never injured our club to benefit any other one...."

Suspicious Boston fans might have thought Ban Johnson wrote a script for Taylor and Collins. Outfielder Bill O'Neil batted .196 in a Red Sox uniform before being traded to Washington with cash on July 2, 1904, for 11-year veteran outfielder Kip Selbach. (Selbach almost went to the Yankees in early May—the deal being called off by Washington manager Patsy Donovan.) Unglaub played in 9 games for Boston, batting .154 and was then hospitalized with blood poisoning. By contrast, Patsy Dougherty's effect on the Yankees was immediate. It seems incredible the Red Sox would participate in any deal that could improve the fortunes of the team chasing them in the standings. Ban Johnson would later sing a "what's good for New York is good for the American League" refrain. Often described as a "pesky" hitter, Dougherty went on to play excellent defense in left field and batted .283 for the Yankees in 106 games, spraying base hits, bunting and stealing bases, leading the AL in runs scored with 113. Other than 2 games at third base, Dougherty only played left field in his career, never appearing at another outfield position.

On Monday, July 11, 1904, Dougherty went 4 for 5 with a home run as the Yankees racked up 16 hits and "slaughtered" (according to the *Boston Daily* newspaper) his old team by a score of 10–1 at Hilltop Park. It was reported that "A big Monday crowd heartily enjoyed the downfall [of Boston]." The attendance total was actually 4,500. Yankee pitcher Jack Powell allowed one run in the first inning but shut the Red Sox out the rest of the way. The Yankees' record now stood at 41-26; they were in second place, 3½ games out of first place, still occupied by Boston. The efforts of Powell (23-19, 2.44 ERA, 390.3 innings pitched) and Chesbro in 1904 were astounding. They essentially served as a two-man pitching staff, keeping the Yankees in the pennant race throughout the summer. Chesbro set many pitching records during the 1904 season that have little chance of ever being broken: 41 wins (an AL record), 48 complete games of 51 games started (#1 all-time), while throwing 455 innings (an AL record). His won lost record for 1904: 41-12, 1.82 ERA. The AL average ERA that year was 2.70. Chesbro, who would be elected to the Baseball Hall of Fame in 1946 along with manager/teammate Clark Griffith, was reportedly anointed with the nickname "Happy Jack" for his affable demeanor while playing for a minor league club in Richmond, Virginia, in 1897. He was a spitball specialist* who imparted his knowledge of this pitch to Powell during the season and the two men formed a powerful winning combination.

Despite the efforts of Chesbro and Powell by July 20th the Yankees still found themselves in second place, still 3½ games out. More support was badly needed from the rest of the Yankee starting pitchers. Was more divine intervention from AL president Ban Johnson in the works?

On the roster of the Washington Senators in 1904 was "Smiling Al" Orth, or—to use a more popular nickname—"The Curveless Wonder." Orth, a 31-year-old veteran—who changed

---

*In December 1920, during the winter meetings, the American and National Leagues voted to ban the spitball except for active major-league pitchers who had thrown the pitch prior to 1920 and were registered to do so by their respective ballclubs. Prior to 1904, Chesbro had supposedly not yet been throwing the spitball on a regular basics. An explanation follows in the following chapter.

speeds on his fastball but never threw a curveball—began his career in 1895 with the Philadelphia Phillies, never winning less than 14 games a year on some terrible teams and notching 20 wins in 1901. Orth signed with Washington for 1902, posting 19 victories in 1902 (losing 18) as the Senators finished in 6th place. The year 1903 brought 10 wins and 22 losses for Orth as the Senators dropped all the way to 8th place—last in the AL. Last is also where the Senators were headed in 1904. Orth, his pitching record at 3-4, hoped for a change of scenery. On July 20th, the Yankees sent pitchers Tom Hughes and Barney Wolfe to the Senators to obtain "The Curveless Wonder." Hughes, at 7-11 with a 3.70 ERA, was considered a disappointment while Wolfe had pitched sparingly for the Yankees—appearing in 7 games—with an 0-3 mark.

The *Washington Post* reported: "It has been known for some time that Orth has not been pleased with playing in Washington, and so far this year he has not been of much value to the club. He is a good pitcher, and would do good work for the Highlanders, but it is felt here that a change would do him, as well as the Senators, good ... as the winds on the heights in New York tend to chill the pitching arm, Hughes has not been worth much to the New Yorkers. A Southern climate would do him much good." The weather differences between Washington Heights, New York City, and Washington, D.C., can be debated. While Ban Johnson might have brokered this deal, at least there were no rationalizations for it in print from the Senators' ownership or management. On the surface it looked to be a simple exchange of disgruntled veteran for younger prospects. Orth picked up some of the badly needed pitching slack for Yankee workhorses Chesbro and Powell, and posted an 11-6 record the remainder of the season. The new combination of Powell, Chesbro and Orth paid immediate dividends for the Yankees as they ran off a five game road winning streak from August 2nd through August 6th, taking 3 games from the Detroit Tigers and 2 from the Cleveland Indians. This vaulted them from 3rd place to first in the standings.

The next four games were not as kind as New York lost four in a row, falling right back where they began the month—3rd place. The Yanks climbed back into first on August 19th, beating the White Sox 6–1 (knocking Chicago out of first) behind the pitching of Chesbro. The Red Sox, meanwhile, sat in 3rd place that day, 1½ games behind, losing to the St. Louis Browns at Huntington Avenue Baseball Grounds in Boston. And so it would remain the rest of the season—a closely contested, agonizing and alternating race to the pennant.

On Wednesday, September 14th, the Yankees, 1½ games out of first, were scheduled to enter enemy territory, traveling to Boston for a double-header, the first of 3 double-headers scheduled against the Red Sox in 3 days.

"Tomorrow will be the biggest day that baseball has ever seen in Boston!" said Mr. John Morrill, of the Boston-based sporting goods company Wright & Ditson, in preparation for buying tickets on the morning of September 13th. "It is only 10:30, a day in advance of the game, and they are lining up to the counter here four deep demanding tickets." There was good reason for the anticipation.

The AL standings were as indicated below.

	Won	Lost		Won	Lost
Boston	79	49	Cleveland	69	55
New York	77	48	St. Louis	53	72
Chicago	73	56	Detroit	52	74
Philadelphia	69	53	Washington	31	96

Yankee owner Frank Farrell was in town for the series and he liked his team's chances, not only in the AL race but for the World Series—if the Yankees reached that far: "I confidently expect to land the pennant this season, and if fortune should so favor me, you can bank on [the Yankees] getting the world's championship in a post-season series with the Giants or any other team the National league cares to put up against us." Unfortunately, the results for the Yankees from September 14–16th, 1904, were mixed at best: 2 wins, 2 losses, and, due to darkness, 2 ties. Two of the starring players, in an ironic twist, were Boston hurler Jesse Tannehill and Yankee left fielder Patsy Dougherty, players that had previously worn the uniforms of the opposition. In the first game on Thursday, September 15th, Tannehill threw a complete game against the Yankees, also hitting a triple and scoring the winning run in a 3–2 victory. Dougherty went to bat nine times in the 2 games, getting 5 hits. Dougherty and Keeler were proving to be an effective combination at the top of the Yankee batting order. The typical Yankee lineup heading into the final games of the 1904 season were as follows: 1. Dougherty, LF; 2. Keeler, RF; 3. Elberfeld, SS; 4. Williams, 2B; 5. Anderson, CF; 6. Ganzel, 1B; 7. Conroy, 3B; 8. Kleinow, C.

Al Orth, at .297, provided additional offensive help in the ninth spot on days he pitched while Chesbro, at .236, posted a decent average for a pitcher. In the first game played on Friday, September 16th, Dougherty led off the game blasting a triple into the standing room only crowd in right field (part of the nearly 25,000 fans in attendance on "ladies day"). He scored on a single by Willie Keeler (still often referred to as "Billy" in newspaper summaries). "Happy Jack" Chesbro gained a 6–4 victory in this game over "Big Bill" Dinneen while Boston ace Cy Young took the second game 4–2 over Yankee right hander Ned Garvin. Garvin was purchased from the National League's Brooklyn team on September 9th to help provide additional pitching support. (Garvin didn't provide much help, this start resulting in a loss, one of only 2 starts Garvin would make for the Yankees. He never again appeared in a major league game.) So after 6 games the Yankees left Boston where they began the series, still in second place, 1½ games out of first.

A series in Washington against the lowly Senators from September 17th through the 21st was just what the Yankees needed: a four game winning streak, taking four out of the five games played with the strong starting pitching trio of Powell, Orth and Chesbro leading the way, while taking first place in the pennant race. As if a higher power (or Ban Johnson himself) had made out the 1904 American League schedule, the Yankees would face Boston in the last games of the season: a total of 5 times from October 7th to the 10th. One game at Hilltop Park on October 7, with double-headers scheduled in Boston on Saturday, October 8th and back in New York on Monday, October 10th.

A long road trip for the Yankees—Cleveland, Detroit, Chicago, St. Louis—ended with 4 wins in a row. They were glad to return home to Hilltop Park and it showed in a close 3–2 win over Boston on October 7th. With this win the Yankees vaulted into first place over the Red Sox. Not surprisingly Jack Chesbro pitched a complete game for the victory. From the October 8th edition of the *Chicago Daily Tribune* ran the story: "Playing with more determination, more nerve, and more dash than Boston, the [Yankees] conquered the world's champions.... The players took more chances on bases.... The batting of Dougherty, Williams, and Anderson accounted for the scoring of Griffith's men, while the splendid pitching of Chesbro was responsible for the scarcity of Boston's runs." And, in a scene that would be prevented today by Yankee Stadium police officers: "The grandstand occupants swarmed on the field after the victory and lifted Chesbro on their shoulders and carried him to the clubhouse." Despite such a celebration the attendance that day was 9,503, less than what Yankee owners Farrell and Devery anticipated for the final days of the pennant chase. Cold weather descended upon Manhattan that day and affected attendance but at least the crowd made up for in spirit what they lacked in numbers.

The celebration was short-lived. It lasted only as long as the trip to Boston from Grand Central Station, and to the bottom of the 4th inning during the first game of the Saturday, October 8th, double-header. Chesbro, insisting to Yankee manager Clark Griffith he could return on no rest, tired early. The Red Sox scored 6 runs in the 4th inning en route to a 13–2 mauling of the Yankees. Sox starter Bill Dinneen threw a complete game, striking out former teammate Patsy Dougherty to end the game. Red Sox ace Cy Young then outdueled Jack Powell in the second game, 1–0. "Nuf Ced" McGreevy, his "Royal Rooters," and the rest of the Boston fans in attendance, reportedly 28,040, roared their approval. Back into second place for the Yankees. After an off-day Sunday, the two teams went back to Hilltop Park for the final showdown—a sweep of the double-header meant the Yankees' first pennant.

The first game featured the same pitching matchup of just two days before—Chesbro versus Dinneen. Starting on short rest and throwing complete games was becoming a habit for these two men as the grueling pennant chase reached its final stages. Over 28,000 people descended upon Hilltop Park that Monday, October 10th, 1904, at least 200 of them being a large contingent of "Royal Rooters" making the trip from Boston, occupying the left side of the grand stand seats. "With the aid of megaphones and tin horns [they] kept up a continual din throughout the nine innings" reported the *New York Times*. The Yankees began the scoring in the bottom of the fifth, with Dougherty batting in catcher Kleinow and Chesbro knocking a single off the outstretched hand of Dinneen. Chesbro scored three batters later after a walk to Elberfeld—2–0 Yankees. The Red Sox tied the score in the 7th, an error by second baseman Jimmy Williams and then a bad throw home allowing both runs. How much more could be expected out of Chesbro? (Supposedly Chesbro wondered the same thing and expected Griffith to send in a reliever.) Chesbro continued into the top of the ninth inning. Red Sox catcher Lou Criger reached first base, just beating the throw by Elberfeld. A bunt by Dinneen and a ground out by left fielder Kip Selbach moved Criger to third. Red Sox shortstop Fred Parent, "the little man from Maine," stepped to the plate. Chesbro quickly worked the count to 0–2. Yankee fans were then stunned as Chesbro fired a spitball

It's standing room only at the Huntington Avenue Baseball Grounds in Boston on October 8, 1904, for the Yankees vs. Red Sox (Library of Congress, Prints & Photographs Division, LC-USZ62-97762).

over catcher Red Kleinow's head. Criger darted home from third with the go ahead run—3–2 Red Sox. Hope remained for the Yankees as the game entered the bottom of the ninth. First baseman John Ganzel struck out but third baseman Conroy drew a walk. Kleinow sent a fly ball near second base for the second out.

Chesbro finally exited the game as catcher Jim McGuire was sent to the plate to pinch hit for Chesbro. McGuire also drew a walk. Yankee manager Clark Griffith was hoping (praying?) for anything that could send the baserunners in motion and sent in the speedy Dave Fultz to pinch run for McGuire. Patsy Dougherty strode to home plate as the Yankees' last hope. It was there he would remain, after swinging through Dinneen's final pitch of the game—a waist-high fastball over the inside corner of the plate. "The New York players acted as if tied to the ground for several seconds, then they started for the bench," said the *Boston Globe*.

Top: Yankee ace Jack Chesbro in 1904. His record that season, and his importance to the Yankees, speaks for itself (Library of Congress, Prints & Photographs Division, LC-DIG-ggbain-10102). *Bottom*: The Red Sox win the pennant! A cartoon that appeared in *The Boston Globe* on October 11, 1904, drawn by Frank Collier, commemorates the Red Sox victory over the Yankees to capture the AL pennant. Note the character labeled "N.Y." in the Scottish kilt (a reference to the "Highlander" nickname) and the New York fans by the fence crying, their tears watering the flower labeled "Next Year." (From the article "Boston Champions Capture The Pennant," *Boston Globe*/ProQuest Historical Newspapers.)

Approximate time of the game: 1 hour and 5 minutes. Approximate disappointment for Chesbro, his teammates and Yankee fans: immeasurable. The Yankees won the meaningless second game 1–0, finishing the season right where they began the day, 1½ games back. Losing the pennant race—despite the herculean effort of Chesbro and Jack Powell—was heartbreaking, but no one surrounding the team had anything but positive thoughts for next year. The Yankees had come so close to a possible World Series appearance in only their second year of existence. Surely there would be many more pennant races, and a World Series victory, in the immediate future?

1904—Postscript

Despite the box score of the fateful game indicating a wild pitch, some controversy existed as to whether Kleinow had allowed a passed ball. (The rookie Kleinow spent 62 games catching in 1904 while the more experienced "Deacon" McGuire appeared in 97 games.) Various people who participated in or attended the game offered different opinions. Kid Elberfeld stated: "Hell! That ball went so far over Kleinow's head he couldn't have caught it standing on a step ladder." Manager Griffith later made reference to Kleinow possibly staying out too late the night before and Chesbro's wife Mabel blamed Kleinow for letting the ball get away. She lobbied to have the wild pitch ruled a passed ball. Whether it was a too wet spitball that Chesbro couldn't control or a pitch that Kleinow should have caught will be forever open to debate. Chesbro himself knew where the actual blame should lay (if the entertaining exchange that took place between him and Griffith in the winter following the 1904 season is accurate). Chesbro, an avid fisherman and hunter, joined his manager on a hunting trip and the following conversation supposedly occurred:

Yankee catcher Red Kleinow in a 1904 Yankee road uniform (National Baseball Hall of Fame Library, Cooperstown, N.Y.).

GRIFFITH: "Why don't you look for something to shoot?"
CHESBRO: "I was thinking."
GRIFFITH: "About that wild pitch?"
CHESBRO: "Yes."
GRIFFITH: "Now look here. If you ever mention that wild pitch again, I'll shoot you as I would a muskrat. Now shut up and hunt!"

5

Back to Earth, 1905

Jack Chesbro recuperated on his farm during the winter of 1904-1905. Ironically, Chesbro and his wife, Mabel, resided in Massachusetts—in the town of Conway (Chesbro having been born in nearby North Adams, about 30 miles away). They resided in New York during the summer but it was clear from Chesbro's comments that he enjoyed the more quiet life afforded the couple during the fall, winter and early spring in their smaller town: "Why, there is more fun to be had at one of our Conway dances than there is at the best theatre in New York." Chesbro raised thoroughbred horses at his farm as well as fished and hunted in his spare time, often covering fifteen miles daily, which was said to "keep his wind in good condition." Despite the heavy toll of all his innings pitched, Chesbro's right arm also seemed in good condition. Chesbro had learned the spitball while observing pitcher Elmer Stricklett, who was rehabilitating his sore arm and pitching for a minor league team prior to the 1904 season. Different versions exist as to how Stricklett himself came to learn the pitch that would help send Chesbro, as well as Chicago White Sox pitcher Ed Walsh, Stricklett's teammate, to the Hall of Fame.

You may need a scorecard for this: An accepted theory is that Stricklett was shown the pitch by teammate George Hildebrand. Hildebrand, an outfielder, had seen what the pitch could do while trying to hit spitballs thrown to him by his minor league teammate Frank "Fiddler" Corridon. Corridon found that applying moisture on a baseball could make it break in odd ways, shooting or dropping as it nears the plate. This revelation occurred as Corridon toiled for the International League Providence Grays, and he retrieved a ball that had landed in a puddle, the wetness on one side making the baseball swerve oddly as he threw it. Stricklett taught the spitball to Walsh, his teammate on the White Sox in 1904, Stricklett's rookie season. Saliva applied to the first two fingers and letting the thumb touch the ball last as it leaves the hand was the key to throwing the spitter.

The speed of the spitball was dependent on the swing of the pitcher's arm, with little wrist action, other than guiding the general direction of the pitch. Walsh's success with the spitball was not as immediate as was Chesbro's, but in a few years he had mastered it completely, and, by 1908, he also won 40 games, while losing 15 and compiling a stellar 1.42 ERA.

Chesbro himself was hesitant to expound upon his knowledge of the devastating pitch for the benefit of the public. When asked about the pitch by a reporter from the *Boston Daily Globe*, Chesbro responded: "Tell the readers of the Globe that [when the spitball is mentioned] Chesbro lights his pipe and smokes." Chesbro was more revealing about his thoughts on his own career in baseball and realistic plans for the future: "The genuine ball player has a love for his work. He loves the zest and sport of ball playing. Naturally he likes a good salary, too, for all of us must live and the sensible player should put something by for a rainy day and when his age will take him out of the game." Worth noting is the fact that Chesbro is the only player enshrined in the Hall of Fame in Cooperstown who actually pitched for a team from Cooperstown. In 1896, Chesbro played with the Cooperstown Athletics, a semi-pro team. Although he was a native of Massachusetts and began his major league career with the Pirates, Chesbro's path to stardom certainly began in New York. He started his minor league career with Albany, in the now defunct New York State League, eventually climbing the minor league ladder back to his home state, playing in the Eastern League in Springfield, Massachusetts.

While Chesbro enjoyed his off-season time on the farm, things were brewing for the Yankees in their upcoming plans for the 1905 season. Some of the optimism of the fans hinged on the arrival of two players signed from the Los Angeles Angels of the Pacific Coast League. The Angels were commonly called the "Looloos." Left-handed pitcher Doc Newton and first baseman Hal Chase were the two Los Angeles imports of which good things were anticipated.

Spring training was held in Montgomery, Alabama, and Griffith was happy to have Chesbro, Powell and Orth returning as the core of his pitching staff. They were supplemented by Newton, second-year Yankee Walter Clarkson, rookie Bill Hogg, and Ambrose Puttmann, who was seeing limited duty with the team, pitching an increasing number of innings since arriving in 1903, but with few wins. According to the *Los Angeles Times*, the consensus regarding the right-handed Clarkson going into the new season was: "He has everything that a pitcher should have ... including one of the best curve balls ever seen." Clarkson also specialized in a change-up, and was said to be mixing up his pitches and throwing everything he had in his arsenal upon arriving in Montgomery, much earlier than usually done by the other pitchers. In addition, while Chesbro didn't care to inform the public about the mysteries of the spitter, he apparently did a good job of explaining and teaching it to his teammates. The *Los Angeles Times* reported: "from the Southland comes the report that Newton and Hogg ... have thoroughly mastered the famous "spit" ball, ... many suggestions are thrown out that the "spit" ball be done away with entirely, for fear of its awful effect upon batting."

Griffith himself would appear again as a starter for his team in 1905. Technically no "bullpen" existed at this stage of baseball, pitching staffs were smaller and additional starters were used in a support role—eventually evolving into the "relief" pitcher. Griffith had gone 7-5 with a 2.87 ERA in 1904 and this season, at the age of 35, he would post a 9-6 record with an excellent 1.68 ERA. However, the main interest of Griffith during spring training of 1905 was not on the performances of the Yankee pitching staff.

6

An Enigma at First Base

"Hal Chase was the greatest first baseman of all time."
—Frank Graham, writer

"Chase was completely and congenitally amoral. Many years ago a doctor should have taken him in hand or he should have been committed to some kind of institution."
—S.L.A. Marshall, "Border League" president

For the Yankee offense of 1905 great things were expected of Hal Chase. Chase would go on to have a very good/almost great career while being dogged by allegations of gambling on and "throwing" games (intentionally mishandling a play to benefit the opposing team, on which Chase had supposedly placed a bet to win that day's game against his team). The problem developed over the years to the point that Chase was reported to have been greeted by opposing players with the question: "What are the odds?" Chase earned the nicknames "Peerless" and "Prince Hal" for his baseball skills as well as his social standing as a New York athlete. Chase moved in a vastly different social circle than a player such as the quiet Chesbro. The "Prince" enjoyed the nightlife of Manhattan and his other major league destinations to the fullest. While this lifestyle provided entertaining anecdotes of Chase racking up big winnings in card or pool games and entering nightclubs with one or more chorus girls on his arm, it caused more than one manager concern that Chase's after hours habits and company he was keeping were creeping into his daytime duties at first base—while certainly taking a heavy toll on Chase's two marriages, both of which ended in divorce. He was an enigmatic personality, baseball hero and villain, a superstar and an outcast. Chase was regarded as the best fielder of his day, but universally despised for supposed game throwing activities. He did admit to gambling but not on his own team: "I could have made a million dollars out of baseball on bets and gambling. I used to bet on games. My limit was $100 per game and I never bet against my own team. That was easy money."

Chase, born in Los Gatos, California, grew up in the foothills of northern California. Too free-spirited for academics, he left high school in the tenth grade. A natural left-hander who insisted on batting right-handed, Chase played on semi-pro teams in the Santa Cruz Mountains and the Santa Clara Valley. At age nineteen, Chase attended the University of Santa Clara, supposedly studying to be a civil engineer (no academic record for Chase exists and he admits to never attending classes). Chase played on the school baseball team, appearing primarily as a second baseman. A left-hander at second was unusual but it apparently held no problems for Chase. The Redwood, the University of Santa Clara yearbook, contained the notation: "Hal Chase played second base, Hal Chase would be difficult to replace."

Santa Clara was playing against St. Vincent's college on March 5, 1904, in Los Angeles. Jim Morley, the president of the Los Angeles Angels of the Pacific Coast League, was earning additional income umpiring the game. Morley observed up close as Chase blasted a double, stole 3 bases and went 3 for 6 for a 13–8 win. Chase's "college days," so to speak were over. Morley signed Chase to a contract with Los Angeles, switching him to first base. As his signing bonus, Chase received a .22 caliber rifle. His debut in the Pacific Coast League came on March 27, 1904. It was an inauspicious start as he went hitless in three trips against Oakland. In the field, however, he showed the dazzling moves that foreshadowed greatness. On March 29, the *Los Angeles Times* reported: "Chase has a future before him that any ball player might look forward to. He plays first base as well as anyone would care to see." Luckily for Yankees manager Clark Griffith, Yankee scout Dan Long wrote to him about the young phenomenon. In October 1904, during the baseball winter meetings, Chase was drafted by New York for the reported sum of $800. This transaction ignited a firestorm between the Coast League and major league baseball.

The "peace agreement" or "hands off" policy that existed between the two was broken, Morley said, since the agreement cited that no P.C.L. player could be drafted prior to November 1. After much dispute between the Pacific Coast League, Chase, and the Yankees management, a contract was finally signed. Chase accepted $200 advance money and joined the Yankees in time for a game on March 29, 1905, in Jackson, Mississippi. The Yankees had broken camp and were making their trek north from Montgomery, first heading west to Vicksburg before proceeding north to Jackson, playing games against Cotton States League teams of both cities.

Griffith was known for running a tough training camp, while allowing the team plenty of freedom once the work was done. A player that allowed himself to fall out of condition over the winter months was rudely awakened and soon back in shape through running, various drills and numerous exhibition games. Compared to today's more centralized schedule, the team took a more circuitous route back then, with many exhibitions or warm up games scheduled along the trip back to New York. In the game against Jackson, a 5–0 win, Chase was 1 for 3 with a single.

As spring training ended, thoughts turned back to the Yankee team as a whole and their hopes for the 1905 season, with writers making their 1905 American League predictions: "Now we come to the dangerous club," said Tim Murnane, popular baseball writer/editor for the *Boston Globe*. "[The Yankees] have a fine leader in Griffith and a liberal owner in Frank Farrell. Farrell could improve the work of his team, however, by keeping away from too close connection with the boys during the playing season. Farrell broods over defeat and shows a disposition to find fault with the umpires. This sort of business is a handicap for the club to carry, as championships are seldom won by clubs whose owners interfere with the umpires...."

Murnane saw the Yankees battling the Red Sox again for supremacy, with the Philadelphia Athletics posing few problems: "...Connie Mack must be counted on to make trouble for all, with very little chance of winning from two 'cracker-jack' clubs as New York and Boston."

Griffith and his "cracker-jack" team opened the season at American League Park in Washington on Friday, April 14th, in front of 9,161 people—quite a crowd for a Senators game. Their average home attendance in 1905 was 3,273 people as Washington's 7th place

Hal Chase (National Baseball Hall of Fame Library, Cooperstown, N.Y.).

finish this year translated into low attendance figures. Many more people might have been in the stands for the 2 P.M. game had rain not fallen around noon, later giving way to sunshine coupled with a cold wind. The Yankees won 4–2 behind the pitching of Chesbro and a home run blast by Jimmy Williams deep to left field. In his major league debut Chase, batting seventh, was 1 for 4 with a double in a game described as a "thrilling affair" by the *Washington Post*.

According to Yankee manager Griffith: "Right away we knew we had come up with the fanciest first baseman we ever saw ... especially on bunts. Those were the days of bunting in baseball, you know, and Chase would start creeping in toward the plate with the pitcher's wind up, daring the hitter to lay one down. I've seen him go all the way to the third base foul line from first, and throw batters out on bunts.... He had a little old-fashioned, round mitt, not much bigger than a pancake, but he could get ground balls or pick throws out of the dirt like no other man who ever lived."

Many of Chase's defensive tactics were learned from Fred Tenney, a star first baseman for the National League's Boston Beaneaters (later the Braves). Chase explained how he emulated Tenney: "I noticed the position of his feet near the bag in fielding plays on ground balls to the infield. Tenney never planted one foot on the base in such a situation, but, instead, straddled the bag, placing one foot to the left and one foot to the right. This enabled him to stretch either way for a wide or a high throw. If he stretched to the left, he dragged his right foot across the bag and rested it against one side of the sack. If he stretched to the right, he dragged the left foot. Most first baseman rush to the bag at the crack of the bat, plant one foot on it and wait for the throw. But suppose the left foot is on the bag and the infield throw is high and wide to the left?

"The first baseman then loses precious seconds shifting both his feet and executing what amounts to a 'hop' across the bag. The tactic of straddling the base, which I learned from Tenney, I consider the most valuable single lesson I ever received in first-basing.... The hardest part of the program is the fact that a first baseman has to study the batters all the time. If he gauges their hits rightly he can calculate the particular part of the diamond they are likely to hit to and be pretty well on guard for the throw [from the fielder]. It is a great study, this study of the batter, and no one has begun to learn it yet."

Despite the tips taken from Tenney, Chase was an originator, not an imitator. Tenney's tactics, coupled with Chase's aggressive defensive posture, set a daring standard for first base play that few could emulate.

The play of Chase might have opened eyes in 1905 but the performance of the Yankee team as a whole proved not worth the price of admission. Chesbro could not be expected to duplicate his heroics of 1904 and he didn't—although he and Orth still posted solid records (at 19-15, 2.20, 303 innings pitched and 18-16, 2.86, 305 innings pitched respectively). Jack Powell fell off badly from his 1904 contribution and little help came from Newton, Hogg, or the highly-touted Clarkson. Clarkson's appeared in 9 games, winning 3 and losing 3. In mid-May he was sent to the minors joining the Jersey City Skeeters of the Eastern League. Rookie Bill Hogg struggled to the tune of a 9-13 record.

On Saturday, June 24, the Yankees were mired in 6th place, 12 games out of first, losing to the Red Sox 3–0. An uncharacteristic note of alarm, supposedly from Chesbro, appeared in the *Washington Post*: "Clark Griffith has himself to blame for a lot of the poor work of all his club. He has an idea that all of his pitchers should work just as he does, and he has given me orders before every game for the past two weeks not to throw a curve nor a spitball, but to use only fast ones. How on earth is a pitcher going to win when he can't mix them up on the batters?"

The 1905 offense provided little help to offset the pitching issues. Keeler batted .302 and second baseman Williams made the most that he could from his .228 average (6 home runs and 62 RBI). Elberfeld batted .262 but the rest of the regular lineup lacked punch—Dougherty hit at a .263 clip but Anderson batted .232 (before his contract was sold to Washington on May 30th). By September the New York team had risen to 4th place, only to fall back to 6th by the end of the month. Baseball Notes, a regular column in the *Washington Post*, stated: "Baseball writers traveling with the Yankees say Griffith's men are playing in a 'don't care sort of a way.' Then count them out of the race."

Center fielder Dave Fultz still seemed to care, despite batting .232. He was knocked unconscious at Hilltop Park on September 30th in a collision with Elberfeld as both men raced to catch a ball hit to short center field. Along the way the 1905 version of the Yankees scored 586 runs, allowed 622 runs and finished in 6th place. Overall attendance at Hilltop Park also went downhill, plummeting to 309,100 from 438,919 in 1904. The sniping and player discontent that was reported in the *Washington Post* was in contrast to Griffith's own 1905 comments regarding his club: "Harmony on a ball team is one of the things necessary to a winner. I have never had any trouble with my men and they have always been able to get along with each other."

On a lighter note, Hal Chase—who struggled with a .249 average in his rookie season—searched for ways to improve his average next year. He tried a unique method for choosing his bats, one not without health hazards. The secret was revealed as Chase had a splinter in his tongue one day: Bystander: "How did you get that in?" Chase: "Well, I'll tell you. I was downtown this morning sampling some new sticks. I can tell a new bat by tasting the wood." Chase went on to hit .323 in 1906. Bat tasting had worked.

7

Dave Fultz, a Man for All Seasons

Dave Fultz's collision with Kid Elberfeld near the close of the 1905 season also brought a close to his baseball career (though the Yankees would trade Fultz's contract to the Athletics on April 29, 1906, to acquire outfielder Danny Hoffman, Fultz decided to retire at the age of 31). To say that Fultz was active in other areas, pursued many interests and achieved much in his lifetime is an understatement. Fultz, a graduate of Brown University in 1898, was captain of the football team and a star running back from 1894 to 1897 as well as captain of the Brown baseball team. His records for points and touchdowns at Brown, 174 and 31 respectively, stood until 1997. Fultz did not post outstanding numbers during his brief, injury-plagued Yankee career from 1903 to 1905 — with batting averages of .224, .274 and .232 respectively — but he was the team's first center fielder (albeit sharing that position with Herm McFarland). In 1903, Fultz had the first extra base hit in Yankee history.

During the off-seasons Fultz attended law school at Columbia University, a short distance from Hilltop Park, and passed the New York state bar exam in 1905. Fultz set up an office on Wall Street, later moving to 165th Broadway, and was also a noted painter in his off-work hours. His legal background as well as experiences in the major leagues led to his forming an organization called the Players' Fraternity in September 1912. It served as essentially the first organized players' union and counted Ty Cobb and Christy Mathewson among its officers. The original goals of the organization were to oppose contract violations and perceived player injustices. On February 14, 1917, a strike was set to begin due to the demand of the Players' Fraternity to abolish the ten-day clause, in which a team ceases to pay any injured player who has been impaired or unable to play for ten days. Fultz called off the strike but major league baseball severed all communications and relations with the union. The Players' Fraternity was disbanded in 1918. Major league baseball players were then left without formal representation until the formation of the Major League Baseball Players Association (MLBPA) in 1965.

Fultz also served as a first lieutenant in the U.S. Army Air Service in World War I and later became president of the International League, serving from 1919 to 1920. In addition, Fultz coached football at Brown, Columbia, New York University, and the United States Naval Academy.

An interesting interview with Fultz took place early in 1904, in which he offered some thoughts on his first sport — football — and predicted a possible strategy for the future of the game: "As to the football rules of today, I think they might be bettered. I have been

THE BASEBALL PLAYERS' FRATERNITY

A Monthly Department Devoted to the Activities
of the Organized Ball Player

Edited by DAVID L. FULTZ, President of the Ball Players' Fraternity

OFFICERS

David L. Fultz, Pres.　　Michael J. Doolan, Vice-Pres.　　Edward Sweeney, Vice-Pres.
Tyrus R. Cobb, Vice-Pres.　　Christopher Mathewson, Vice-Pres.　　Jacob E. Daubert, Secy.

DIRECTORS

Tyrus R. Cobb	Richard J. Egan	John Miller
Raymond Collins	David L. Fultz	R. E. Myers
Samuel E. Crawford	Robert Harmon	Derrill B. Pratt
Michael J. Doolan	John P. Henry	Morris Rath
Jacob E. Daubert	Christopher Mathewson	Victor Saier
Edward Sweeney	Ira Thomas	Fred Falkenberg

ADVISORY BOARD

Tyrus R. Cobb　　Michael J. Doolan　　David L. Fultz
Edward Sweeney　　Christopher Mathewson

Some Minor League Legislation Which is Grossly Unfair to the Players

As there is no provision in the minor league contract requiring ten days' notice of release, a player may be unconditionally released without any notice whatsoever and the National Commission, in a recent bulletin has upheld the clubs in this practice.

Notwithstanding this fact, the player is bound for a period of ten days, unless his release takes place within a period of thirty days prior to the expiration of the season, to hold himself in readiness to sign with any team in his league that may want him.

This legislation is found in Article 25 of the National Association Agreement and Rule 27 of the Rules and Regulations of the National Association which read as follows:

Article 25. Upon the release of a player during a playing season from contract or reservation with any club member of an association then acting under this Agreement the service of such player shall at once be subject to acceptance by any club belonging to the same association, expressed in writing or by telegraph to the Secretary of the Board, for a period of ten days after notice of said release, and thereafter, if said services be not so accepted, said player may negotiate and contract with any club.

Rule 27. Any player released by any National Association Club within a period of thirty (30) days, prior to the close of the current playing season, shall immediately become a free agent and can sign with any National Association Club, except the releasing club.

It is therefore seen that when a player receives what is called an "unconditional release," when his contract has come to an end, when he owes no obligation to his team and is receiving no salary from it, still he is not permitted for a period of ten days to play for, nor to contract

78

An issue of *The Baseball Players' Fraternity* newsletter reprinted in the October 1913 issue of *Baseball Magazine* (courtesy LA84 Foundation, 2141 West Adams Boulevard., Los Angeles, California 90018).

Dave Fultz, taking a break from attending to Players' Fraternity business matters or possibly reviewing a case at his law firm (Library of Congress, Prints & Photographs Division, LC-DIG-ggbain-16675).

thinking over the rule requiring the team with the ball to make 8 yards in 3 downs.... The time is coming when the light backs will be a thing of the past. Every year colleges are placing heavier men behind the line and if necessary weakening the strength of the line in order to affect this. The tactics of opposing teams (with the ball) is to smash the line."

In 1935 Fultz was a candidate for Assemblyman from the 21st District of Brooklyn, representing the Flatbush area. He retired to Florida with his wife Marjorie, purchasing the estate of Henry A. DeLand, founder of the city of DeLand, a magnate from upstate New York who made his fortune in the baking soda business. Dave Fultz passed away in DeLand at the age of 84 on October 29, 1959.

8

ALMOST THERE, 1906-1907

Yankee right fielder "Wee Willie" Keeler, who stood 5'4" and weighed 140 pounds, would turn 34 heading into the 1906 baseball season. In deference to a Reggie Jackson quote about 71 years later: Keeler didn't need New York to be a star—he brought his star with him.

Keeler was born on March 3, 1872, and raised on the streets of Brooklyn, New York. As a youngster he played baseball on the fields of Prospect Park and the public began to take notice of his exceptional batting and great fielding. After playing for various semi-pro teams Keeler joined the New York Giants in 1892. He was acquired by the old Baltimore Orioles of the National League in 1894 and thrived as a lead-off hitter. At this time, in the "dead-ball" era, Keeler exemplified the qualities needed to score runs by hitting singles, stealing bases, and being part of the hit and run. Keeler pioneered the "Baltimore chop," swinging downward and bouncing the ball off the hard infields over the heads of opposing fielders. Keeler's batting averages during his years with Baltimore are mind-boggling: .371 in 1894, .377 in 1895 and .386 in 1896. In 1897, Keeler compiled a stunning .424 average and uttered a famous line in relation to his batting skills. Questioned by a reporter as to how he managed the feat: "Mr. Keeler, how can a man your size hit .424?" Keeler smiled. "Simple, I keep my eyes clear and I hit 'em where they ain't." Keeler produced these amazing statistics while using one of the shortest, yet heaviest bats in major league history. It was 30 inches long but weighed 46 ounces. Keeler's batting averages with the Yankees were not at the stratospheric levels of previous seasons but he batted .343 in 1904 and .302 in 1905. Keeler was also a good right fielder for the Yankees—and an outfielder that was not without his superstitions—especially in relation to how many chances he would have in the outfield before missing a fly ball. According to *The Sporting News*: "He swears by the teeth of his mask-carved horse chestnut, that he always carries with him as a talisman."

Keeler commented: "All of us fellows in the outworks have got just so many of them in a season to drop and there's no use trying to buck against fate." He also had one other cautionary bit of advice: "Keep your temper cool." Some of Keeler's Yankee teammates, and even manager Clark Griffith, could have profited from this advice in the upcoming season.

Keeler, along with Chesbro, remained the star attraction of the team, with Hal Chase gaining in popularity as 1906 spring training opened—this year in Birmingham, Alabama.*

---

*The Yankees' spring training exodus varied in its destination almost each year in this early period. Unlike today a formal working agreement with a specific city, and/or stadium accommodations, were not firmly in place. Economics, as well as availability, determined the spring training site each year.

The *Atlanta Constitution* reported: "Hal Chase, the youngster who was imported from the Los Angeles club year before last, will be on the initial bag. He was considered the great find of the year and this year he promises to be the most sensational first baseman in the game ... [one of the] outfielders [is] Willie Keeler, credited with being the most scientific batter the national game ever produced...." So on the same squad the Yankees had the most scientific hitter as well as a man who tasted bats!

Clark Griffith stopped short of predicting a pennant but still spoke highly of his team's chances during an interview with the *Atlanta Constitution*: "You can say for me that the team is in fine condition, and that we will be in the fight for the flag from the first day of the season until the finish." What were the reasons for Griffith's optimism?

In essence, little roster overhaul occurred from 1905, but the 1906 results were far better. Chesbro, 32, and Orth, 33, were still the workhorses of the pitching staff, throwing 325 and 338 innings respectively, in 1906. Chesbro posted a 23-17 record while Orth had his greatest season—a 27-17 record with a fine 2.34 ERA (far below the league average ERA of 2.96). Red Kleinow, in his third season with the Yankees, had taken over as full time catcher with 42-year-old Deacon McGuire as backup.

The major changes were in the New York outfield, Fultz being replaced by Danny Hoffman as starting center fielder. The 23-year-old Frank Delahanty, referred to as "Pudgie" despite a 5'9", 160 lb. frame, was in camp for his second year, vying for an outfield job. Infielder Frank LaPorte (holder of another unfortunate nickname: "Pot"), was also in his second year with the team. LaPorte would win the starting job at third base, previously handled by Wid Conroy and Joe Yeager. LaPorte's contribution to the offense in 1906: a .264 average with 2 home runs and 56 RBI—seemingly modest totals but those numbers exceeded the statistics posted by most major league third basemen in 1906. Williams at second base and Elberfeld at shortstop were again the glue of the infield, a strong double-play combination as well as being two of the most productive batters on the team. Williams led the team in RBI in 1906, knocking in 77 to go along with 3 home runs and a .277 batting average. Elberfeld missed time with minor injuries, appearing in 99 games and batting .306. He missed additional games for another reason: suspensions. Some background is in order.

Elberfeld was one of the most intense competitors in baseball history, an aggressive, tobacco—and expletive—spewing player. He earned the nickname "The Tabasco Kid" for his competitive play. When opposing players slid in to bases, slashing him with their spikes, Elberfeld poured whiskey on his wounds to cauterize them. Ty Cobb stated that Elberfeld gave as good as he got when he covered the second base bag as Cobb tried to steal: "On my first attempt I slid into second head forward. In a flash it seemed that Elberfeld gave me the knee. Stepping on the bag to receive the ball from the catcher he blocked my slide by coming down on my head with his knee. My forehead and face were shoved into the hard ground and the skin peeled off just above the eyebrows. The clever way in which he did this completely blocked me.... I had run into a real big leaguer."

A real big leaguer for certain—though not one without "baggage." On June 9, 1903, the Yankees sent 37-year-old shortstop Herman Long and infielders Ernie Courtney and Paddy Greene to the Detroit Tigers for Elberfeld and pitcher John Deering. This transaction was the first trade in Yankees history. Ed Barrow, later the Yankee general manager and president for 24 years, was Elberfeld's manager at Detroit. According to a newspaper report of June 3, 1903, "[Elberfeld] was fined $200 and indefinitely suspended for disgraceful actions on the ball field on June 1 and for indifferent playing during the games of May 20–30 and June 1." According to Barrow: "He utterly disregarded the rules and regulations, refused to

Willie Keeler, practicing to "hit 'em where they ain't" (National Baseball Hall of Fame Library, Cooperstown, N.Y.).

1, Powell; 2, Chesbro; 3, Kleinow; 4, Puttmann; 5, Dougherty; 6, Clarkson; 7, Yaeger; 8, Williams; 9, Fultz; 10, Griffith, Mgr.; 11, Newton; 12, Starkell; 13, Duff; 14, Chase; 15, Keeler; 16, Anderson; 17, Hogg; 18, McGuire; 19, Orth.   Copyright, 1905, by Pictorial News, New York.
NEW YORK BASE BALL TEAM—AMERICAN LEAGUE.

A page from the 1906 *Spalding Official Baseball Guide*. Willie Keeler hit .304 in 1906, his last major league season above .300. Hal Chase batted .323, the second highest total of his career (Library of Congress).

obey the orders of his captain and manager to such an extent that we feel called upon to put a stop to it." Needless to say, Detroit was happy to unload Elberfeld and, despite Barrow's admonition, the Yankees were happy to acquire the 5'7" 158 pound sparkplug. Elberfeld was known for leaning into pitches, purposely getting hit to reach first base, a quality admired by his teammates. He would rage against umpires (and occasionally teammates)

Norman "Kid" Elberfeld (Transcendental Graphics/ruckerarchive.com).

during his career but Elberfeld provided a badly needed aggressive quality to the fledgling Yankee team.

Elberfeld's aggressiveness, such as spitting tobacco juice in an umpire's face, provided anxiety for owners Farrell and Devery and manager Clark Griffith, as well as entertainment for the crowds.

The Yankees also provided entertainment for their fans in 1906—and proved Griffith's fight for the pennant prediction was a correct assessment—but it was a definite struggle at the beginning of the season. Eventually, the New York team was in the middle of the pennant race, battling against the White Sox and the Indians.

"Battling" would also apply to relations between the Yankees and the umpiring crews. It started as they sunk from 4th to 6th place in the middle of May, 5½ games out of first. On Monday, May 7th, Tim Hurst was the umpire at first during a game at Hilltop Park against the Senators. Griffith was coaching at first when Frank LaPorte hit a ground ball to the Senator shortstop and seemed to beat the throw to first base. Hurst yelled "Out!" Griffith exploded with anger over the call. Hurst grabbed Griffith by the arm and yelled, "Get out of the game!" An on-field brawl between the two men was prevented with Elberfeld (of all people) holding Griffith back. Hurst and Griffith finally ended up at the New York bench, Hurst slugging Griffith in the mouth. They were both suspended for five days by AL president Johnson. To describe Hurst as "pugnacious" would be an understatement. He joined the American League in 1900 and once spit in the eye of Philadelphia Athletics second baseman Eddie Collins after hearing Collins complain about his umpiring. A riot in the stands ensued. Hurst was fired by the AL, eventually becoming a boxing referee (possibly a more suitable venue). He died of "acute indigestion" in 1915.

Elberfeld, not to be outdone, clashed with umpire Billy Evans in next day's game and was fined $50. The year 1906 was Evans' first in major-league baseball, joining the AL crew at age 22, becoming the youngest major league umpire in the process. According to the *New York Times* of May 16, 1906, these eruptions and the Yankees' poor early-season record supposedly led to a "dissensions in the ranks." Griffith had an immediate response also quoted in the *New York Times*: "There is no trouble between my men and myself. I called my men together today and they gave me their assurance that they were heart and soul with the club...."

Griffith's words rang true. By the end of August the Yankees had climbed all the way to 2nd place, 3 games out. A long home-stand at Hilltop Park was punctuated by a 3 game sweep of the 5th place St. Louis Browns and 2 double-header sweeps of the lowly Senators (7th place) on Thursday, August 30th and Friday, the 31st. Home attendance, and profits for owners Farrell and Devery, soared this year to a total of 434,700 people (the league average being 367,260). Unfortunately, this home-stand was also punctuated by another suspension for Griffith and another $50 fine for Elberfeld. Griffith argued that Browns base runner Harry Niles was out on a close play. Elberfeld chimed in and they were both ordered off the field by umpire Jack Sheridan. Sheridan was known for establishing the practice of crouching while calling balls and strikes, a seemingly innocuous move at first but it was quickly adopted by all umpires because it afforded a more accurate view of the plane of the pitched ball. He also used no protective gear other than a mask, his agility was said to be enough to avoid being hit by foul tips. Two man umpiring crews were the standard in these times and the Yankees certainly had "issues" with Sheridan as well as Evans, who worked with Sheridan observing the senior umpire.

The August 29, 1906, edition of the *New York Times* ran the story: "Yesterday

[Griffith] was notified by President Ban Johnson that he had been suspended indefinitely ... Elberfeld ... escaped without any penalty other than the customary fine attending dismissal from the grounds."

On Monday, September 3, 1906, Elberfeld found himself in the midst of another flare-up. In the first game of a double-header against the Athletics at Hilltop Park, he made a permanent enemy out of home plate umpire Silk O'Loughlin by running after O'Loughlin and attempting to spike the umpire after a disputed call went against New York. Elberfeld was forcibly removed from the game by police. Elberfeld still refused to leave the park premises so Griffith ushered him out of the Hilltop Park gate. An afterthought to all that excitement is the fact the Yankees won the game 4–3. They also won the second contest under unique circumstances. In the 9th inning with the A's leading 3–1, the Yankees rallied to win (by forfeit). With Willie Keeler on second and Wid Conroy on third, second baseman Jimmy Williams strode to the plate. Home plate umpire O'Loughlin called two strikes and then Williams hit a ground ball towards third.

John (Schoolboy) Knight, the Athletics third baseman, stepped back to field the ball—right into the path of Keeler who was racing towards third. Keeler fell onto the dirt as the ball rolled into left field and Conroy crossed the plate. Keeler got up and also scored, tying the game. Philadelphia's players ran towards O'Loughlin, screaming for Keeler to be called out on runner's interference. O'Loughlin, never one to tolerate excessive complaining, ordered the A's at least two times to stop their argument and leave the field. When they refused to comply O'Loughlin ended the game, awarding the Yankees a 9–0 victory by forfeit. Elberfeld must have at least been happy with the turn of events—despite receiving a suspension from AL president Ban Johnson. The Yankees were certainly pleased. It was their ninth win in a row. They would not stop there.

The next day the Yankees won another double-header up in Boston (the amount of double-headers played in this early period is astonishing compared to today's schedules). The Yanks blasted the Red Sox 7–0 in the first game in support of pitcher Walter Clarkson. Al Orth was in total control in the second game as New York shut out the Sox 1–0. Bill Hogg kept the Red Sox in check on Wednesday, September 5th, and the Yanks rolled on 6–1. They returned to the friendly confines of the Hilltop on Thursday and continued their winning ways against the Red Sox and the Athletics, capping it off with an 11–4 rout against Philadelphia on Saturday, September 8th, behind the pitching of Chesbro. The Yankees had won 15 games in a row! Their record stood at 77-48 and they were in first place. Was the juggernaut that Ban Johnson wanted to create in Manhattan, and the winning team which Farrell and Devery hoped they were getting, finally in full formation? Was the 1906 American League pennant within the Yankees' reach?

Unfortunately, the second place White Sox went on a winning streak of their own, taking 7 games in a row from September 12th to the 18th, vaulting from second place to first with an 83-51 record. The Yankees visited Chicago on Friday, September 21, and struck back, sweeping yet another double-header by scores of 6–3 and 4–1 with important pitching contributions from Chesbro in the opener and Bill Hogg in the second game, placing and keeping New York in first place. A brief setback occurred on Saturday. "Smiling" Al Orth didn't have his best stuff and the White Sox took the contest 7–1. The Yanks found themselves half a game out of first. Sunday's game was a pitcher's duel between Bill Hogg and Chicago right-hander Ed Walsh (on his way to a 17-13 record). Hogg limited the White Sox to two hits and the Yankees prevailed 1–0. "There were over 30,000 maddened fans on the field, packed like barrels of mackerels in the stands," said the *Washington Post* the next day. A

Umpire Billy Evans was one of the many men in blue involved in "disagreements" with Kid Elberfeld. Evans umpired in the American League from 1906 to 1927 and later served as the Cleveland Indians general manager from 1927 to 1936. He was also director of the Red Sox farm system from 1936 to 1940, president of the Southern Association from 1942 to 1946 and general manager of the Detroit Tigers from 1947 to 1951. He was elected to the Baseball Hall of Fame in 1973. This photograph was taken long after the 1906 season, when the Yankees played at the Polo Grounds (note the later-style Yankee jacket hanging in the dugout) (Library of Congress, Prints & Photographs Division, LC-DIG-ggbain-01979).

look at the box score reveals that the 31-year-old Elberfeld, batting lead-off, at .306, and the veteran Keeler, the second place hitter, at .304, were an effective combination. First baseman Chase batted third, with 76 RBI, second to only the Yankee clean-up hitter and most valuable cog in the lineup—Jimmy Williams, with 77 RBI.

The White Sox, on the other hand, were well on their way to earning the nickname "The Hitless Wonders," the game Hogg pitched against them being indicative of their typical offensive attack for the season. While the overall Yankee team batting average in 1906 was .266 (second only to the Indians at .279), the team batting average for the White Sox was only .230. A .300 batting statistic was an unknown to any starting player on the Chicago team. Second baseman Frank Isbell came closest with a .279 average. Veteran shortstop George Davis, 35, contributed 80 RBI, 23 more than any other player on the team. The Chicago pitching staff more than made up for the lack of offensive firepower—left-hander Nick Altrock and right-hander Frank Owen won 20 and 22 games respectively, Ed Walsh won 17 and lefty Doc White went 18-6 (with a microscopic 1.52 ERA). Overall, the White Sox starters had an ERA of 2.13.

8. Almost There, 1906–1907

Fourteen more games remained in the 1906 season and the Yankees' hopes for capturing the pennant burned bright. Then came the Detroit Tigers. As a 6th place team, the Tigers did not appear to pose a problem in New York's quest for the AL championship. Yet they did. Three losses in a row at Detroit, and a 10–1 rout by the Indians over Chesbro crushed the Yankees' pennant hopes. While they were losing the White Sox were winning—at precisely the right time, taking 5 in a row as of September 30th. By Tuesday, October 2nd, the Yankees had fallen to second place, 4½ games behind Chicago. Requiem for Yankee pennant chances in 1906. Despite a hard-fought 90-61 record, they ended the 1906 season in second place, 3 games behind Chicago. "Tearing of hair, gnashing of teeth and other high signs of distress are common occurrences now in the home of the New York [team] since the Chicago White Sox have snatched the rag away from Clark Griffith.... It is reported that Griffith is pretty sore over this losing business." The White Sox pitching staff obviously made the difference. Despite the efforts of Orth, 27 wins, and Chesbro, 23 wins, the rest of the Yankee pitchers could not compete—Bill Hogg's 14-13 record being the best Griffith received from among his other starters.

During the 1906 season, Chesbro was removed from games by Griffith a total of 16 times, revealing his arm might have been tiring from all the innings pitched. Walter Clarkson, in his third year, went 9-4, but Griffith again depended far too much on Chesbro and Orth while the other starters fell below expectations. Better numbers were hoped for, but not received, from Doc Newton, who posted a 7-5 record for 1906. Newton had not helped matters when he was suspended in mid-season by Griffith for failing to stay in condition.* What would be different going into the 1907 season? How could the Yankees avoid the same fate next year?

What changes were in store as the New York club prepared for their spring training trip to Atlanta in 1907? Not many, according to manager Griffith. "Although just back from his Montana ranch, [Griffith] took hold of affairs yesterday at the club headquarters.... One thing that Griffith was emphatic about was that the greater New Yorks would not be materially changed from last year," reported the *New York Times* on February 10, 1907.

Griffith continued: "I don't see where anybody has got the better of us in the infield or outfield. Now as to pitchers, I am pretty confident that we will be stronger than last year.... If Chesbro takes twenty games or better, and Al Orth is sure to duplicate that performance, I will have Hogg, Clarkson, Doyle, and Brockett to help make up the necessary victories to place us dangerously near the top ... [Doyle and Brockett] are certainly good for five or ten games a piece."

Doyle was "Slow Joe" Doyle (birth name Judd Bruce Doyle), a rookie in 1906. His debut that year was a strong one as he tossed a 2–0 shutout against the Cleveland Indians. He followed that up by beating Washington in his next start and becoming the first 20th century pitcher to begin his career with two shutouts. Doyle's nickname was well earned. He conducted his baseball career at a leisurely pace—catching naps on the tarpaulin and becoming known for delaying tactics on the mound, driving opposing batters to distraction with an assortment of pitches—including, naturally, a change-up as well as a sinker and spitball. His own fielders were also frustrated as Doyle seemingly made time stand still

---

*The exact nature or severity of Newton's transgression was not known but it could have involved alcohol. It was supposedly said the more he drank the better he pitched, and Newton did post a 15-14, 2.42 ERA record for Brooklyn in 1902. In 1903 with the Los Angeles Angels, during one of Newton's winning—and possibly drinking—streaks, he reportedly fell off the mound, unable to throw the first pitch of the game. However, Newton's 1903 won-lost record was 35-12.

A photograph from the *Atlanta Constitution* of March 14, 1907, shows rookie Lew Brockett, Kid Elberfeld, and another rookie, right-handed pitcher Bobby Keefe. Keefe, from California, went to Santa Clara University as did Hal Chase, but had far less success than Chase on the major league level. He went 3-5 for the Yankees in 1907, did not return to the majors until 1911 with the Cincinnati Reds, and ended a 3-season career in 1912 with an overall 16-21 record.

without ever throwing a pitch. Griffith was also counting on 26-year-old right-hander Lew Brockett for 1907. Brockett, of Brownsville, Illinois, was signed from the minor-league Buffalo Bisons, after a season in which he won 23 games and the Bisons won the minor-league "Little World Series" under manager George Stallings. "I have great faith in Brockett" said Griffith.

Lew Brockett could not reward Griffith's faith in 1907 (though he was given little opportunity to do so—appearing in eight games and ending the season with a 1-2 won-lost record). In 1907 the entire team did little to place themselves "dangerously near the top" to quote Griffith. In fact, New York was closer to the bottom in 1907, finishing at 70-78 and falling to 5th place, 21 games behind the pennant winning Detroit Tigers.

The Tigers rode to the AL pennant by combining the highest team batting average in the American League with outstanding pitching from George Mullin (20-20), Ed Killian (25-13), and Bill Donovan (25-4).

Donovan would later become important in the fortunes of the Yankees—albeit not on the pitching mound—but they certainly could have used a pitcher of Donovan's caliber in 1907. Griffith's continued reliance on veterans Chesbro (10-10 with an ankle injury) and Orth (14-21) meant that more was expected of mostly untested pitchers such as Brockett and Doyle. Hal Chase continued to hit well (.287 with a team-leading 68 RBI) but down years at the plate from Keeler (.234) and Wid Conroy (.234) spelled poor offensive production from the Yankee outfield. The 35-year-old Keeler could not be expected to hit above .300 forever. He also missed some time after his finger was "smashed" by a pitch from Cleveland left-hander Otto Hess during a 2–1 loss to the Indians in Cleveland on July 5th: "...gives him much pain, and makes it difficult for him to sleep" went the newspaper report. No major deal to add another starting pitcher—or an additional bat—doomed the Yankees this season. Instead, stopgap trades for pitchers Earl Moore and Frank Kitson did little to help the Yankees reach the top of the standings. Where was Ban Johnson? The AL president might have been worried about cries of favoritism, or been annoyed by Elberfeld's tantrums. In any case, no behind the scenes assistance was forthcoming to help the 1907 New York team. The lack of real—or even perceived—help from Johnson in building up the New York team is evident in the later seasons of Griffith's tenure as Yankee manager. Griffith severely overestimated the talent level of his team heading into the 1907 season. The Yankees floundered at 32-34, in 5th place, 11 games out in early July during the Cleveland road-trip in which Keeler was injured. Sunday, the usual off-day, led the now desperate Griffith on a scouting trip to nearby Erie, Pennsylva-

(From Photo by Will F. Nelson.
"KID" ELBERFELD,
The Greatest Shortstop in the Game.

A photograph/cartoon of Kid Elberfeld titled "The Greatest Shortstop in the Game" appeared in the *Atlanta Constitution* on March 31, 1907. The fact that such an image exists, literally and figuratively, shows that—despite his combative nature—Elberfeld's importance to the early Yankee teams could not be underestimated and his popularity more than rivaled the other star players of the day. He was by this time the Yankee "captain," having been referred to as such in newspaper articles.

nia, searching for new additions. On Monday, July 8, the *Boston Daily Globe* reported: "Among the men he has his eyes on is John Cosma, first baseman of the Erie team of the Interstate League. Cosma ... was a good pitcher ... [but] his batting was so good that the manager played him regularly at first base, and Cosma practically gave up pitching. If Griffith decides to give him a trial he likely will play him in the outfield."

Griffith's time spent on the shores of Lake Erie was spent in vain. Cosma never appeared on a major league roster—although he did spend time with the minor league Toledo Mud Hens in 1914.

By the end of July, beginning a long home stand at Hilltop Park, the Yankees were fading fast. They lost 4 in a row and were still stuck in 5th place, now 12 games out of first. However, the prospect of a losing season didn't preclude a lack of interesting and volatile events. "Big Shake-Up predicted in New York Americans" proclaimed the *Atlanta Constitution* on July 30, 1907. Elberfeld, having a decent season at the plate (.271), was posting a slightly below average fielding percentage (.930) when compared to the American League total for shortstops (.935). Elberfeld's error problems were shared by the entire Yankee club this season, as the .947 fielding percentage they produced was the lowest in the league (while their 336 errors were the highest). Griffith, frustrated by the sour turn of events, and Yankee owner Frank Farrell—seeing home attendance nosedive to 350,020 from 434,700 in 1906—took decisive action. The *New York Morning World* stated: "Manager Clark Griffith ... under instructions from President Frank Farrell ... yesterday indefinitely suspended 'Kid' Elberfeld, who has played shortstop for the team since its organization in 1903."

Farrell was quoted in the story saying: "Elberfeld has been 'laying down' on us during the last few weeks, and in spite of all that Manager Griffith could do or say Elberfeld refused to give his best services to the club. I have almost been on my knees to him myself and asked him to play the ball he is capable of.... His slouchy, indifferent playing has been plain to the spectators since the team returned home. We don't want anybody on this team who isn't trying, and for that reason we have given Mr. Elberfeld what he has been working for—an indefinite suspension."

Despite Elberfeld's continued antics while in a Yankee uniform, the team's pennant hopes for the 1907 vanished mainly due to lack of pitching depth. Criticism of Griffith's management of his pitching staff was evident in another article printed in the *Atlanta Constitution* on September 1st. The Georgia paper followed the events of it's spring training guest as closely as the northern-based papers throughout the season, and it had sympathy as well as harsh words for Griffith: "In his efforts to turn out a winning combination on the Hilltop the pitching problem has caused Manager Clark Griffith more worry than anything else. The Old Fox has had the hitters and the fielders, but he has been unfortunate in obtaining and developing box talent, though he has experimented industriously.... One criticism that has been made of Griffith's handling of his pitchers is that some men received too many chances to work and others too few. This indictment is brought because this year Keefe would be put in to finish games and lose them when the man who started the contest might have pulled through a winner. Keefe now is in Montreal, and is not setting the Eastern League on fire by his work."

Pinning the Yankee pennant hopes on veterans on the downside of their career—Chesbro, Orth, Keeler—and untested minor league pitchers was not the answer for Griffith and his team. What was the answer? What improvements could be made for 1908? Owner Frank Farrell, always more active in baseball matters than co-owner Bill Devery, was wondering the same thing long before the ashes of the 1907 season fell to earth. The Yankees had made a profit of about $90,000 for the two owners in 1906, but that profit decreased to about $30,000 less in 1907.

Rumors surfaced, quickly denied by Farrell, that Griffith would be let go at the close of the 1907 season. Someone did take the fall for the Yankees' shortcomings in 1907. It was not Griffith. Joseph Gordon, "Vice President, Greater New York Baseball Club," as referred to by the *New York Times*, was dismissed by Farrell prior to the 1908 season. Gordon, with the team since its inception in 1903, and well-liked by associates as well as the general public, had brought a wide range of business knowledge and an association with and love of baseball to his job. He had a long history in the game, first gaining notice as a youngster pitching for Public School #49, and helping them win the New York City championship in games played in Central Park. A sore arm led to Gordon involving himself in the business matters of the game instead of competing on the field. Late in the 1907 season, while the Yankees sunk in the standings, Gordon journeyed by ocean liner to Europe and returned to New York in a happy frame of mind. As the *New York Times* reported: "He was positively fat as a result of his long trip and as voluble as he was rotund." Gordon stated: "I simply had a glorious time." As for the state of his team: "As well as I could I kept in touch with happenings at home, and especially on the diamond. I have watched the Yankees with the liveliest interest, and while I wish they could have stood higher in the race on my return, I am satisfied they have made a good fight considering the handicaps they have had to labor under. I am hoping with the rest of you for better luck nest year." Better luck indeed. Farrell was annoyed that Gordon enjoyed his vacation as the 1907 season went down in flames. Could Griffith avoid the same fate as Gordon if the 1908 season brought similar results?

9

GOODBYE GRIFF (TWO VERSIONS), 1908

Off to Atlanta again went the Yankees for spring training. Elberfeld, seemingly forgiven for past transgressions, was given a contract for 1908 with a disclaimer: "Elberfeld's salary will be about $2,700 for the season, with the provision that if he does satisfactory work all next season he will receive a $1,000 bonus in the fall. Elberfeld agreed to these terms willingly, which means that the little shortstop will probably play better ball for New York than ever before." Adding Elberfeld's contract to the total, Yankee secretary Abe Nahon revealed the entire Yankee roster would total $65,000 in contracts. Some of the regulars, Chesbro, Orth, Hogg, Keeler, Elberfeld and catcher Kleinow, came to Georgia from Hot Springs, Arkansas. Hot Springs was a popular stopover and spring training site for many major league teams. Direct from New York came Doc Newton, Wid Conroy and Mrs. Conroy as well as rookie pitcher Joe Lake. Lake was signed from Jersey City, and "will be a fixture with the Yankees" according to the *Washington Post*. "...Lake will prove the best pitcher that has come out of the minor leagues in many years," commented that paper. The *Washington Post* covered the seasonal activities of two New York teams—both Yankees and Giants—very well, possibly owing to the fact that Washington's own team was awful, typically finishing 7th or last in the 8 team AL from 1903 to 1911. "First in war, first in peace, and last in the American League" went a later saying regarding the Washington club and only the presence of some bad St. Louis Browns teams during this period kept Washington from additional last place finishes.

Joe Lake, as well as Mrs. Lake, joining Joe for his first big-league spring training, certainly hoped the glowing predictions were accurate. Long-time Yankee trainer Mike Martin also made the trip in hopes of keeping the team injury free. New additions other than Lake included first baseman Jake Stahl, pitcher Fred Glade, second baseman Harry Niles and outfielder Charlie Hemphill.

In its 1908 season preview, the *Washington Post* took a positive outlook on Yankee fortunes: "Griffith has been [cited] by some critics for mismanagement, but while he has undoubtedly made mistakes ... [he] has adopted radical measures to place the New York Americans on a winning basis this year. He has made several sensational deals by which some new and fast men will wear New York uniforms. When he traded Second Baseman Jimmy Williams [and] Center Fielder Danny Hoffman to the St. Louis Americans for Second Baseman Harry Niles, Center Fielder Charlie Hemphill, and Pitcher Fred Glade, Griffith completed a deal that will doubtless benefit the New York Americans to a marked degree."

While trying to shake up the club with new additions, it was clear Griffith still placed

A horse-drawn carriage helps the Yankees navigate their spring training trip near Atlanta, Georgia, 1908 (National Baseball Hall of Fame Library, Cooperstown, N.Y.).

hope, possibly far too much, on his old standbys on the pitching staff: "He is banking on Al Orth, a veteran, who is one of the greatest boxmen in the profession, to be the team's mainstay. But Griffith is also confident that Jack Chesbro, who has cut out the injurious spit ball delivery, will show much of his former effectiveness." Doyle, Hogg, and Brockett returned to compete for a spot on the pitching staff. Also in camp were some pitchers of the "glad just to be here" variety that journeyed south with the Yankees each spring. They were part of Griffith's continued insistence and hope on discovering major talent among some obscure minor league candidates: Rube Zeller, Roy Castleton, and Ira Plank. Ira was the brother of Athletics left-hander Eddie Plank. Eddie would be inducted into the Baseball Hall of Fame in 1946. Suffice to say Eddie was the only Plank brother so honored. As usual Griffith took a positive view of the proceedings: "I like the team very much, and am satisfied that our pitching staff will be one of our strongest points," he commented to the *Washington Post*.

The Yankees brought 23 players in all to their training camp, where the Atlanta Crackers again provided competition in exhibition games played at Ponce de Leon park. By April 7th, the New York team was on its way north, stopping on the way in Lynchburg, Virginia, facing the Class C Lynchburg Shoemakers minor league team. It was a homecoming for pitcher Al Orth, who resided in Lynchburg, and he treated the hosts badly, limiting them to 5 hits and 1 run. The Yankees, on the other hand, impressed the 1,000 fans in attendance by smashing 14 hits and scoring 8 runs. In a true sign of an exhibition game, Griffith played second base (not until 1912 would Griffith take the field again at second—the only other time he would ever play that position). Wid Conroy was the batting star for the Yankees, going 3 for 3 and Al Orth contributed 2 hits in 4 at-bats. (Offense from Orth was not surprising considering his career batting average of .273.)

The 1908 season began with promise at Hilltop Park. The Yankees defeated the Athletics 1–0 and took five out of six games during the home-stand. Too bad this was essentially the highlight of the season. A seven game losing streak in mid–June and a six game losing streak to close the month left the Yankees in 7th place, 10 games out of first place. What went wrong? Everything. Fourteen hits against the Lynchburg Shoemakers more than two months ago was now a distant memory. The 1908 Yankee lineup produced a pathetic team batting average of .236 and it's 2.96 runs per game was the worst in the American League. Center fielder Charlie Hemphill, at .297, had the highest average of any starting position player. Keeler, still soldiering on in right field, was second in BA at .263 and Hemphill's 44 RBI led the team. A spiking injury to Elberfeld—who appeared in only 19 games—and his substitute Neal Ball batting a less than robust .247 only worsened the proceedings. As for the pitching staff, Chesbro, 34, and Orth, 35, had toiled long and hard for the Yankees but this year the doors on their baseball careers slammed shut in succession. Chesbro (14-20) and Orth (2-13) never won another major league game after the 1908 season. Right-handed pitcher Fred Glade, called "Lucky," was not aptly named. He had won 18 games for St. Louis in 1904, 15 games in 1906 and 13 games in 1907. This year, his sore arm threw a wrench into the Yankee pitching staff hopes and ended his career at age 32.

The inconsistency of the Yankee teams under Griffith produced a strain in the relationship between the manager and owners Frank Farrell and Bill Devery. Farrell was always more active in team matters than Devery, with a constant eye on the bottom line. The Yankees were well on the way to more sagging attendance figures this year—down to 305,500, well below the league average of 451,421. In bad times, deposed team president Joseph Gordon had been a buffer between the owners and Griffith. Griffith was actually a close friend of Farrell, but was frustrated and disgusted by the poor showings of his team. The end of the line came on Wednesday, June 24th. Clark Griffith resigned as Yankee manager stating: "In justice to Mr. Farrell and myself, I think a change in management will give better results. Whenever the team had a chance to win the pennant luck broke against us ... I want it distinctly understood that Mr. Farrell and myself are good friends. He has always treated me fine and has spared no expense to get a winner."

Another version of the story was revealed in the *Chicago Daily Tribune* after the 1908 season—that Griffith was actually fired. Griffith had apparently been managing without an actual written contract, further evidence of friendly relations between him and Farrell. Supposedly, a conflict arose between Griffith and Farrell due to an ongoing "feud" between Griffith's long-term double-play combination of second baseman Jimmy Williams and shortstop Elberfeld. Poor communication between the two and bad play in the Yankee infield was the direct result. Elberfeld's suspension in 1907 kept the two feuding fielders apart briefly (Elberfeld played 120 games while Williams appeared in 137) and Griffith then sought to trade either one of the disgruntled players for the good of the club—Williams being sent to

Opposite top: Pitcher Rube Manning takes the easy route during spring training (National Baseball Hall of Fame Library, Cooperstown, N.Y.). *Opposite bottom*: In this rare in-game action photograph taken circa 1908 at Hilltop Park, the Red Sox are playing the Yankees. Willie Keeler is the batter, Lou Criger is the catcher and Frank "Silk" O'Loughlin is the umpire. O'Loughlin, of Rochester, New York, was abrupt when a player argued one of his calls. He responded: "I have never missed one in my life and it's too late to start now!" (Library of Congress, Prints & Photographs Division, LC-DIG-ggbain-01981).

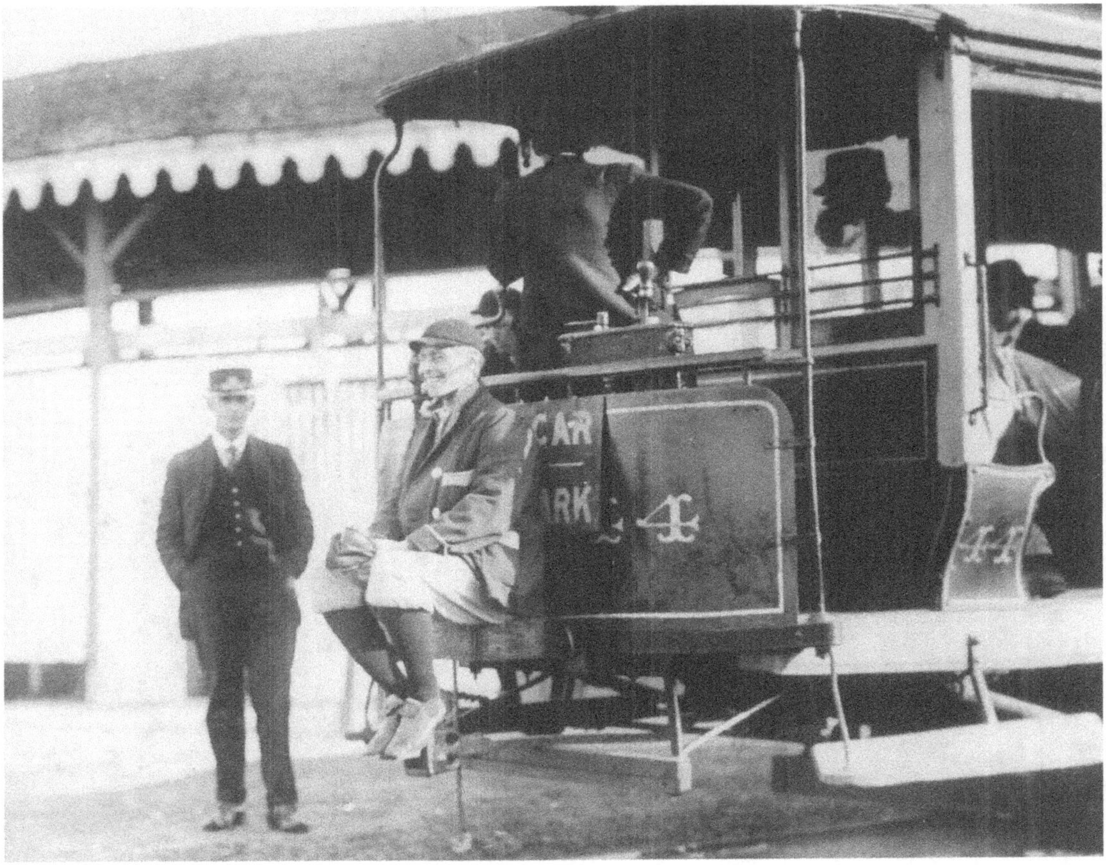
CAR
4

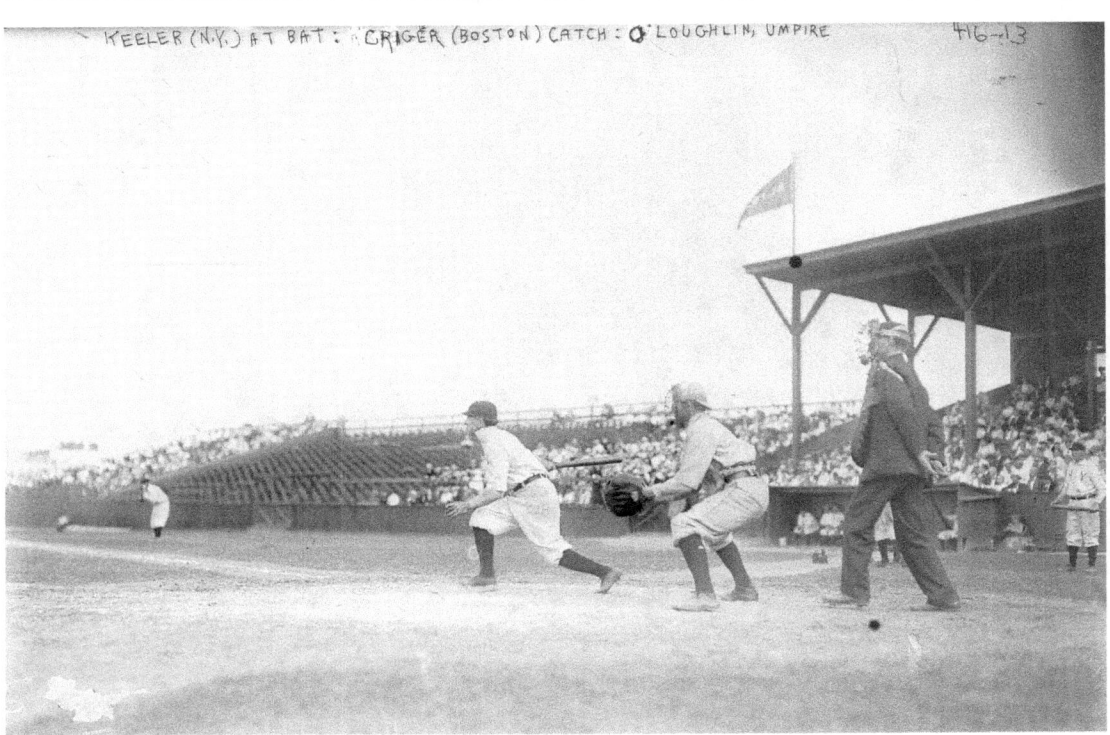

KEELER (N.Y.) AT BAT : CRIGER (BOSTON) CATCH : O'LOUGHLIN, UMPIRE
416-13

56 Greatness in Waiting

the St. Louis Browns in the acquisition of Niles, Hemphill and Glade. Harry Niles' poor batting coupled with a .928 fielding percentage prompted severe criticism of Griffith from a "minor" official of the Yankees.

The criticism, the continuing conflict with Elberfeld and poor team record in 1908 reportedly led Farrell to send Griffith packing. In any case, whether through resignation or dismissal, ruptured relations between Farrell and Griffith led to the appointment of a new manager, a man capable of pouring gasoline on any fire: "Kid" Elberfeld himself.

Clark Griffith in civilian attire. Despite never winning a pennant, Griffith was the manager who put the Yankee franchise on the major league baseball map (Library of Congress, Prints & Photographs Division, LC-DIG-ggbain-06462).

Clark Griffith's record as Yankee Manager

Year	Won	Lost	Percentage	Standing
1903	72	62	.537	4th
1904	92	59	.609	2nd
1905	71	78	.477	6th
1906	90	61	.596	2nd
1907	70	78	.473	5th
1908	24	32	.429	incomplete
6 Years:	419	370	.531	0 pennants

Opposite top: A shot from Opening Day, April 14, 1908. The Yankees take the field for warm-ups and fielding practice. Rookie A's pitcher Nick Carter faced Yankee starter Slow Joe Doyle. George Grantham Bain, born in St. Louis in 1865, was a full-time photographer in New York from the late 1800s through the early 1900s and is responsible for these great photographs. He established one of the nation's first news photograph agencies, the Bain News Service, in 1898, providing engaging visuals to coincide with newspaper stories (Library of Congress, Prints & Photographs Division, LC-DIG-ggbain-00316). *Opposite bottom*: In-game action from Opening Day, 1908, with an innovative low camera angle from George Bain. The batter, Kid Elberfeld, was possibly attempting to bunt and A's catcher Syd Smith prepares to throw. The Yankees won the extra inning contest, 1–0. Catcher Red Kleinow had 3 hits in 5 at-bats and scored the winning run in the bottom of the 12th inning on a sacrifice fly. This was a rare offensive outburst for Kleinow, who was the starting catcher in 1908, sharing time with Walter "Heavy" Blair and 19-year-old rookie Ed Sweeney. Kleinow batted .168 in 1908, with 1 home run and 13 RBI. Blair batted .190, and Sweeney hit .146 (Library of Congress, Prints & Photographs Division, LC-DIG-ggbain-00274).

10

Apocalypse

The results of Kid Elberfeld's reign as manager were disastrous. Soon after he took charge, the Yankees lost 6 games in a row. Then they lost 7 more, beginning with the second game of a Saturday, July 4th, double-header in Washington and ending in an 8–2 loss to the Tigers back in New York on Friday, July 10th. Worse was soon to come. A 12-game losing streak from July 18th to August 6th deposited the Yankees into last place (8th) in the American League. They were 28½ games out of first place. "Yankees Lose Once More" became an appropriate newspaper headline.

The qualities that Clark Griffith exhibited as a player—shrewd, competitive yet personable, slowly morphed into temperamental and high-strung outbreaks when the Yankees lost. On the other hand, the fiery Elberfeld completely deteriorated—throwing volatile and annoying tantrums as the losing continued. Elberfeld was a wild field manager, berating his team as much as the umpires. This led to problems with the easy-going first baseman Hal Chase, on his way to becoming the most popular player in Yankee uniform as Chesbro and Keeler faced the end of their careers. A full-blown feud developed between Chase and Elberfeld. Chase was envious of Elberfeld being named manager, but truly felt his bitter style was ruining the team. Chase, calling Elberfeld "unbalanced," complained about the manager to Frank Farrell, who listened but did not act. As his team was hovering in the basement and he struggled with a .257 average, rumors surfaced that Chase's performance on the field was a reflection of the managerial reins being handed to Elberfeld. A newspaper review of the events on August 27, 1908, follows. "Gradually we are getting a line on the real cause of the Yankees' slump. It began to leak out that Mr. Chase's head has been swollen so much within the last year that he has been causing trouble on the team. Mr. Chase is a grand ball player ... but he is getting $5,000 for his season's work and recently he has shown such a disposition to sulk and shirk that not only the fans have roasted him openly, but Manager Elberfeld has also taken notice. They tell me that the young Californian, when he saw himself pictured and boomed in the newspapers, became so inflated that he thought he was [the greatest ever] ... Mr. Chase decided that he alone was the natural successor to the "Old Fox." He went around kidding himself that he would be the new manager and consequently he was ready to explode with surprise and indignation when he learned that Farrell decided on Elberfeld ... it is a sure thing that the great first baseman is disgruntled.... A player who, for petty reasons, does not give his full value to his employer is not fit to remain in professional baseball. He is of no service to his team and manager and by retaining such a player, a club-owner merely adds fuel to the fire."

Chase, who could be as sensitive as he could be petulant, broke from the team. He departed for California on September 3, stating: "I am not satisfied to play under a management that sees

Intensity personified: Yankee manager Kid Elberfeld surveys his domain along the first base coaching box at Hilltop Park in 1908 (Library of Congress, Prints & Photographs Division, LC-DIG-ggbain-01978).

fit to give out a story detrimental to my character and honesty. I feel that I could not do myself justice under such conditions, and therefore I have decided to quit. I never had managerial ideas." However, Chase's protestations about not wanting to manage seemed only to apply to the Yankees, as he became the manager for the Stockton club of the California State League shortly after he arrived in California on September 7. He batted .385 and led Stockton to the California State League championship (perhaps Farrell was reconsidering the choice of Elberfeld?). For jumping the Yankees, according to Baseball Commission rules, Chase could have been suspended for five years. Frank Farrell began pleading on his absent star's behalf with American League President Ban Johnson.

Farrell and Devery wanted Chase back as soon as possible, but had other pressing concerns. The Yankees finished the 1908 season 39½ games back, in last place for the first time in their short history. That was more than enough to prove to Farrell and Devery that the Elberfeld managerial experiment should be abandoned. Elberfeld was shown the door, at least as manager, at the close of the 1908 season. "The Tabasco Kid" would return to the playing field in 1909, where it was hoped he could cause more damage to the opposition than to his own team (or the umpires).

11

WITH A LITTLE HELP, 1909

The Yankee owners sought a proven commodity as the new field leader. On November 5th, 1908, George Tweedy Stallings, of Augusta, Georgia, stepped into the void. Farrell didn't look very far for his choice. Stallings had managed the Newark Indians of the Class A Eastern League in 1908 and partially owned the club with Farrell. (They sold the club before the 1909 season began.) Stallings owned a large plantation, just outside Macon, Georgia, which he dubbed "The Meadows," where he raised cattle and tended to peach crops. He typically appears in photographs managing in a suit, as was his signature, and smiling broadly. Despite outward appearances, Stallings—who also guided the Phillies and Detroit Tigers prior to his minor league managing days—was a far cry from a southern gentleman. He was known for savagely and profanely excoriating his players. First on Stallings' "to do" list was finding a solution to the Elberfeld/Chase flare-up. Chase was still out of sight in California, but not out of mind. Also, the Yankees had recently acquired shortstop John "Schoolboy" Knight,* 23, so the 34-year-old Elberfeld was considering a shift to third base, and a new team, as the American League winter meetings began on December 8th.

Stallings commented, "We are not doing anything with reference to Chase, because he is at the present time ineligible because of his having jumped the team last season ... but I consider him the best first baseman in the business today.... He will play right here or not at all." As for Elberfeld: "I don't believe there is room on the same team for both Elberfeld and Chase ... Elberfeld has written to me that he would like to go to Washington because he can play third base there, and that is the position he wants to cover." Elberfeld also suggested Washington, D.C., for other reasons. Elberfeld was born in Mason City, Virginia. Though he and his wife spent winters at their farm in Chattanooga, Tennessee, and he had recently purchased similar land in upstate New York, Virginia was still home to close friends and family. In the end, Elberfeld remained with the Yankees and the 1909 Yankee spring training contingent descended upon Macon, Georgia. Stallings obviously had a hand in choosing the location. In hopes of finally solving the problematic Yankee starting pitching issues, Stallings hired Charley Farrell (no relation to Yankee owner Frank), a native of Marlboro, Massachusetts. Farrell was dubbed "The Duke of Marlboro," a former major league catcher and very good hitter for 18 seasons, cited as "one of the best informed baseball men in the country" by the *New York Times* on Feb, 21, 1909.

In another move to break with the Clark Griffith era, veteran Yankee trainer Mike

---

*Knight attended the University of Pennsylvania and was thus tagged with this nickname in an era when a great number of major leaguers had not gone to college.

Martin was dismissed in favor of James Burke, formerly an assistant trainer at the University of Pennsylvania. Athur Irwin continued as chief Yankee scout, and signed some new young talent for Stallings in addition to shortstop Knight. Outfielder "Birdie" Cree and pitcher Jack Warhop were some of the new recruits. Third baseman Jimmy "Pepper" Austin, a rookie at age 29, was also in camp. Pitcher Bill Hogg was released, being sent to the minor league Louisville club of the American Association. Hogg, who suffered a kidney ailment during the 1907 season, died mysteriously in New Orleans, Louisiana, in 1909 at the age of twenty-eight.

Hal Chase, meanwhile, was missing the spotlight of Manhattan. He applied to the National Commission—baseball's ruling body prior to the appointment of Commissioner Kenesaw Mountain Landis in 1920—for reinstatement. A $200 fine was levied and Chase again joined the team, at a salary of $4,500. In early March, Chase arrived in Macon. His first act was to walk up to "Kid" Elberfeld and shake his hand. Thus ended the feud between the teammates. Stallings was quite pleased with the makeup of his team. In a letter sent to the *Washington Post* from Macon on March 13, 1909, Stallings wrote: "I believe that we now have as strong a set of young players as any team in the country, and some most valuable veterans. The combination is an ideal one, and I feel confident that some team besides New York will be last." Not exactly a ringing endorsement. More drama was still to occur before the Yankees headed North. It again involved Hal Chase. It came in a rather disturbing form.

Smallpox, an acute infectious disease, is not well known—or well feared—today. It is characterized by high fever, severe headaches, fatigue, delirium and a horrible rash that turns into raised lesions on the skin. The disease, only evident in humans and not carried by animals, was declared eradicated from the earth by the World Health Assembly in 1980 due to a program of vaccinations. In 1909 things were much different. During the 17th and 18th centuries smallpox was a deadly disease with mortality rates approaching 90 percent in America and, despite it's decline in the 19th century, it was still a real threat in the early 20th century. Hal Chase became ill in early April, as the Yankees played their last game in Georgia, against the Augusta Tourists of the South Atlantic League. A smallpox outbreak had occurred in Macon and it was determined Chase had contracted the feared disease, albeit a lesser form called variola minor. "Minor" in this case meant a low mortality rate on the order of 1 percent but the symptoms were still severe. Chase recovered after a month of battling the neurological effects of the illness but the skin lesions etched permanent scars on his face. In the interim, George Stallings was alarmed not only for Chase's welfare but for the health of everyone connected with the team. The entire Yankee squad, making its way to Lynchburg, Virginia, for exhibition games, received vaccinations but were quarantined before finally being allowed to the team hotel. Crisis averted, the Yankees continued north to New York for the last exhibition game, played against Newark, Stallings' former team, at Hilltop Park. Elberfeld, who was vaccinated twice as a precaution, watched the game from the press box with sportswriters. The double dose of vaccinations gave Elberfeld a different version of the baseball term "sore arm." Lacking Elberfeld and "Prince Hal" Chase, still recovering in an Augusta hospital, a Yankee lineup featuring Hemphill, CF, Keeler, RF, Austin, 3B, and Knight, SS, produced 11 hits, but few New York runners crossed the plate at this well attended game. In front of 7,500 people the Yankees lost by a 6–1 score. "George Stallings' Old Crew Thumps His Vaccinated Hopefuls" ran the newspaper headline.

The 1909 season began on a sour note. The Yankees lost at Washington 4–1 with lefty Doc Newton closing out his erratic eight-year major league pitching career. (The left-hander would go 0-3 before finally being discarded as a player unable, or unwilling, to harness his talent.) Chesbro and Orth were also fading out of the Yankee picture, Chesbro appearing in only 9 games with an awful 6.34 ERA. Orth had even less an effect on Yankee fortunes—one game pitched after joining the team in July, after a stint managing his hometown minor league team. Orth, who ran a tobacco farm in Lynchburg, retired but he was not through with baseball.

"The Curveless Wonder" served as an umpire in the Virginia League and the National League from 1912 to 1917. He later coached several college teams, including the Virginia Military Institute. During World War I, Al Orth worked with the YMCA in France, training soldiers and civilians in athletic competition.

The 1909 season, in which the Yankees went a seemingly insignificant 74-77 to finish in fifth place, was a vast improvement from 1908. Despite the mediocre record, this year's edition of the team was a huge hit with fans. Home attendance at Hilltop Park soared to 501,000, well above the AL home park average of 467,484. The Yankees drew an average of 6,549 fans per game at home in 1909. Replacing Orth and Chesbro as front-line starting pitchers were Joe Lake (14-11, 1.88 ERA), Jack Warhop (13-15, 2.40 ERA), Rube Manning (7-11, 3.17 ERA), and Lew Brockett (10-8, 2.12 ERA). The won-lost records were not

George Stallings, center, sits with the Yankee troops during spring training. This photograph was taken in Gray, Georgia, not far from the Yankee spring training base in Macon. First baseman Hal Chase stands third from the left (no cap) in the back row (National Baseball Hall of Fame Library, Cooperstown, N.Y.).

outstanding but the earned run averages, except in the case of Manning, were well below the 1909 AL average of 2.52. Tom Hughes (7-8) and Slow Joe Doyle (8-6) also took their turns. Out of the "bullpen" emerged 25-year-old Jack Quinn, appearing in 23 games and finishing with a 9-5 record and 1.92 ERA. Quinn was discovered by Al Orth in 1908, as Quinn played for the Lynchburg Shoemakers. The Yankee offensive attack in 1909 was weak at best—including a team batting average of .248. The few bright spots included second baseman Frank LaPorte's .298 average, which led all regulars, Hal Chase's .283 average and rookie left fielder Clyde Engle's 71 RBI.

Despite the rather uninspiring on-field events of 1909, another mediocre season would not pass into the early Yankee record book before things became a lot more intriguing. Opposing teams noticed Yankee hitters produced more offense at Hilltop Park than they did on the road. The Yankees scored an average of 4.39 runs per game at home while scoring 3.30 runs per game away from Hilltop Park. It was reasonable the team would perform better at home but this was a greater run scoring disparity than 6 of the remaining 7 AL teams. The Washington Senators had been blasted by Yankee batters to the tunes of 8–1 and 17–0 wins at Hilltop Park in April, and Senators manager Joe Cantillon suspected the Yankees were stealing the signs of the visiting teams' catchers. He informed Detroit Tigers

Action from Thursday, April 22, 1909, at Hilltop Park, home of the Yankees from 1903 to 1912. The batter is Otis Clymer of the Washington Senators, the catcher for the Yankees is John "Red" Kleinow, and the umpire is Tim Hurst. The Yankees won, 8–1 (Library of Congress, Prints & Photographs Division, LC-USZ62-111962).

manager Hughie Jennings. Slugging outbursts were not a common theme on the 1909 Yankees but on July 29, 30 and 31 they defeated the Tigers by scores of 11–2, 6–0 and 7–2. The 7–2 victory was the first game of a Saturday double-header. Though the Yankees lost the second game 7–4, Jennings had already decided it was time for detective work. Prior to the game, he sent pitcher Bill Donovan to the outfield fence of Hilltop Park to investigate. Donovan returned "without having shown any ability as a Sherlock Holmes" according to the *Washington Post*.

Enter Detroit trainer Harry Tuthill. Tuthill was a wise man, well-rounded in athletic training, a "specialist in knees and ankles" who had previously supervised boxers and who would later become the first trainer at West Point. It was said that an Army coach observed Tuthill's handiwork on the Tigers—particularly the bandaging of Ty Cobb's legs after various collisions with opposing infielders—and decided Tuthill was the right person for the job on the Army football team. After conferring with Jennings, the two men reasoned that sending another Detroit player to examine the fence would make the New York team suspicious while Tuthill would generate less interest. It was up to Tuthill to find the evidence of sign stealing. What Tuthill discovered was reported in full by the *Washington Post* after the end of the 1909 season: "Tuthill watched closely, and finally he saw a movement in one of the letters of a big hat sign painted on the fence in deep center. Gluing his eyes on the sign he noticed that the crossbar in the letter 'H' turned over at times and now showed a white surface and again a black surface. He tried to climb the fence but was prevented by the barbed wire which protects it. The next day Tuthill went out and took a close observation, and his suspicions were confirmed. He found a place where he could raise a strand of wire and climb over the fence, which he did in a hurry, and just in time to see a man running away at full speed. Dropping over on the outside of the fence he found that there was an open space between the fence proper and the big hat sign and two holes had been bored in the sign at this point for the accommodation of a pair of field glasses [binoculars] which were lying on the ground where the signaler had left them in his haste. He also discovered that the crossbar on the letter 'H' was so constructed that it could be turned around. The method of signaling was as follows: First, the operator would detect the catcher's signs by the use of his field glasses. It would not take him more than an inning or two to find out what was the sign for a fastball and what for a curve.... If the catcher signaled for a fast ball the cross bar would be turned to show white. If a curve was signaled for, the bar would be black. Thus the New York batters were always aware of just what kind of ball was coming.... It has been a noticeable fact all season that [New York] always hit like fury at home and were punk batters on the road, and the reason has now been explained."

Tuthill broke the crossbar lever and turned the field glasses and lever over to Jennings. In actuality, Tuthill did not intend to reveal his discovery. The Tigers ended up winning the 1909 AL pennant, finishing 98-54. Manager Hughie Jennings and Tuthill agreed Detroit was not affected by Stallings' sign stealing scheme and they were unwilling to embarrass the Yankees.

Washington Senators manager Joe Cantillon had other ideas. The Senators finished in 8th place—dead last—in 1909 (after finishing 7th in 1908 and 8th in 1907). Cantillon was fired as manager after the 1909 season and had no thought of leaving the scene quietly. He addressed a letter to AL president Ban Johnson that stated in part: "The present system being worked in New York shows the caliber of the men behind the club. You can get all the proof necessary to convict New York of the crime of 'tipping' the opposing team's signs

Detroit trainer Harry Tuthill examines the arm of pitcher Ed Summers, one of the many types of examinations Tuthill was performing in 1909. Detroit first baseman Del "Sheriff" Gainer observes. Summers posted a 19-9 record for the AL champion Tigers in 1909. They lost the World Series in 7 games to the Pittsburgh Pirates (Library of Congress, Prints & Photographs Division, LC-DIG-ggbain-10297).

through the aid of a hired and long-experienced man with glasses." Wanting to know all the details Johnson telegrammed Tuthill telling him to divulge what he had discovered.

The "tipper" in the sign stealing operation was pitcher Gene McCann, formerly with Brooklyn in the National League and most recently with the Jersey City Skeeters of the Class A Eastern League—well known to Stallings as well as Yankee owner Farrell due to their previous involvement in the same league with Newark. The 33-year-old McCann was hired as a "scout" by the Yankees and paid $75 a week for his "work." Despite the headline "Ban Johnson will insist on removal of Stallings" in the *Washington Post* on October 17, 1909, Stallings was retained as manager. Yankee owners Farrell and Devery met with Johnson, trying to convince him to allow Stallings to remain until his contract expired in 1910. Johnson, fearing an embarrassing situation for his league agreed and hoped the whole mess would be forgotten. The final resting place of the field glasses and other evidence presented is unknown.

The whole sign stealing affair, as well as Cantillon's letter of condemnation to Johnson regarding "the caliber of the men behind the club," speaks to a greater truth. The Yankees

The scene of the crime: Action at Hilltop Park against the White Sox, circa 1909. Note the Bull Durham tobacco sign along the outfield fence near the sign for "Young's Hats" in center field, part of the mechanism for the Yankees "sign stealing." Also note the fielding position of Hal Chase, far from first base. It's possible a runner is on at third base, cropped from the photograph, and Chase anticipates a play at home plate (National Baseball Hall of Fame Library, Cooperstown, N.Y.).

at this time were not a bunch of choirboys. That owners Farrell and Devery knew about the sign stealing maneuvers can safely be assumed.

While Stallings remained, two of the more outstanding—and some might say upstanding—players on the team were no longer around at the end of the season. Jack Chesbro's contract was sold to the Red Sox on September 11th and Willie Keeler was released. The 37-year-old Keeler appeared in 99 games and batted .264—one of only 3 seasons in which he batted under .300 during his 19 year career. Chesbro and Keeler would both be elected to the Baseball Hall of Fame. A later well-known owner of the Yankees aptly used the term "warrior" to describe right fielder Paul O'Neill. Keeler—also chasing down fly balls in right and destroying the pitching of opposing teams—and Chesbro, with his superhuman pitching endurance (in a wool-flannel uniform) were the first "warriors" of the Yankees. As events unfolded, it proved near impossible to find suitable replacements. Also leaving the Yankee scene was Kid Elberfeld, his contract being sold to Washington on December 14, 1909. The Tabasco Kid, a warrior in the literal sense, eventually retired with a .271 career batting average. The pugnacious Elberfeld later returned to managing in the minor leagues, terrorizing umpires and the personnel of other teams along the way. In 1912, Elberfeld was leading a Montgomery,

Left fielder Arthur Clyde "Hack" Engle in 1909. The Yankee uniform this year featured the second incarnation of the interlocking "NY" logo, on the left sleeve (the logo first appeared on the left chest in 1905). The cap was blue with a red "NY" logo while the socks were blue with red horizontal stripes. Engle, while not a star, was a capable player who produced a .265 career batting average in 8 seasons. Engle joined the Red Sox in 1910, becoming an infielder. He later coached at Yale University (Library of Congress, Prints & Photographs Division, LC-DIG-ggbain-03332).

Alabama, AA team with future Hall of Fame manager Casey Stengel on the roster. Elberfeld had these ironic words of advice for Stengel: "If you're going to be a big leaguer, act like a big leaguer." From 1915 to 1916, Elberfeld managed the Chattanooga Lookouts and then proceeded to Little Rock, winning a minor league pennant in 1920. Elberfeld passed away in Chattanooga on January 13, 1944, at the age of 69.

12

THE EMERY BALL, 1910

Given the misadventures of 1909, it's easy to think the Yankees prepared for the 1910 season with a collective cloud over their heads, humbled by the experience. But embarrassment was not the order of the day for this crowd. In fact, Stallings was not only forgiven, but had a clause in his 1910 contract that would further reward him financially dependent on the final standings in 1910. The *Washington Post* reported on January 6, 1910: "Frank Farrell, owner of the local American League club, is anxious for a winner and has offered Stallings $2,500 if he captures [the pennant], $2,000 for second place, $1,500 for the third honors, and $1,000 if the manager lands the club in fourth position." Receive $1,500 for third place? As a comparison, Ray Fisher, a rookie pitcher who joined the Yankees for 1910, made $1,500 in total salary for the season.

Further insight into New York Yankees—and American League—financial matters at the time was brought out in a newspaper report prior to the 1910 season. It indicated the Philadelphia Athletics, who previously had "inadequate" stands, would now receive the same percentage of the gate receipts as other clubs in 1910, due to the improvement in seating at Shibe Park, the Athletics' home field. In short, it spelled out the fact the Yankees now took in twelve and a half cents for each twenty-five cent bleacher seat admission at Hilltop Park and twenty-five cents on all other seats sold. Those percentages and the alternating attendance figures at the Hilltop due to inconsistent showings by the team meant the New York club faced a precipitous financial situation. Owners Farrell and Devery were hoping for a quick change in the team's fortunes heading into 1910.

One other off-field occurrence of note—a humorous one in retrospect—came prior to spring training of 1910. Spikes would remain in use on baseball shoes. "To discontinue the present style of spikes would slow up the game," noted Chicago White Sox owner Charles Comiskey at the annual American League meetings. "None of the substitutes that we have examined would have the effect of the old spikes. I admit that they are dangerous, but I think it would be better to adopt safeguards, such as shin guards, or something like that, instead of doing away with the spikes." Shin guards on infielders? Kid Elberfeld must have been laughing out loud in Washington.

Georgia was again the destination for Yankee spring training, this time in Athens. Hal Chase—now the "face" of the franchise after the departures of Chesbro, Keeler and Elberfeld—was appointed captain, the third Yankee to be so honored after Griffith and Elberfeld. With Chase at first, LaPorte at second, Knight at shortstop and Austin at third, Stallings had the entire starting infield returning from 1909. It was a solid core, the closest thing to a stable foundation to build the team around, despite occasional fielding lapses from Knight and low batting averages from Knight and Austin the previous season (.236 and .231 respectively).

The other vital component of the team—one that brought an infusion of youth Stallings hoped could mean the pennant—was the pitching staff. In the most significant departure from the Clark Griffith days, seasoned veteran pitchers were nowhere to be found. Instead, an abundance of youngsters and a significant rookie, Ray Caldwell, were not just auditioning to fill out the staff, but were being counted on to become the next versions of Chesbro and Orth.

The 1910 Yankee pitching staff featured the following players: RHP Russ Ford, 27, RHP Jack Quinn, 26, RHP Jack Warhop, 25, LHP Jim "Hippo" Vaughn, 22, RHP Tom Hughes, 26, and RHP Ray Fisher, 22. To handle the young pitching corps, Stallings was counting on veteran catcher Lou Criger, obtained on December 16, 1909, from the St. Louis Browns for pitcher Joe Lake and center fielder Ray Demmitt. Criger played for the Red Sox from 1901 to 1908, catching Cy Young. "Criger, it is believed, will be a great help to the inexperienced pitchers, and with his coaching they will be able to weather a campaign far better than with less capable men on the receiving end," proclaimed the *Washington Post* on April 10th. The acquisition brought an end, albeit temporarily, to the Yankee coaching career of Charlie Farrell, who was no longer needed to guide the pitchers with the experienced, 38-year-old Criger on the scene.

Vaughn, nicknamed "Hippo" due to a pounding running style, stood 6'4", and weighed 215 pounds. He was born April 9, 1888, in Weatherford, Texas, west of Fort Worth, and began pitching in the Texas League in 1906. By 1907 Vaughn was in Hot Springs of the Arkansas State League, posting a 9–1 and generating notice from the Yankees. They purchased Vaughn's contract for $5,000. Vaughn had a brief tryout with New York in 1908 but was back in the minors in 1909 at Macon in the South Atlantic League. It was there that Vaughn blossomed, throwing a no-hitter, and posting a 1.95 ERA for the season. He found additional success upon moving to Louisville in the Class AAA American Association later that year, where he threw another no-hitter, going 8–1 with an ERA of 2.05. Vaughn's career trajectory is a microcosm of players that appeared on the Yankees and many major league teams at this time. Prior to drafts featuring million dollar signing bonuses thrown at highly-touted high school and college players, the formula for acquiring the next possible major league star was less distinct. Small scouting staffs, even consisting

Manager George Stallings faces the camera (Library of Congress, Prints & Photographs Division, LC-DIG-ggbain-17329).

1, Hemphill; 2, Vaughan; 3, Austin; 4, Brockett.
Conlon, Photo.
A GROUP OF NEW YORK AMERICANS, 1909.

Page from the 1910 *Spalding Guide*, **with photographs of outfielder Charlie Hemphill, pitchers Hippo Vaughn and Lew Brockett (a holdout in 1910) and infielder Jimmy Austin. Brockett reappeared briefly in 1911 and faded from the scene (Library of Congress).**

of one person, were responsible for roaming the countryside, taking notice of decent performances, signing the player to a contract and hoping for the best. The disparate backgrounds of players on the 1910 Yankee pitching staff bear witness to a wide-ranging search for mound talent and the varied minor league and semi-pro paths that brought them to the Yankees: Ford—Brandon, Manitoba, Canada; Quinn—Janesville, Pennsylvania; Warhop—Hinton, West Virginia; Hughes—Coal Creek, Colorado; Fisher—Middlebury, Vermont; and Caldwell—Corydon, Pennsylvania.

Vaughn was selected by Stallings as the Yankees' opening day pitcher in 1910, the youngest Yankee pitcher ever to start the opening game. The Boston Red Sox were in town that day and Vaughn squared off at Hilltop Park against emerging Red Sox ace Ed "Knuckles" Cicotte on April 14. Cicotte featured his "shine" or spitball in addition to the knuckler.

Two Paths to Stardom: Jack Quinn, right, and Jim "Hippo" Vaughn were mainstays on the early Yankee pitching staffs. Quinn was a spitballer who won 18 games for the Yankees in 1910. He pitched for 23 years, winning 247 games, losing 218 with a 3.27 ERA. Quinn had two stints with the Yankees, from 1909 to 1912 and from 1919 to 1921. In 1932, at the age of 49, Quinn became the oldest man to win a major league game while pitching for the Brooklyn Dodgers. Vaughn's highest win total as a Yankee was 13 in 1910, but he blossomed soon after being acquired by the Chicago Cubs, posting five 20-win seasons from 1914 to 1919 and winning 19 games in 1920 (Library of Congress, Prints & Photographs Division, LC-DIG-ggbain-07936).

This plaque in a courtyard at Manhattan's Columbia Presbyterian Medical Center* commemorates the site of home plate at Hilltop Park, the Yankees' home field from 1903 to 1912.

Vaughn gave up three quick runs in the first three innings and one more in the fifth. He settled down thereafter, matching Red Sox relief pitcher Joe Wood in shutting down the opposing batters in a game that lasted 14 innings. It was called on account of darkness with the score tied 4–4.

"Hippo" Vaughn posted a 13-11 record with a 1.83 ERA in 1910. However, "Hippo" was not the feature story on the team. That designation belonged to Russ Ford. In 1909, the Canadian-born Ford appeared in 1 game, pitched 3 innings and ended the season with a 9.00 earned run average. Ford was sent to the minor leagues in Jersey City. The year 1910 presented an entirely different story for Ford: one of the most stunningly successful years seen in baseball history. Ford posted a major league rookie pitcher record of 26 wins and 6 losses, with a 1.65 ERA with 8 shutouts.

Why the sudden success? Ford used emery paper to scuff his pitches—making the ball break sharply towards the plate. Ford discovered the effects of scuffed pitches while he toiled at Atlanta of the Southern League in 1907. He threw a warm-up pitch prior to the game that sailed past the plate and hit a rough concrete pillar. "...[A]fter that I noticed the ball breaking in a peculiar way," explained his catcher Ed Sweeney. Sweeney was signed to a contract by the Yankees that summer. One day owner Frank Farrell asked Sweeney who the best pitcher in the Southern League might be and upon Sweeney's suggestion the Yankees signed

*Now Columbia University Medical Center.

The still-standing apartment buildings appeared beyond the center field fence at Hilltop Park (courtesy Matt Fulling).

Ford. During the 1910 spring training in Athens, Ford took Sweeney into his confidence and explained the procedure and qualities of the "emery ball": "Russ showed me a little leather ring that he slipped over a finger on his left hand. Like most player's gloves, his mitt had a big hole in it. All he had to do was to scratch the ball with the emery, which was pasted on to the leather. The concrete had given ... the tip." Sweeney continued: "The bigger the scratch, the greater the freak jumps the ball would take. But Russ merely scraped a part of the ball. And he never used it except in a pinch. He would fake a spitter and nobody ever got wise. When he pitched he always requested that I catch him. When Russ threw the ball, with runners on, or in pinches, no batter in the world could hit it. Once in a while somebody did, but it was by accident. Ford could break the ball in two ways—in and down and out and up. I've seen batter after batter miss the ball by a foot." Teammates Eddie "Kid" Foster, a shortstop, and second baseman Earl Gardner also "knew the secret" according to Sweeney, since he and Ford had been roommates with those two players.

Ford started his first game on Thursday, April 21, at Shibe Park, beating the Philadelphia Athletics 1–0, pitching a 5 hitter. During his remarkable season Ford threw 29 complete games. He was the first Canadian-born pitcher to win 20 games in a season.

Behind Ford and the young pitchers the Yankees reached early heights that owners Farrell and Devery could not have expected. By mid–June they were in first place, one game ahead of the Philadelphia Athletics. The offense was sputtering along (producing a team batting average of .248 just as in 1909), but the Yankees were demons on the basepaths,

Russ Ford in on the mound at Hilltop Park. Note the apartment buildings beyond the outfield fence (National Baseball Hall of Fame Library, Cooperstown, N.Y.).

leading the AL in stolen bases with 288. Stallings proclaimed: "I have a better team than most people give me credit for having.... We are on top now. I don't know how we will stand when the season is finished, but I know that we are hustling hard and trying to win as many games as possible." The typical starting lineup from mid-season 1910 on was as follows: Daniels LF; Wolter RF; Chase 1B; Knight SS; LaPorte 2B; Cree CF; Austin 3B; Sweeney C; Pitcher.

In an unfortunate case of best laid plans going astray, Lou Criger was not the Yankees' primary catcher in 1910. Catcher Ed Sweeney, 21, who served as a fireman in his hometown of Chicago, inherited the starting role as Criger became ill with appendicitis. While Criger's playing time with the Yankees was insignificant, his influence was not as he helped instruct Sweeney on defensive techniques and handling the New York pitchers. "No, he hasn't caught many games for us but he has served the purpose for which I obtained him," was Stallings' comment. Criger's major league playing career came to an end but he contributed to baseball in far greater ways than could have been anticipated. Criger became ill again in 1914, falling victim to tuberculosis, and was hospitalized in Boston. Criger's health issues ruined him financially, forcing him out of his farm in Indiana, which was "mortgaged to the limit." A fund was started to help pay for Criger's medical care with former Yankee Dave Fultz and the Players' Fraternity taking part. The *Boston Daily Globe* reported: "It is hoped that a sufficient amount will be raised to provide for Criger's immediate needs, and, if his ailment yields to treatment ... to send him for a time to Arizona or to some other place where the climatic conditions are such that he will have a fair chance of ultimate recovery." That was achieved—but not without the help of AL president Ban Johnson and his league.

By 1923 the first steps of creating a pension fund for former major league players in need began. The American League initially set aside $50,000. Criger was relocated to Arizona and received medical assistance from this fund. Johnson's care and interest in Criger was fostered 20 years earlier, when he revealed an attempt by gamblers to "fix" the first World Series in 1903. Prior to the first game, Criger received a letter from the representative of a group of gamblers, indicating much money could be made for Criger and Red Sox pitching ace Cy Young should they take part and help lose one of the games. Criger turned the letter over to Johnson, and the plot was thwarted—thus major league baseball avoided a major gambling scandal years before the infamous "Black Sox" World Series of 1919. Criger recovered from the tuberculosis in Arizona and lived far longer than deemed possible when he was first hospitalized. He died at Tucson on May 14, 1934, at age 62, leaving his widow Belle, a daughter and four sons.

While Sweeney benefited from Criger's defensive tutorials, Criger, who held a lifetime .221 batting average, could not help Sweeney improve his hitting. Sweeney batted .200 in 1910. In this early era a catcher's defensive skills were valued over offensive statistics and Sweeney's pitiful performance at the plate could be tolerated when other Yankee batters were taking up the slack. Despite a .248 team average in 1910, notable contributions at the plate came from some of the players. Shortstop John Knight was the Yankee clean-up batter for good reason. Knight posted the best batting average of his 8-year career at .312. First baseman Hal Chase batted .290 and tied for the club lead in RBI with 73. Outfielder William Franklin "Birdie" Cree also knocked in 73 runs and posted a .287 average.

Birdie Cree was one of the bright spots on the roster during his tenure with the Yankees, the only major-league team for which he played. Of dispute is how he actually received the nickname "Birdie" that remained and essentially became his first name during his career. Educated as well as athletically-inclined, Cree obtained a teaching certificate prior to college in his native state of Pennsylvania and won a football scholarship to Penn State. A dislocated collarbone led to his playing baseball in college instead. Cree hit for the cycle in one game, supposedly causing a teammate to shout, "He's a bird!" as Cree rounded the bases.

Another version reports that Cree played semi-pro ball under the assumed name of "Burdee" and the name stuck. He graduated with a degree in forestry and joined the Yankees in 1908. Cree primarily played left field for the team from 1910 to 1911, batting .287 and .348, respectively, then .332 for the first 50 games of the 1912 season before sustaining a broken wrist courtesy of a fastball

Russ Ford, father of the Emery Ball (Library of Congress, Prints & Photographs Division, LC-DIG-ggbain-09132).

thrown by Walter Johnson, a future Hall of Fame pitcher for the Washington Senators. Cree returned in 1913 to lead all American League outfielders in fielding with a .988 average but appeared in only 77 games in 1914 while batting .309. Getting hit by the pitch seemed to affect Cree and he became less aggressive at the plate. Cree retired at the age of 32 in 1915, compiling a .292 batting average. Of the well-spoken, well-educated Cree, one writer has said: "He possessed an excellent command of the language, which later enabled him to call an umpire the most horrible and inhu-

Birdie Cree in 1910. He played his entire career (1908–1915) for the Yankees (National Baseball Hall of Fame Library, Cooperstown, N.Y.).

From left, third baseman Jimmy Austin, second baseman Frank LaPorte, first baseman Hal Chase, and shortstop John Knight in 1910 (*Chicago Daily News* negatives collection, SDN-056375, courtesy Chicago Historical Society).

man names without the arbiter comprehending." Upon retirement Cree pursued a career in banking.

On the other side of the Yankee outfield, right-fielder Harry Wolter contributed a .267 average. That was fine for Stallings considering Wolter's salary. "Wolter, who is playing right, has turned out a valuable $1,500 man," said Stallings. By mid-season the Yankees were in second place, 5 games behind the Athletics.

Other young Yankee pitchers—ones not named Vaughn and Ford—also contributed to the early season success in 1910. Jack Quinn went 18-12 with a 2.37 ERA and Jack Warhop managed a 14-14 record with a 3.00 ERA. "Managed" is a good word to describe the wins total of Warhop's entire Yankee career. Despite the batting attack of Knight, Chase, Cree and Wolter, a few close losses in 1910 gave Warhop a .500 record and run support would be lacking throughout his 8-year tenure on the Yankees. Warhop was nicknamed "Crab" for his surly disposition and the consistently weak offense of his team could have been a contributing factor.

Stallings' positive outlook in June was being severely tested two months later. By August 30th, the Yankees had fallen to 3rd place with a 68-50 won-lost record, 14½ games behind Philadelphia. The highlight—and lowlight—of the 1910 season came on that day. The first no-hitter in Yankee history was thrown by Tom Hughes, and he lost! Hughes had brief trials with the Yankees in 1906, 1907 and 1909 and was the fifth starter this season, behind Ford, Quinn, Warhop and Vaughn. Hughes posted a 7-9 record with a 3.50 ERA but reached

Tom, Terrific! Right-hander Tom Hughes, who threw the first no-hitter in Yankee history (with one important disclaimer) on August 30, 1910 (Library of Congress, Prints & Photographs Division, LC-DIG-ggbain-22481).

Veteran catcher Red Kleinow, the last remnant of the Yankees' 1904 pennant loss to the Red Sox, warms up at Hilltop Park. Kleinow had suffered a broken finger in 1908, leading to catcher Ed Sweeney seeing more playing time. In 1910, Kleinow had a sore arm, which meant he became the third-string catcher behind Sweeney and Fred Mitchell, a former pitcher who saw his only action as catcher in 1910. On May 26, 1910, Kleinow's contract was sold to the Red Sox. Kleinow's career ended in 1912, and he returned to New York as a resident, not a player. He lived at 570 West 156th Street, not far from his old stomping grounds at the Hilltop (National Baseball Hall of Fame Library, Cooperstown, N.Y.).

immortality (or mortality?) with his losing no-hitter. Hughes faced the 6th place Cleveland Indians in the second game of a double-header and didn't allow a hit or a walk for 9⅓ innings, but began to tire in the 10th and ended up losing 5–0 in the 11th. Fourteen thousand people had packed into Hilltop Park that Tuesday. Other than second baseman Nap Lajoie, batting .384, and first baseman George Stovall, at .261, the Indians lineup was not strong but all things considered Hughes' effort was noteworthy—at least through nine innings, and he was helped by some great fielding by the 6'2" shortstop Knight, considered quite tall for those days. The *New York Times* summed it up in this way: "Tom Hughes usually has one bad inning. Never did he come so close to ducking it as yesterday. Lucky for him that Jack Knight is as tall as two ordinary shortstops, because Long John went skyward for hoppers that most any other shortstop could only get by standing on a soap box....

"Hughes heaved the game of his life in the second clash, mowing down the enemy in order for nine innings. In that time twenty-eight men faced him, Austin's nightmarish toss to Chase in the seventh being the only reason why [a Cleveland baserunner] got to first base. In the tenth, Hughes weakened, and just got through by an eyelash. The eleventh saw [the Indians] rise in their might and whale the no-hit man for five singles and five runs. Hughes deserved a better finish after the way he had bent the Cleveland backs in their effort to bang the ball." This game was not Tom Hughes' only brush with glory. He resurfaced for the National League's Boston Braves in 1914 and won 16 games in both 1915 and 1916, leading the NL in relief wins each year. On June 16, 1916, Hughes pitched a second no-hitter, winning 2–0 over the Pittsburgh Pirates and striking out Honus Wagner to end the game.

The season slowly unraveled for the Yankees after Hughes' loss. The setting was Chicago, Monday, September 19th, as the Yankees were set to face the White Sox at Comiskey Park (the original Comiskey Park—recently opened on July 1st of this season, with a huge seating capacity for 32,000 compared to the 16,000 plus confines at Hilltop Park). The Yankees, in a game started by Jack Quinn, lost 1–0. They were in second place, but were 16 games out. Stallings was losing patience, not only with the team's poor record, but with first baseman Hal Chase, the team's star attraction. For his part, Chase was losing patience with the manager, and his growing dictatorial style as the Yankees failed to gain ground in the standings. Tension had been building for some weeks, as Stallings suspected Chase was working behind the scenes to undermine his authority in subtle, and not so subtle ways. Chase hoped owner Frank Farrell would fire Stallings. The manager thought Chase was "laying down" and giving a poor effort on the field. Things exploded after the loss to the White Sox as detailed in the *New York Times*: "Dissensions and open quarrels have split the team into factions. Last night the row took on a decidedly serious aspect when the players rode home from Comiskey's park, the men nearly coming to blows over the defeat at the hands of the White Sox.... Chase has been accused of quitting the team several times during the summer because he did not like the way Stallings was running things.... The charge that Chase is trying to oust Stallings has been going the rounds for some weeks, but in St. Louis ... Stallings openly accused Chase of double-crossing in the signals of the team. In order not to be interfered with from the bench Chase changed the signals of the team for certain plays and worked in a set of signals and called for the squeeze play when it proved fatal."

Considering these extracurricular events it was a miracle the New York team was only 16 games out. That would not be the case for long. By Wednesday, September 21, they lost 3 games to the White Sox, falling to 3rd, 17½ games out.

At that point George Stallings was no longer running the team. He had gone to New York to plead his case with owner Farrell, that Chase was detrimental to the Yankees and Chase should be traded or Stallings would resign. Following is the summary of a newspaper report that leaves no doubt Stallings fought a losing battle against the star first baseman: "When Mr. Stallings accused Hal Chase, the captain and first baseman of the New York Americans, of laying down, or deliberately losing games for the purpose of preventing the team from becoming a pennant winner, he made a very serious charge against Chase. One that demanded a most thorough and careful investigation. That has been conducted by the owners of the club, whose good name were at stake, assisted by the president and vice-president of the American league. President Johnson, the head of the American League, said: 'Stallings has utterly failed in his accusation against Chase. He tried to besmirch the character of a sterling player. Anybody who knows Hal Chase knows that he is not guilty of the accusations made against him, and I am happy to say that the evidence of the New York players given to vice-president Somers this morning showed Stallings up.'"

Stallings' accusations that Chase was not giving his best effort on the field were a charge that would echo throughout the career of "Prince Hal," gaining in pitch, and unfortunately in substance. It culminated in his involvement (if only on the periphery) in the Black Sox Scandal and his leaving organized baseball under a cloud of suspicion. At the time, American League president Ban Johnson was obviously eager to disbelieve any charges against Chase. He didn't want the prize jewel of the New York franchise tarnished and along with owners Farrell and Devery sided with Chase against Stallings. By Sept. 26, the Yankee owners forced Stallings to resign. He was replaced as manager by—Hal Chase! "What a way to run a ball club," was third baseman's Jimmy Austin's assessment of the situation years later. Chase led the team to a 9-2 record to end the season, where the Yankees sat 14½ out, finishing in second place to the Philadelphia Athletics.

Stallings' departure from Farrell's employment seemed to end amicably despite the controversy and strange turn of events. His contract technically did not expire until October 15th and he was paid in full through that date. "He expects to leave in a few days for a rest at his plantation in Georgia," reported the *New York Times*. Though Stallings was dismissed, he was not entirely disgraced. Stallings returned to lead the 1914 Boston Braves, who were in last place in the National League, to a World Series triumph—supposedly by slightly mellowing his managerial style and not through any dubious means this time—earning the nickname "The Miracle Man."

Chase's managerial appointment was rumored to be on an interim basis, with longtime Yankee scout Arthur Irwin directing the team's fortunes in 1911, but Chase's appointment soon became permanent. The captain was now the manager too. Could Prince Hal transform his team into the pennant-winning squad that fans, and management, were so eager to see take the field at Hilltop Park?

13

"Drawing Flies," 1911

Hal Chase was paid $6,000 to guide the Yankees in 1911. Under the headline "Big Salaries of Ball Players" the *Washington Post* announced: "Stars and Managers in Major Leagues Get All the Way from $1,000 to $25,000 a Year."

The team assembled in Athens, Georgia, on February 28th. New faces included third baseman Roy Hartzell, acquired from the St. Louis Browns for second baseman Frank LaPorte and third baseman Jimmy Austin. LaPorte was an excellent hitter and fielder in

A classic image of the 1911 team, forming the letters "NY," possibly taken during spring training. Notable players include pitcher Ray Caldwell (1), infielder/outfielder Roy Hartzell (2), pitcher Jack Quinn (3), outfielder Birdie Cree (4), first baseman Hal Chase (5), pitcher Ray Fisher (6), pitcher Russ Ford (7), pitcher Jack Warhop (8) and outfielder Harry Wolter (9) (Brown Brothers).

Manager Hal Chase wears a Yankee home uniform in 1911. Visible just above the elbow area are button holes for adding detachable sleeves to the uniform (National Baseball Hall of Fame Library, Cooperstown, N.Y.).

his day—posting a .281 average in 11 seasons—but at work in this transaction (other than Austin's .218 average in 1910) were 2 other factors: 1. Neither LaPorte nor Austin were friends of Chase and had been loyal to Stallings in 1909-1910. 2. Chase occasionally ran his patent play of scooping up a bunt and throwing to third to cut down an opposing base-runner only to find that Austin was not covering the bag. Chase addressed the issue of his less coordinated teammates—without humility: "I could make plays like that every day, only I am afraid to turn the ball loose because I might hit one of those dopes in the head." Later allegations of "throwing"

Batting practice at Hilltop Park in 1911, the year the team batting average was .272. Pitching was the major problem (Library of Congress, Prints & Photographs Division, LC-DIG-ggbain-09133).

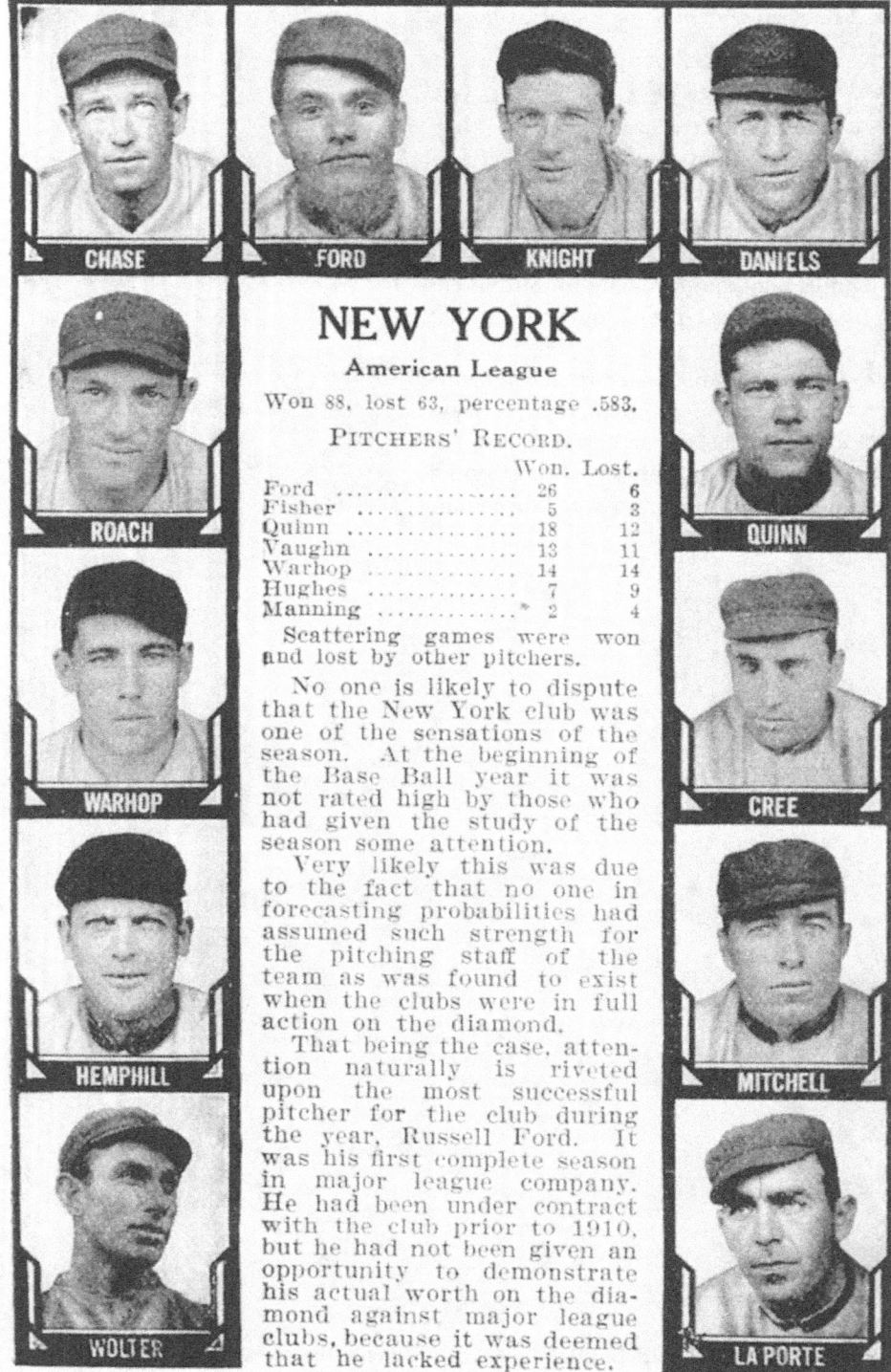

NEW YORK
American League

Won 88, lost 63, percentage .583.

PITCHERS' RECORD.

	Won.	Lost.
Ford	26	6
Fisher	5	3
Quinn	18	12
Vaughn	13	11
Warhop	14	14
Hughes	7	9
Manning	2	4

Scattering games were won and lost by other pitchers.

No one is likely to dispute that the New York club was one of the sensations of the season. At the beginning of the Base Ball year it was not rated high by those who had given the study of the season some attention.

Very likely this was due to the fact that no one in forecasting probabilities had assumed such strength for the pitching staff of the team as was found to exist when the clubs were in full action on the diamond.

That being the case, attention naturally is riveted upon the most successful pitcher for the club during the year, Russell Ford. It was his first complete season in major league company. He had been under contract with the club prior to 1910, but he had not been given an opportunity to demonstrate his actual worth on the diamond against major league clubs, because it was deemed that he lacked experience.

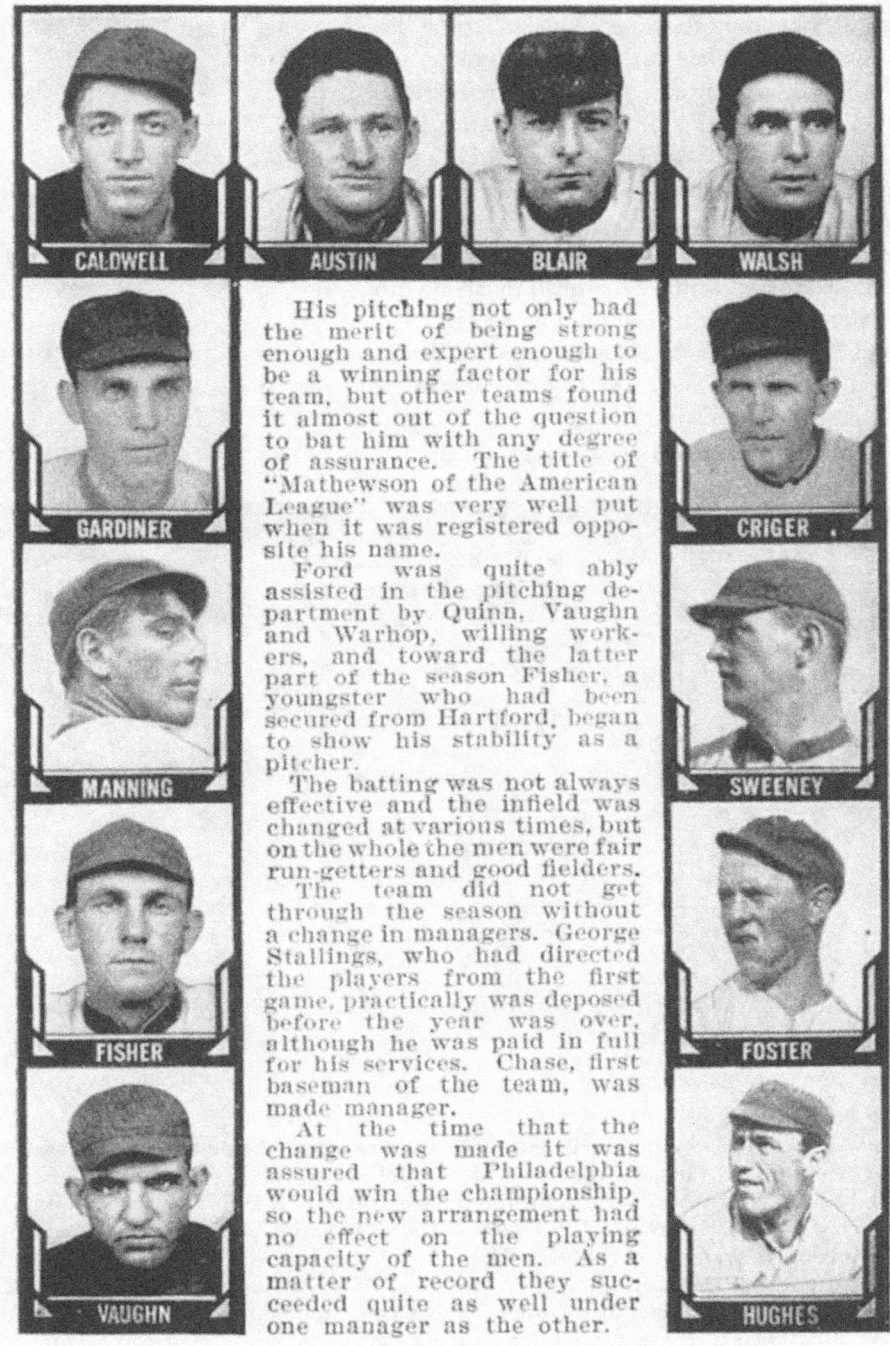

His pitching not only had the merit of being strong enough and expert enough to be a winning factor for his team, but other teams found it almost out of the question to bat him with any degree of assurance. The title of "Mathewson of the American League" was very well put when it was registered opposite his name.

Ford was quite ably assisted in the pitching department by Quinn, Vaughn and Warhop, willing workers, and toward the latter part of the season Fisher, a youngster who had been secured from Hartford, began to show his stability as a pitcher.

The batting was not always effective and the infield was changed at various times, but on the whole the men were fair run-getters and good fielders.

The team did not get through the season without a change in managers. George Stallings, who had directed the players from the first game, practically was deposed before the year was over, although he was paid in full for his services. Chase, first baseman of the team, was made manager.

At the time that the change was made it was assured that Philadelphia would win the championship, so the new arrangement had no effect on the playing capacity of the men. As a matter of record they succeeded quite as well under one manager as the other.

Opposite and above: Yankee team pages from 1911 edition of *The Spalding Guide*, recapping the 1910 season. *The Spalding Guide* was one of two annual guides produced by famous baseball players and sporting goods magnates/manufacturers—Albert Spalding and Al Reach. *The Spalding Guide* began in 1878, and Reach's *Official Baseball Guide* was first published in 1883. The publications merged in 1940 and were replaced by *The Sporting News Baseball Guide* later in the decade (Library of Congress).

games indicated Chase played in a carefree manner for reasons other than showing off his athletic skills.

Fourth-year Yankee Earle Gardner took over at second in 1911 and batted .263 while Roy Hartzell batted .296. Cree, at .348, Chase, hitting .315, and Wolter, at a .304 average, paced the Yankee hitting attack. Chase was ill with bronchitis in mid–May, missing two weeks but otherwise the starting players stayed injury-free. Fielding was a serious detriment, as the 1911 squad finished with a .949 percentage, 6th place in the 8-team AL. sixth was also exactly where the Yankees finished in 1911—with a won-lost record of 76-76. The Yankee mound performances were not up to par and prevented the team from being a serious contender.

Top: American League veteran Charlie Hemphill was nicknamed "Eagle Eye" for an ability to avoid swinging at bad pitches. He spent 4 seasons with the Yankees, providing good batting averages in 1908 (.297) and 1911 (.284) but very little in the interim with totals of .243 in 1909 and .239 in 1910. This photograph was taken in 1909 and shows the Yankees were wearing pinstripes on jackets long before they appeared on their uniforms (in 1912). These are the only pinstripes Hemphill would wear since he retired after the 1911 season (Library of Congress, Prints & Photographs Division, LC-DIG-ggbain-09246). *Bottom*: Pitcher Jack Quinn stands second from left in this 1911 team photograph. Two days after this picture was taken Quinn started a game against Washington Senators pitching ace Walter Johnson, with Quinn and the Yankees winning, 5–3. Quinn got his start in professional baseball as a spectator at a game in his native Pennsylvania. He threw a ball back to the catcher, hitting the mitt dead center. The manager of the visiting team offered Quinn a start in the team's next game and $5 for a win, $2.50 for a loss. Quinn was 18-12 in 1910 with a 2.37 ERA and 8-10 with a 3.76 ERA in 1911, primarily coming in from the bullpen. He won 247 games and saved 57 more during a 23-year career (Library of Congress, Prints & Photographs Division, LC-DIG-ggbain-09092).

Yankee third baseman Roy Hartzell in 1911. He toiled for the early Yankee teams from 1911 to 1916, moving among third base, second base and the outfield. Hartzell batted .296 in 1911, and his 91 RBI that season was the highest RBI total by any Yankee player during the first 13 years of the team's existence (Library of Congress, Prints & Photographs Division, LC-DIG-ggbain-09518).

Left: Harry Wolter was an important contributor to the Yankees in 1911, posting a .304 average in 122 games with 17 doubles, 15 triples, and 4 homers. Like teammate Hal Chase, he attended Santa Clara University and played for the Santa Clara "Broncos" from 1903 to 1906. Wolter first appeared in 1907 with the Cincinnati Reds, Pittsburgh Pirates and St. Louis Cardinals, playing sparingly in the outfield and pitching. He was acquired from the Red Sox before the 1910 season for a waiver fee of $1,500. The Yankees turned Wolter into a full-time outfielder because of his strong throwing arm, and he replaced Willie Keeler in right field. Wolter also set a Yankee record for outfielders by participating in 8 double plays in 1911. In 4 seasons with New York he batted .277 overall. Wolter was a native Californian, twice leading the Pacific Coast League in batting. He coached at Stanford University for 26 years and passed away in 1970 at the age of 86 (Library of Congress, Prints & Photographs Division, LC-DIG-ggbain-13195).
Right: Bob Williams, Yankee backup catcher to starter Ed Sweeney from 1911 to 1913 and one of the ever-changing faces on the roster during the earliest seasons. His first appearance in the major leagues came on Monday, July 3, 1911, at the age of 27, in a loss to the Philadelphia Athletics at Hilltop Park (one of 4 consecutive losses to the A's). Williams appeared in 20 games in 1911, batting .191. He finished his career with a .164 average in 46 games. The Yankees were the only major league team for which Williams would play (Library of Congress, Prints & Photographs Division, LC-DIG-ggbain-12240).

Ray "Slim" Caldwell, a 6'2" spitball specialist, pitched for the Yankees from 1910 to 1918, winning 14 games in 1911, 17 games in 1914 and 19 games in 1915. On August 24, 1919, in his debut with the Cleveland Indians, a bolt of lightning struck Caldwell. He recovered and got the final out of the game, defeating the Philadelphia A's, 2–1 (National Baseball Hall of Fame Library, Cooperstown, N.Y.).

Bobby Wallace, manager of the St. Louis Browns, in a pregame meeting with Yankee manager Hal Chase. The Veterans Committee elected Wallace to the Hall of Fame in 1953. Chase, whose life took more circuitous and tragic turns, will never be enshrined (Library of Congress, Prints & Photographs Division, LC-DIG-ggbain-09306).

Russ Ford, at 22-11, with a 2.27 ERA, was proving the emery pitch was still an effective weapon.

Ray Caldwell produced numbers indicative of a talented pitcher laboring on a mediocre team. Caldwell's won-lost record was 14-14 while he pitched 255 innings, allowing 240 hits. It was reported in the *New York Times* that "Up to June the team traveled along at a clip that threatened to make Chase's first year of management a sensation, but the pitching staff broke down completely...." The collapse included records of 12-13 by Warhop, 10-11 by Fisher, and 8-10 by Vaughn, the remainder of the starting rotation. Jack Quinn was relegated to a lesser role than in 1910, pitching 174 innings and falling to 8-10. Chase the manager was not unlike Chase the player, and he employed a loose reign with the club. Given the team record, it's no surprise attendance at Hilltop Park dropped to 3,954 persons a game, 302,440 total for the season. "They weren't drawing flies" was the comment of famed sportswriter Fred Lieb on the poor attendance at the Hilltop. The Yankees were still locked in competition for fan interest with the rival National League Giants, who were on their way to winning a pennant in 1911 (but losing the World Series to the Philadelphia Athletics in 6 games). Meanwhile, the small attendance and quiet crowds at Hilltop Park were indicative of a Yankee team still searching for its own identity and hoping to generate

Pitcher Harry Ables spent one season with the Yankees, 1911, after brief periods with the St. Louis Browns in 1905 and the Cleveland Indians in 1909. In 1911 he was 0-1 in 3 games with a 9.82 ERA, surrendering 16 hits in 11 innings, contributing to the team's pitching woes and ending his 3-year career (Library of Congress, Prints & Photographs Division, LC-DIG-ggbain-09048).

fan interest, but bordering on second-class status compared with John McGraw's Giants.

Hal Chase's major league managerial career came to a close on November 21, 1911. Chase went to the Yankee offices at 320 Fifth Avenue to resign but Farrell was attending a session of the New York Supreme Court, defending a financial case brought against him by former Yankee president Joe Gordon. Chase met Farrell during an adjournment at noon, saying, "I think managing is not my cup of tea, Frank." The *New York Times* commented: "As a manager Chase failed to show the expected and necessary qualifications. Like Larry Lajoie, Chase is one of baseball's greatest stars, and, like the big Frenchman, he lacks that essential something which makes real managers.

"His rule on the Hilltop, while it proved a disappointment at the finish, can hardly be charged against Chase, other than because he failed to enforce the discipline which was necessary.... [Farrell] realized as much as anybody that Chase was not the right man in the place, being too easy with the players." Knowing Chase's personality that should have been no surprise. Chase commented: "I have been treated most liberally by the club owners and most fairly by the fans, and I would prefer to remain in New York, even as a private in the ranks than to go elsewhere."

For the fourth time in five seasons the Yankees were facing a managerial change. Could anyone step in, take charge and save the sinking Yankee ship? And, more importantly, where would the search for a new "captain" begin?

14

HARRY IN THE HOUSE (OF HORRORS), 1912

Harry Wolverton was born on December 6, 1873, in Mount Vernon, Ohio. Thirty-nine years later to nearly the same day Wolverton was signed as the fifth manager in Yankee history. The 5'11", 205 pound Wolverton earned the nickname "Fighting Harry" for his competitiveness. While he labored in semi-pro baseball Wolverton's contract was once sold for $5. He was a good third baseman, making his major league debut on September 25, 1898, with the Chicago Cubs. He was traded to the Philadelphia Phillies in 1900 and, other than a brief stint with the Senators, stayed with the Phillies until 1904, batting above .300 two times. Wolverton managed the Oakland Oaks of the Pacific Coast League in 1910, bringing the team in with a second place finish. In 1911 the Oaks finished in third place, earning this comment from the *Los Angeles Times*: "Big grouch; sour on the world; sore because he cannot win the pennant, and a lot more stuff they saw about him. Just forget all of this for if he is any of it, which he is not, it may be because he was both a pitcher and a catcher once before he reformed and became a third baseman."

Philadelphia A's manager Connie Mack praised Wolverton when "Fighting Harry" was handed the Yankee managerial reigns for 1912: "Wolverton has a fine personality. He has a way peculiarly his own of getting along with ball players. If a man doesn't hustle, Wolverton will come down on him as hard as any manager. But he isn't a bulldozer by any means. He has just enough executive ability to make him a first-class manager." *Baseball Magazine* commented: "For one thing he has the entire respect and confidence of his men without resorting to the arbitrary methods which some of the managers employ. He is always quiet and pleasant in his ways, but he expects his orders to be obeyed and they are obeyed."

Wolverton dived right into his new job. "Yankee Infield Worries Manager" noted the *New York Times* on December 27, 1911. On paper, the Yankee infield, and their respective 1911 averages, read: Chase, 1B, .315; Gardner, 2B, .263; Hartzell, 3B, .296; and Knight, SS, .268. Not such a worrisome looking group but for Wolverton the main concern was defense. The same article continued: "Wolverton, it is said, wants to get rid of Jack Knight. The long, lanky player has good days and bad days in the infield, and Wolverton wants a more reliable man." Wolverton also believed Earle Gardner could not be relied on to start again at second base—the 1911 season being the only one in which Gardner appeared in more than 100 games. Instead of Gardner, Brooklyn-born George Washington "Hack" Simmons would be Wolverton's starting second baseman in 1912. Simmons was signed from the Rochester

Hustlers of the Eastern (later International) League. Rochester had won the division title in 1911 under the managerial leadership of former Yankee first baseman John Ganzel. Simmons last played major league baseball for the Detroit Tigers in 1910, batting .227. Simmons appeared in 110 games for the Yankees in 1912, batting .239. He returned to Rochester for 1913 and led the International League in batting average (.339), hits (185) and doubles (28), while scoring 99 runs, 54 more than he produced for the Yankees in 1912.

Backup second baseman Gardner appeared in 43 games in 1912, hitting .281 so Yankee fans might have been wondering why Simmons was needed in the first place. As for "Schoolboy" John Knight, he was traded to the Washington Senators for catcher Charles "Gabby" Street. Street would serve as the backup catcher to Ed Sweeney. Sweeney was still soldiering on as the regular catcher and now entering his fifth season with the Yankees. Rookie Jack Martin of Plainfield, New Jersey, was the starting shortstop. As the club prepared for the spring training trip to Atlanta on March 4, Wolverton said: "The club as it now stands looks to me like a pretty fair team. It got a good start last season, but met many reverses—in fact, serious reverses—but we hope to avoid hard luck this season."

Hard luck? Wolverton entered the 1912 season with high hopes (and unrealistic expectations) for success. As fate would have it, the 1912 Yankee club went 50–102, finishing in last place. The season began on a sour note on Thursday, April 11th—a 5–3 loss to the Red Sox at Hilltop Park. Hippo Vaughn, being used by Wolverton as a reliever this year, got into the opener in New York on April 12, 1912, against Boston and Joe Wood, recording the last two outs in the ninth inning after Ray Caldwell surrendered four runs, giving Boston a 5–3 win. From that point on, Vaughn was 2–8 with an ERA of 5.14 and one shutout, until June 26, when New York sold him to Washington for the waiver price.

While the 1908 New York team had more losses (103) the pitiful 1912 edition set a club record for lowest winning percentage with .329 (a statistic that seems to have no chance of being eclipsed). Pitcher Russ Ford had the dubious distinction of losing 21 games (winning 13) while pitcher Jack Warhop won 10 and lost 19. Frightening statistics as these men were the top starters on the team.

A fastball thrown by Senators pitcher Walter Johnson broke outfielder Birdie Cree's wrist. Cree, batting .332 at the time, was limited to 50 games played in 1912. Harry Wolter's finger injury left the team without another potent bat for just about the entire season. Hal Chase* and outfielder Bert Daniels both batted .274 to lead all starting players while Wolverton found it necessary to play 8 games at third base and pinch-hit 26 times. Wolverton batted .300 in his limited duty and might have started at third base if not for Roy Hartzell batting a capable .272 while also taking his turns in the Yankee outfield. The 1912 Yankee squad did establish a major league record for steals of home plate, with 18 overall. Steals were needed as the team batting average was .259—far below the .272 pace of 1911—and 5th place in team batting average for 1912 in the 8 team AL. The 50 cent asking price for grandstand seats at Hilltop Park must have seemed like highway robbery for fans being subjected to the nightmare-like 1912 season. In fact, attendance fell to 242,194 in 1912.

As the 1912 season developed into a hell for Harry Wolverton and the New York team plunged to the depths, owner Frank Farrell was daydreaming about replacing ancient Hilltop Park—with a new baseball field in the Bronx. Farrell had found a site in the Kingsbridge

---

*Wolverton later said he had a trade in place involving Chase going to the Chicago White Sox in exchange for star players. The deal somehow disintegrated and Wolverton, out of "respect" for the players involved, did not reveal the identities of the probable players from the White Sox.

section at West 225th Street and Broadway. In fact, it was much more than daydreaming. The lease on Hilltop Park was expiring and Farrell was eager to build an improved park to accommodate and bring in more fans. Of course, both the team as well as the field they played upon were in dire need of improvement before Farrell could hope for an increased fan base. According to the *New York Times*: "President Frank J. Farrell of the Yankees said yesterday that work on grading the site for his new baseball park at 225th Street and Broadway would be resumed next week. Some work was done last fall in filling in a creek which runs through the grounds, but the work was stopped when cold weather set in. Temporary tracks will be built to the edge of the site for the accommodation of the dirt trains. The dirt which is to be used for filling in will be taken from the excavation at the Grand Central Terminal, on Forty-second street."

What might have been: Frank Farrell's proposed site for a baseball field for the Yankees near the bank of Spuyten Duyvil Creek, a mile-long channel connecting the Hudson and Harlem rivers, which separates Manhattan from The Bronx. Spuyten Duyvil is Dutch in origin, seemingly translated as either "devil's whirlpool," because of the rough current during high tide, or "to spite the devil." The latter translation emanates from a story by writer Washington Irving. It featured a Dutch trumpeter vowing to swim across the creek's treacherous waters during the British attack on New Amsterdam (New York) to "spite the devil." The neighborhood, Marble Hill, was formerly part of Manhattan island. The canal was constructed in 1895, separating the Marble Hill area, and additional filling in of a creek attached Marble Hill to the mainland of The Bronx. It is still considered part of Manhattan for political and administrative purposes (Library of Congress, Prints & Photographs Division).

Giants manager John McGraw and Yankee manager Harry Wolverton on Sunday, April 21, 1912, before an exhibition game between the Yankees and the rival NL Giants. McGraw looks positively jovial in comparison to his usual expression in later photographs taken with members of the Yankees (McGraw with Babe Ruth being a notable example). Since the Yankees were fielding a succession of lousy teams, McGraw perceived them as less of a threat to the Giants' New York fan base. In this particular instance, Wolverton is the one with the grim expression, reflective of the awful 1912 season (Library of Congress, Prints & Photographs Division, LC-DIG-ggbain-11221).

The state of the Yankee franchise in 1912—as well as that of his own career—is captured by the expression on Pat Maloney's face. Maloney, an outfielder, logged a .215 average in 25 games played in 1912, his only season in the major leagues (Library of Congress, Prints & Photographs Division, LC-DIG-ggbain-12162).

Second baseman Hack Simmons didn't do much "hacking" for the Yankees in 1912 or in his one other AL season with the Tigers or two seasons with the Baltimore Terrapins of the Federal League. He ended a 4-season career with a .246 average (Library of Congress, Prints & Photographs Division, LC-DIG-ggbain-13407).

So ongoing construction at a now-famous New York landmark was proving useful in Farrell's plan to escape the old wooden confines of the Hilltop. An older version of Grand Central terminal existed but it was demolished in 1910, with a temporary station in the Grand Central Palace at Lexington Avenue and 43rd Street being used until 1912. The "new" Grand Central Terminal officially opened at 12:01 A.M. on Sunday, February 2, 1913.

Farrell's planned new ballpark for the Yankees was another story. The Yankees did not become "The Bronx Bombers" under Farrell's reign, but the end for Hilltop Park came in 1912. The Yankees played their last game in the old field on October 5th, defeating the Senators 8–6 behind a 3-run homer from Chase, the last home run ever hit on that field. During his eight year career at the Hilltop, Chase hit 14 home runs. A modest statistic by today's standards, but it stands for all time as the top home run total at Hilltop Park.

Yankee veteran Hal Chase in 1912. He was the first star of the franchise to appear in the now-famous pinstriped uniform (National Baseball Hall of Fame Library, Cooperstown, N.Y.).

Yankee co-owner Frank Farrell and manager Harry Wolverton (National Baseball Hall of Fame Library, Cooperstown, N.Y.).

DANIELS

MALONEY.

One other notable event occurred among the wreckage of the 1912 season: pinstripes first appeared on the Yankee uniform (in black as opposed to the navy blue of future seasons). The modern interlocking "NY" logo was on the left side of the uniform shirt in blue (it's first appearance in that location since the original "NY" design in 1905). The home uniform consisted of a white shirt and pants, a white cap with a blue "NY" monogram, and blue stockings with maroon stripes. The 1912 road uniform was of a grey color shirt and pants without pinstripes.

Harry Wolverton had a "woe is me" approach to the sad showing of 1912. "If the New York team had not been broken up from the start of the season, the Yanks would be right up at the top now...," he lamented. Despite some unexpected setbacks, Wolverton would not be managing the Yanks in 1913. Realizing the sour turn of events was not entirely the fault of the manager, Farrell deliberated for a while before finally dismissing Wolverton on November 6, 1912. The 1912 Yankees were the only major-league team Harry Wolverton managed. He returned to the Pacific Coast League, taking the helm of the Sacramento Wolves in 1913 and 1914. That team went bankrupt in 1915 and, staying in the vicinity, Wolverton signed on to manage the San Francisco Seals for two more years. "Fighting Harry" died in Oakland, California, on February 4, 1937. He was 63 years old.

Postscript: Another Ty Cobb?

Regarding outfielder Guy Zinn, former teammate Chet (Red) Hoff said: "I thought he was going to be another Ty Cobb! He had everything [going for him]." Zinn was born on February 13, 1887, in Hollbrook, West Virginia. He first appeared in the big leagues on September 11, 1911, debuting with the Yankees at the age of 24. Hoff and Zinn only appeared in a handful of games in 1911 but Hoff's prediction for the left-handed hitting Zinn seemed to hold true leading into the 1912 season. An article in *Baseball Magazine* contained a picture of Zinn on page 2 entitled: "New Stars in Baseball." The subheading read in part: "Every Season has its Particular Prodigies, Its Miniature Ty Cobbs and Christy Mathewsons."

Zinn was the starting right fielder for the Yankees in 1912, batting .262 with 6 home runs and 55 RBI, also hitting 15 doubles, 10 triples, drawing 50 walks and swiping 17 bases. His 6 home runs tied the then-existing Yankee club record (first baseman John Ganzel in 1904 and second baseman Jimmy Williams in 1905 also hit 6). It is not surprising to see

Opposite top: A busy man: Outfielder Bert Daniels played left, center and right field for the Yankees from 1910 to 1913. In 1912, Daniels became the first Yankee player to hit for the cycle. It happened on Thursday, July 25, during a 6–4 loss to the White Sox at Hilltop Park. Daniels starred in football and baseball at Bucknell University, the University of Notre Dame, and Villanova University under his birth name while simultaneously playing semipro and minor league ball under assumed names. Daniels had trouble hitting curve balls in 1910, finishing with a .253 average, but he rebounded to bat .286 in 1911 and .274 in 1912, the highest averages of his 5-season career. After leaving baseball, Daniels became a building inspector in New Jersey (Library of Congress, Prints & Photographs Division, LC-DIG-ggbain-13805). *Opposite bottom*: Pat Maloney, warming up. The highlight of Maloney's career occurred on June 30, 1912, at an exhibition game the Yankees played in Providence, Rhode Island, against a Class B team called the Brockton Shoemakers. A local dignitary presented Maloney, who also resided in Rhode Island, with a gold watch. Maloney had a modest career but lived a long and full life, passing away at the age of 91 in Pawtucket, Rhode Island (Library of Congress, Prints & Photographs Division, LC-DIG-ggbain-12164).

Top: Harry Wolverton, who was a playing manager at times in 1912, warms up with the team in pregame drills at Hilltop Park (Library of Congress, Prints & Photographs Division, LC-DIG-ggbain-10419). *Bottom*: Dismissed! Harry Wolverton leaves the Yankee offices at 320 Fifth Avenue after his firing on November 6, 1912 (Library of Congress, Prints & Photographs Division, LC-DIG-ggbain-06464).

Top: Outfielder Guy Zinn at Hilltop Park in 1912 (Library of Congress, Prints & Photographs Division, LC-DIG-ggbain-11313). *Bottom*: Utility infielder Bill Stumpf (his name is misspelled on the photograph) warms up before a game in 1912. Stumpf appeared at first base, second base, shortstop, third base, and, for one game, in the outfield during the 1912 season, batting .240. His overall fielding percentage of .876 means he wasn't helping with his bat or glove in his brief appearances. Stumpf did prove useful to the Yankees on May 13, 1913, when they traded him and outfielder Jack Lelivelt to Cleveland for shortstop Roger Peckinpaugh. The 22-year-old Peckinpaugh became one of the few star players for the Yankees in the midteens and would remain with New York through the 1921 season (Library of Congress, Prints & Photographs Division, LC-DIG-ggbain-11311).

Zinn's name in the cleanup spot in Yankee box scores from the 1912 season. On Friday, May 24th, at Hilltop Park, Zinn hit a first inning home run that began the scoring in an 11–6 Yankee victory against the Washington Senators. The *New York Times* described the action this way: "Zinn started the Hilltoppers to victory when he collided with one of [pitcher] Walker's slants and gave the ball a ride into the centre-field bleachers, chasing Quinn and Daniels home ahead of himself. This splash upset the nerves of [third baseman] Eddie Foster and Catcher Ainsmith, and they made bungles which, with two more Yankee hits and a sacrifice fly, made the Washington disaster complete." On August 15, 1912, Zinn stole home twice in a 5–4 win against Detroit—two stolen bases of the previously mentioned Yankees' major-league record of 18 steals of home for the 1912 season. Zinn shares the record of stealing home twice with 11 other players—Joe Jackson, Honus Wagner and Vic Power among them.

For all his accomplishments, Zinn was sold to the National League's Boston Braves in December 1912. In 1913 Zinn was batting .297 for the Braves but a salary dispute resulted in Zinn "jumping" to the Federal League's Baltimore Terrapins before the 1914 season—where he played left field and batted .280 in 61 games. On July 12, 1914, Zinn broke his left leg while sliding into third base. Typically, the productive Zinn had just doubled a run home in the ninth inning and attempted to make third base on the hit. The *Washington Post* described the injury: "His foot caught in the bag, and he was twisted in such a manner as to snap the bone at the ankle ... [Zinn] was one of the best players on the Baltimore club." Yankee teammate Chet Hoff recalled: "There was a ballplayer I felt sorry for ... he broke his leg and that was the end of Guy Zinn." Zinn did play one last season in 1915 for the Terrapins, batting .269—the exact total batting average for his 5 year career. He toiled for a variety of minor league teams upon retirement. Ty Cobb? Not quite, but Zinn accomplished a great deal in his short, injury marred tenure in the major leagues.

15

"A Bunion and an Onion," 1913

Change was in the air for the Yankees in December of 1912—in the dugout as well as on the field. During 1911, a fire had destroyed much of the Polo Grounds, the home of the NL's New York Giants. They temporarily played at Hilltop Park that year, sharing home field with the Yankees through the end of May. In 1913, the favor was returned. While Frank Farrell's new dream site for his team at 225th Street and Broadway was being prepared, the Yankees left their old field at the Hilltop to become co-tenants with the Giants in a newly refurbished Polo Grounds. The field in which both New York teams would now play was the fifth version of the Polo Grounds—built of concrete and steel in place of the wooden-seated structure that previously existed.

As for the dugout change, Frank Farrell (co-owner Big Bill Devery is hardly ever cited in the team's business transactions) enlisted Frank Chance—a former star first baseman of the Chicago Cubs and future Hall-of-Famer—for Yankee manager. Chance was a tough player who earned the nicknames of "The Peerless Leader" and "Husk" while winning four NL pennants and two World Series titles in 1907-1908. He planned to retire in California but was lured back to the major leagues by a lucrative offer first reported to be in the $20,000 range for the season. That figure was disputed by Farrell. Most likely it was $18,000 plus some percentage of the New York club profits. Reports that those percentages were 10 percent of the club's stock plus 5 percent of the net profits of the team were "pipe dreams pure and simple" according to the *Boston Globe* of January 12, 1913. AL president Ban Johnson, while not brokering the deal outright, had a hand in the Yankees' acquisition of Chance. Chance was technically still property of the Cubs, and the AL and NL—working in rare harmony—met at the Waldorf-Astoria hotel to arrange an agreement, albeit a sort of back alley deal that was somewhat typical of the way baseball business could be run in those days.

Essentially it was resolved that all AL teams waived claim to shortstop Red Corriden, who played with Detroit in 1912, so that Corriden was acquired by the Cincinnati Reds, owned by August "Garry" Herrmann, for $8,000. Herrmann was also president of major league baseball's National Commission from 1903 to 1920, serving as a de facto type of baseball commissioner before that position became official in 1920. Cincinnati then sent Corriden to the Cubs. For allowing Corriden to fall into the NL's hands in the first place, Chance was allowed to leave the NL and jump to the AL to negotiate with Farrell.

"The Peerless Leader" was expected to jump-start an anemic Yankee team. On a suggestion by Yankee business manager/chief of scouting Arthur Irwin, Chance held spring training drills in Hamilton, Bermuda. In doing so, his club became the first major league baseball team to train outside the United States. Chance was in great shape to make the trip—which had not been the case months earlier. The right-handed hitting Chance was known for crowding the plate. He had been hit by so many pitches that he suffered from intense headaches, causing him to remove himself from the Cubs' lineup late in his career. These problems led to a visit to Dr. W.G. Frolich, a "nerve specialist and surgeon" at 83 East 60th Street in Manhattan. After an operation on Chance, Dr. Frolich declared: "I will stake my reputation in asserting that Frank Chance is in better health now than for six years. The operation I performed ... completely cured him of a nervous trouble which had caused frequent headaches and compelled him to give up ball playing. This ailment had been caused by being hit on the head by pitched balls." No word exists on the exact nature of the procedure. Judging by the following comment, Dr. Frolich's surgery certainly had a major effect on Chance's brain: "I will win the pennant for you before I get through in New York," Chance declared to Frank Farrell soon after the operation. With the team Chance inherited even a .500 record seemed unlikely.

There were new faces on the pitching staff—right-hander Ray Keating being one—obtained by scout Irwin from a minor league club in the New England League. Keating's presence, and that of left-hander Al Schulz, was due to the fact two familiar faces among the Yankee pitchers had left the club: Jack Quinn's contract was sold to Rochester—one of many transactions between the Yankees and the upstate International League team—and Hippo Vaughn's contract was sold to the Washington Senators, after former Yankee manager Clark Griffith, now guiding Washington's club, put in a waiver claim. Keating was referred to as a "saliva" ball pitcher, meaning yet another spitball pitcher had joined New York's AL team. Keating joined a Yankee staff that included spitballers Ray Caldwell and Ray Fisher, also right-handed pitchers. The Yankees seemed to be cornering the market again on starting spitball throwers, just like the days of Chesbro and Orth.

Chance and the first group of Yankees, including Ford, Warhop, Fisher, Keating, Sweeney and Chase, set sail from Pier 42 on the Hudson River and arrived in Bermuda on February 24th. A second group including Cree, Wolter, Daniels, and pitchers Chet Hoff and Schultz, departed on March 1st. The Yankees played games in Bermuda against the minor-league Jersey City Skeeters, who had leased the playing grounds at Hamilton, Bermuda. The field was actually designed for playing the British game of Cricket, and Cricket itself shared with baseball a supposed origin in the older English game of Rounders. The Yankees took six games against the Skeeters, against three losses, and Chance anticipated more practice for his pitchers on the steamship journey home, owing to a large area that allowed throwing. Rough waters on the return trip led to seasickness for almost every member of the team and no practice at all.

Unlike Harry Wolverton's worry over the Yankee second base and shortstop combination a year earlier, Chance found an in-house solution to the Yankee starting infield alignment. Chance himself would play first base, with Hal Chase shifting to second, really the first time at the position since Chase's "college" career. Twenty-seven year-old Claud Derrick, who showed "great improvement in both batting and fielding" according to the *New York Times*, was selected to play shortstop. (Derrick batted .241 for the Philadelphia Athletics in limited duty in 1912 so Chance and the New York team as a whole hoped the *Times*' assessment proved accurate!) The Yankees "lifted the lid"—in the words of the *New York Times*—on the 1913 season not in their home borough of Manhattan but across the East River, in Brooklyn. The reason? The Yankee and Dodgers were playing

15. "A Bunion and an Onion," 1913

Yankee owner Frank Farrell signs Frank Chance to manage the Yankees (*Chicago Daily News* negatives collection, SDN-058117, courtesy Chicago Historical Society).

an exhibition game to celebrate the opening of Ebbets Field, the Dodgers' new $750,000 ballpark.

The Brooklyn team was known as the Superbas (no kidding) in the late 1890s, before being re-christened as the Robins in 1914, finally becoming known as the Dodgers (a shortened version of the term "trolley dodgers"—an early reference by dwellers of Manhattan to their Brooklyn neighbors, due to all the surface street car lines that ran through the Brooklyn borough by 1890). The new field was named after Brooklyn owner Charles Ebbets. Considering the interior features—such as a floor tiled with the likeness of the stitches of a baseball plus a chandelier consisting of 12 baseball-bat arms holding 12 globes shaped like a baseball—a construction cost estimated at $750,000 sounded like a real bargain. There were 25,000 fans in attendance. The Yankee lineup for that game was as follows: Bert Daniels, RF, Harry Wolter, CF, Roy Hartzell, 3B, Birdie Cree, LF, Hal Chase, 2B, Frank Chance, 1B, Ed Sweeney, C, Claud Derrick, SS, Ray Caldwell, P. According to the *Times*: "Caldwell has been chosen to oppose Nap Rucker and Brooklyn is confident that the Yankees will be unable to hit the Dodger southpaw." Dodger fans went home happy as 28-year-old George "Nap" Rucker, of Crabapple, Georgia, stifled the Yankee hitters and Brooklyn won 3–2.

Things did not improve for New York once the regular season began. After the home

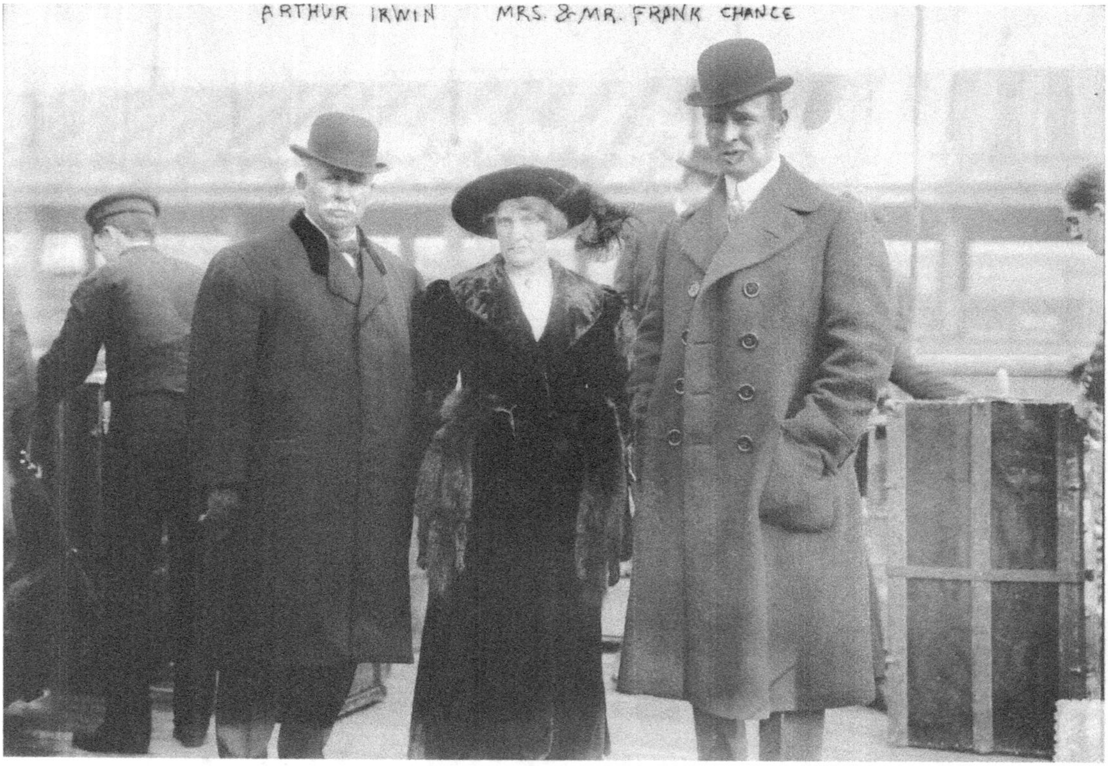
ARTHUR IRWIN
MRS. & MR. FRANK CHANCE

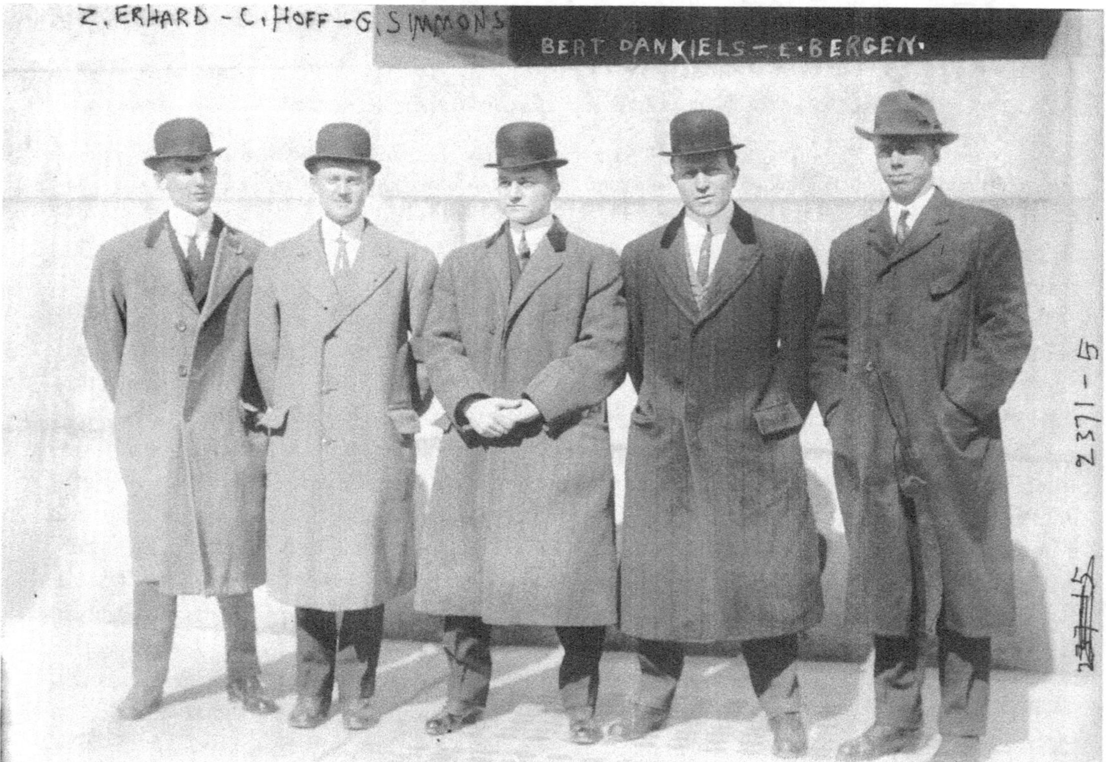
Z. ERHARD - C. HOFF - G. SIMMONS
BERT DANIELS - E. BERGEN.
2371-5

15. "A Bunion and an Onion," 1913   107

Bird's-eye view in Brooklyn: It's a tough to see him but that's Yankee starting pitcher Ray Caldwell on the mound, pitching the first game ever at Ebbets Field in Brooklyn. The Brooklyn lineup that day included future Yankee manager and Hall-of-Famer Casey Stengel, leading off and playing center field. Stengel scampered around the bases in the 1st inning, hitting an inside-the-park home run for Brooklyn, the first home run in the history of Ebbets Field and the run that helped defeat the Yankees, 3–2 (Library of Congress, Prints & Photographs Division, LC-DIG-ggbain-12804).

opener at the Polo Grounds on Thursday, April 17th, a 9–3 loss to the Senators, the Yankees were in 7th place, though only 2½ games out. The next day brought another loss to Washington, 7–5, and the Yanks were in 8th place, dead last in the AL. In last place they would remain, until July 13th (whereupon they would elevate themselves to 7th for two days before returning to last place again on Tuesday, July 15th—a 3–0 loss to the Browns in St. Louis with Ray Keating starting). They were 33 games behind the first place Philadelphia

Opposite top: Yankee scout/business manager Arthur Irwin and Mr. and Mrs. Chance prepare to sail to Bermuda for spring training (Library of Congress, Prints & Photographs Division, LC-DIG-ggbain-12469). *Opposite bottom*: Left-handed pitcher Chet Hoff, second from left, pitched sparingly for the Yankees from 1911 to 1913. Regarding spring training in 1913, Hoff said the temperature difference between New York harbor and Hamilton, Bermuda, was noticeable. He recalled: "When we got off that boat, about 7 o'clock in the morning, we had all of our heavy coats. When we hit that Hamilton field, up the steps, they had a big thermometer there—it read 90 degrees!" While it is representative of the attire, this photograph was likely taken the previous year of 1912, indicated by the presence of second baseman Hack Simmons, middle, and Hoff's friend, Eddie Bergen, far right, who joined the team for spring training in Atlanta during 1912. Hoff and Bergen previously played together on a semipro team in Yonkers, New York (Library of Congress, Prints & Photographs Division, LC-DIG-ggbain-10171).

This photograph was taken on Thursday, April 17, at the home opener at the Polo Grounds. Manager Frank Chance is being honored with a floral wreath centered around a framed print of Chance with the words "Frank Chance, The Peerless Leader, New York Americans, 1913." It is presented by men in uniforms that reveal the political background of Yankee co-owner Big Bill Devery. Note the word "TAMMANY" printed on the pinstriped uniforms. The Yankees lost to the Senators that day, 9–3 (Library of Congress, Prints & Photographs Division, LC-USZ62-133639).

Athletics. Philadelphia featured the baseball crushing skills of third baseman Frank "Home Run" Baker, .337, 12 home runs, 117 RBI and great pitching from left-hander Eddie Plank, 18–10, 2.60 ERA, and Charles "Chief" Bender, 21–10, 2.21 ERA. The Yankees, meanwhile, were not crushing anything, except their fans' spirits, as they were on their way to a team batting average of .237.

The lack of talent on the New York roster and Frank Chance's managerial style combined to make 1913 an awful footnote in Yankee history—forgettable for both players and fans alike. Following is an excerpt from an interview with former major league pitcher Chet "Red" Hoff, who played on the Yankees for parts of the 1911–1913 seasons. I conducted this interview on November 18, 1995. Hoff received his nickname due to his hair color and provided an engaging and entertaining afternoon of remembrances...

> Q: In 1913 Frank Chance was your manager. What do you remember about Chance?
> A: He was no good. He was no good to me and he was no good to the players. The players didn't like him. None of the ballplayers got along with Chance. They did everything to discourage him. In practice, if they did get on base, they'd never get further than second base. They'd start to steal second and would overrun [the base], slide over. I didn't think he would last a year.

Q: So Chase and Chance didn't like each other very much?
A: They didn't get along. No.
Q: Do you remember spring training in Bermuda that year?
A: I went to Bermuda. Oh, that was a wonderful trip. What a beautiful trip. Everything was perfect. We were there thirty days, and we didn't see a drop of rain.

Anyway, first thing—Chase kidded him [Chance]. Chase made a bluff that he hurt himself out at practice. He had to get a bicycle. He couldn't practice. He said he had to have that bicycle to ride around and get in shape. He did that to get Chance mad, to get his goat. So that's the way it went on.
Q: Do you believe any of the stories about Chase gambling or throwing games on the team?
A: I never heard anything about that. I never saw anything suspicious going on. I never saw him make an error.

Poor pitching records (a ongoing theme) in 1913 were only part of the problem. Ray Fisher and Russ Ford posted the most wins on the Yankee staff, with 12 each. Unfortunately Fisher lost 16 and Ford lost 18 (while posting a 2.66 ERA). Double-figure defeats were common on the 1913 Yankee pitching staff as the following numbers attest: Al Schulz: 7 wins, 13 losses; Ray Keating: 6 wins, 12 losses; George McConnell: 4 wins, 15 losses. The Yankees were on their way to a 57-94 record and 7th place finish in 1913. The Hal Chase experiment ended with Roy Hartzell taking over at second base. In essence, the Hal Chase experiment ended in a more definitive way as well. Chance, a disciplinarian by nature, clashed with the free-spirited first baseman Chase on and off the field. Chase and Chance did not hide their hatred for each other. Chance also suspected Chase was mishandling plays for the purpose of "throwing games," and accused him of this in front of newspaper reporters. In addition, while Dr. Frolich's surgical procedure had cured Chance's headaches, there was a residual problem—deafness in his left ear. Chase openly mocked Chance in front of the other players, always when the manager's deaf ear was turned. Chance was alerted to this by catcher Ed Sweeney. Enraged, Chance told Chase: "Get out. You'll never wear that uniform again!"

On the night of Saturday, May 31, 1913, in one of the worst trades in Yankee history, Chase was sent to the Chicago White Sox for first baseman William Baker "Babe" Borton and infielder Rollie Zeider. Zeider appeared in only 50 games due to bunions (a swollen, painful bump in the joint that connects the big toe to the foot) batting .233. Borton was even worse—a .130 average in 33 games as Yankee first baseman. Sportswriter Mark Roth, later a business assistant for the Yankees, wrote this immortal line: "Chance traded Chase for a bunion and an onion."

In analyzing the trade of Hal Chase to the White Sox, two things are clear: 1. Frank Chance believed in addition by subtraction. 2. The two players obtained—no matter their statistical contributions—could never be equal to Chase in the eyes of New York fans. The New York sportswriters knew Chance and Chase could not peacefully co-exist, and that Chase's career trajectory in Yankee uniform had reached it's nadir, but the trade could only make their task more grim, as they were faced with the prospect of covering a bad team bereft of talent and hope. In fairness to Chance, Chase was batting .212 at the time of the trade but in Rollie Zeider and Babe Borton Chance misjudged badly on what he thought the Yankees were obtaining from the White Sox. In limited duty in 1912, his first year in the major leagues, Borton batted .371 and fielded well at first base. Zeider, who entered major league baseball and joined the White Sox in 1910, had compiled batting averages of .217, .253, and .245 leading up to the 1913 season.

Zeider's average at the time of the trade (.350), and Chance's anger toward Hal Chase, blinded Chance into making the deal. Borton was batting .275 with Chicago before the trade, but his .130 contribution to the Yankees only added to backlash from the fans who still held Chase in high esteem. As Zeider's "disability" from bunions became evident and Borton proved to be far from another "Prince" Hal, Frank Chance issued a complaint—one that claimed damaged goods were received from Chicago. The *Washington Post* reported on July 22, 1913: "No official action will be taken by the American League in connection with Frank Chance's complaint, charging the Chicago Americans with misrepresenting the physical condition of Zeider and the playing ability of Borton, for whom Chance traded Hal Chase, [American League] President Ban Johnson announced today. 'It will be impossible to take action compensating New York for alleged loss,' said Johnson, 'for the simple reason that Chance wanted Zeider more than any other [player]. He had his choice of at least six Chicago players, and picked Zeider and Borton. Zeider was playing regularly with the Sox at the time of the trade.'"

Why is this man smiling? Frank Chance had little reason to do so during his tenure as Yankee manager (National Baseball Hall of Fame Library, Cooperstown, N.Y.).

Both Zeider and Borton lasted with the Yankees only through the end of the 1913 season, Zeider joining the Chicago Federal League team for 1914. Borton closed out a brief 4 season major-league career in 1916, leaving behind a .270 batting average, 4 home runs and 136 RBI. Chase, despite being referred to as a "temperamental prima donna" in a *Chicago Daily Tribune* headline in mid-season, batted .286 for the White Sox. Meanwhile, rumors flew that Chance would quit the Yankees when the season ended. His response: "I have not the slightest inclination of resigning as manager of the New York club. Instead, I am working and planning to put a real pennant contender into the American League next season. It's slow work to be sure, for I have to go into the bushes for new material, and then develop it for the big league."

On a lighter note—if such a thing was possible amidst the disaster—Chance found time to become an actor, playing a "leading part in a moving picture scenario." The film was titled *Baseball's Peerless Leader* and featured actress Gwendolyn Pates as well as Yankee players Ed Sweeney, Bert Daniels and Roy Hartzell in cameo roles. English-born Leopold Wharton helmed the film, which was shot at the Polo Grounds and a studio in Jersey City, N.J., where Chance rehearsed his role. The 35 mm silent film is described as a 2-reel romantic drama. (Highlights of the 1913 season were certainly not an option.) Wharton went on to direct slightly more significant films, and, in 1914, he and his brother Theodore established "The Whartons, Incorporated" at Ithaca, New York, becoming the first directors to establish their own studios as independent producers. It is not known if any copies of *Baseball's Peerless Leader* survive to this day.

While the Yankee team was in disarray, hope for a new permanent home field burned bright. Basic construction at the site of the proposed new park in the Bronx continued into the 1913-1914 off-season. On January 12th, 1914, the *New York Times* reported: "The grading has been finished and the infield has been built. The area of President Farrell's new park will be the largest in the major leagues. The outfield fences will be so far from the home plate that it will be impossible to bat the ball out of the park. The distance from the home plate to the center field fence will be more than 300 yards ... the builders plan for a seating capacity for 30,000 people." Building such a colossal stadium was a huge venture and it could not be completed before the 1914 season began. So the Giants would continue to help the Yankees, their second-class citizen, co-tenant at the Polo Grounds.

As reported in the *Washington Post*: "When it became evident that Farrell could not have his new park in readiness for the opening of next season, he conferred with President Johnson, of the American League, and the latter wrote to President H.N. Hempstead, of the New York Nationals, asking that Farrell's club be allowed to play at the Polo Grounds in 1914, agreeing that the Yankees would remove to their own grounds at the earliest possible moment." While Farrell's vision of a gargantuan new field was progressing, the Yankees lost another one of their prominent players to bad relations with Chance. In this case it was Russ Ford. Ford "jumped" to Buffalo of the Federal League, a newly-formed rival to the

Grim Days: A group photograph of the 1913 Yankees taken at the Polo Grounds, the large stadium making recently vacated Hilltop Park look like a Little League field by comparison. Starting players and pitchers flanking a dour looking Frank Chance, sitting middle in sweater, include mainstays Ray Caldwell (1), Ed Sweeney (2), Birdie Cree (3), Roy Hartzell (4), Ray Keating (5), Ray Fisher (6), Russ Ford (7), Jack Warhop (8), Roger Peckinpaugh (9) and Harry Wolter (10) (Brown Brothers).

Frank Farrell and Bill Devery's box at the Polo Grounds. The two Yankee owners and their wives take in a game, possibly in early spring during the 1913 season (Library of Congress, Prints & Photographs Division, LC-DIG-ggbain-13259).

15. "A Bunion and an Onion," 1913   113

Ray Keating, another Yankee pitcher who threw the spitter, faces the camera at the age of 21 on April 18, 1913. The Yankees had an outstanding line of spitball pitchers through the years—Chesbro, Orth, Caldwell, Fisher, Quinn. Keating never had a winning season in 6 years with the Yankees but later found great success in the Pacific Coast League (Library of Congress, Prints & Photographs Division, LC-USZ62-133660).

First baseman Babe Borton records one of his few base hits for the Yankees. This came against the Chicago White Sox, possibly in midsummer 1913, during a poorly attended game at the Polo Grounds. The Yankees drew 357,551 people in their first year at the Polo Grounds. While that total was far below the AL average crowd of 440,851, it was more than might have been expected for a seventh place club (Library of Congress, Prints & Photographs Division, LC-DIG-ggbain-13528).

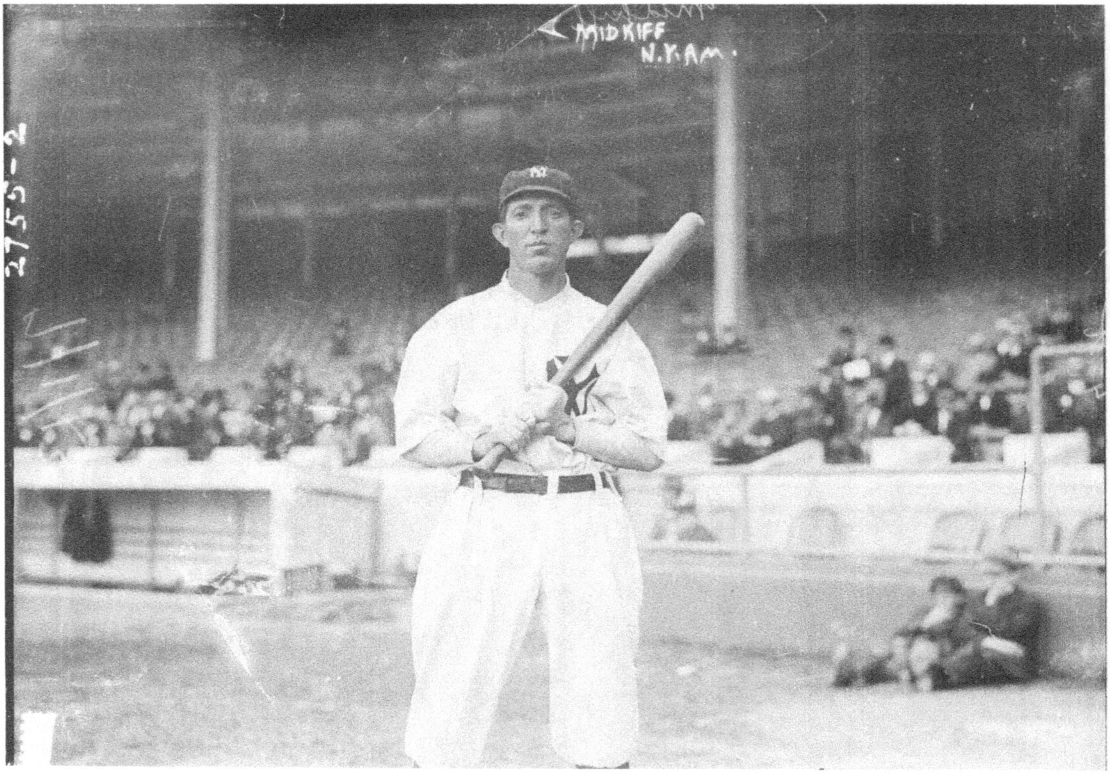
MIDKIFF
N.Y.AM.

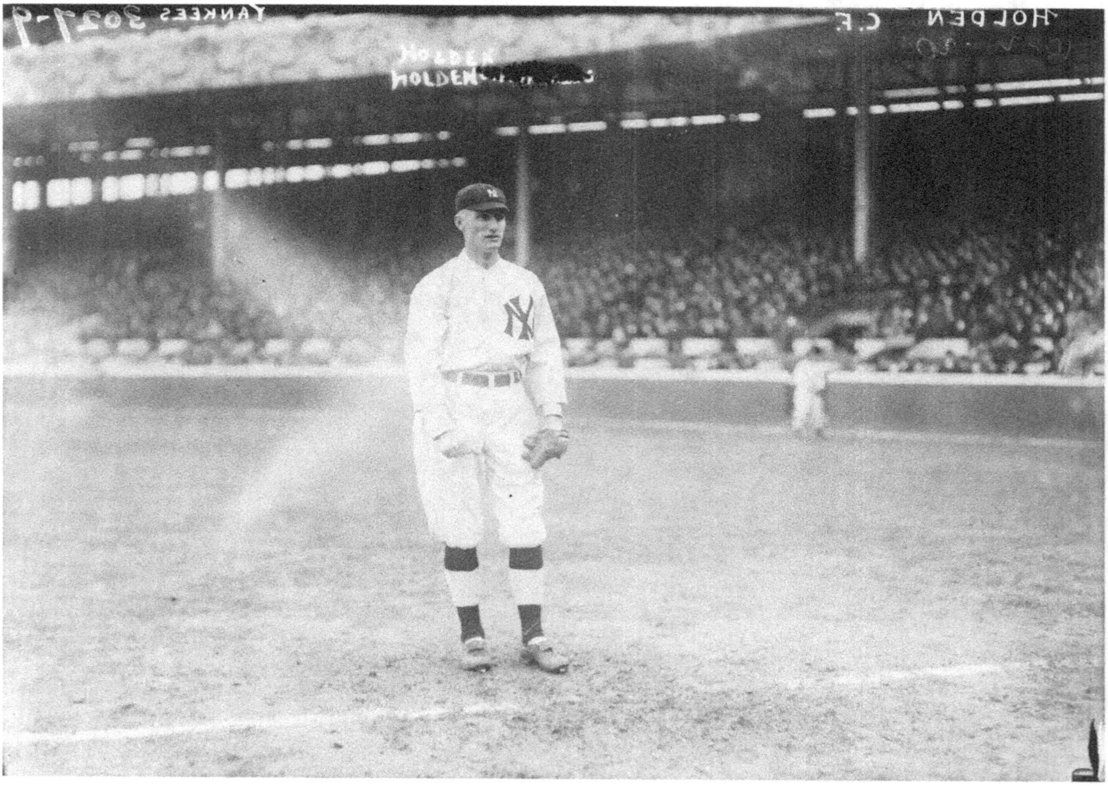
HOLDEN
HOLDEN

15. "A Bunion and an Onion," 1913

This photograph of right-hander George McConnell at the Polo Grounds shows the wide expanse of the concrete and steel baseball field compared to Hilltop Park. McConnell, a right-hander from in Shelbyville, Tennessee, first appeared with the Yankees as a 31-year-old rookie in 1909 (Library of Congress, Prints & Photographs Division, LC-DIG-ggbain-13644).

established major leagues. American League president Ban Johnson was concerned, but not surprised, that a star pitcher like Ford had left the American League. He explained: "Ford had a reason for jumping as he was not satisfied, being in the ill graces of Farrell and Manager Chance. Chance, being a stern taskmaster, kept after Ford throughout last season trying to get him to pitch to his usual speed, but it was of no use. This constant warring between the two resulted in open friction and Chance didn't care what Ford did." What Ford did was produce his last great season (21-6) in 1914, retiring after the 1915 season as the Federal League

Opposite top: Third baseman Ezra Midkiff in a 1913 Yankee home uniform. Midkiff was nicknamed Salt Rock because he was born in the West Virginia town of the same name. He began his career in 1909, playing in one game with the Cincinnati Reds, getting no hits in 2 at-bats. He improved slightly upon joining the Yankees in 1912, batting .244 in 21 games but dropped to .197 in 83 games in 1913. Midkiff typified the "journeyman" baseball players that populated the Yankee roster in the Frank Chance years as Chance scrambled, in vain, to find a winning combination (Library of Congress, Prints & Photographs Division, LC-DIG-ggbain-13523). *Opposite bottom*: Outfielder Bill Holden had a great year for the Yankees in 1913, batting .302 (unfortunately it happened in only 18 total games). Holden, born in Birmingham, Alabama, appeared in his first major league game for the Yankees on September 11, 1913. He batted .182 in 50 games for the Yanks in 1914 and was traded to the Reds (where he batted .214 in 11 games), finishing a less than illustrious 2-year career with a .211 average (Library of Congress, Prints & Photographs Division, LC-DIG-ggbain-15775).

Left: Yankee shortstop Claud Derrick in 1913. Derrick, who attended the University of Georgia, appeared in 23 games for the Yankees in 1913, batting .292 in 65 at-bats with 1 home run and 7 RBI. Derrick was the starting shortstop during the April 5, 1913, exhibition game at newly opened Ebbets Field but left after being spiked on his throwing hand by Brooklyn outfielder Zack Wheat. Derrick was sent to Sacramento of the Pacific Coast League but returned the next month, playing sparingly. He joined the Reds for 3 games in 1914 before being traded to the Cubs, closing out a 5-season career with a .241 average, playing in 113 games (Library of Congress, Prints & Photographs Division, LC-DIG-ggbain-13193). *Right*: In this photograph George McConnell seems somewhat dazed, possibly owing to his 15 losses in 1913. McConnell did the best pitching of his 6-season career after leaving the Yankees, going 25-10 with 2.20 ERA in 1915 for the Federal League's Chicago Whales, helping them win the Federal League Championship (Library of Congress, Prints & Photographs Division, LC-DIG-ggbain-12734).

dissolved due to monetary problems. Ford passed away in Rockingham, North Carolina, at the age of 76 in 1960. His lifetime record was 99 wins and 71 losses and he was elected to the Canadian Baseball Hall of Fame in 1989.

John "Schoolboy" Knight was back with the Yankees in 1913, playing 50 games at first base as Frank Chance searched, without success, for a replacement for Hal Chase (Library of Congress, Prints & Photographs Division, LC-DIG-ggbain-13894).

16

No Chance, 1914

New ballpark plans to the contrary, the nondescript group of journeymen and untested youngsters that populated the New York spring training camp in Houston, Texas, in 1914 was a great indicator that owners Farrell and Devery had lost interest in their Yankee plaything that seemed so new and fascinating back in 1903. Manager Frank Chance had told Farrell one year earlier: "I will win the pennant for you before I get through in New York." How "The Peerless Leader" was going to accomplish the task with untested recruits like Harry Williams, Lute Boone, Frank Truesdale, and Jimmy Walsh vying for playing time was unknown. Boone started at second base in 1914 and batted .222 with Truesdale the backup at .212. Williams, a first baseman, batted .192 overall in a 2-year career (1913–1914 with the Yankees) while Jimmy Walsh had a less than stellar 6-year career finishing with a .232 career batting average.

Despite a definite lack of star quality on his roster, Frank Chance still remained moderately hopeful, but realistic, heading into the 1914 season. He offered this message: "A place at the head of the second division will be satisfactory to all, I think, but the players insist that there is room for a team such as the Yankees in the first division." Not exactly an awe-inspiring assessment from the Yankee skipper. An early season newspaper prediction for the 1914 squad was actually quite positive in light of the mostly pedestrian crew in Yankee camp but it also warned of a severe lack of offensive ability: "Taken as a whole, the team appears to be a fast fielding and base running combination.... Offensively the squad does not appear at this time to be overstrong in batting, but Chance believes that this department of the game will improve with more practice and play." It didn't. The Yankees batted .229 as a team in 1914, the lowest average of any team in the AL, NL and Federal League, producing the lowest slugging percentage in Yankee history with .287. For what it was worth, the team did lead the AL in stolen bases with 251.

Roger Peckinpaugh, a shortstop obtained from the Cleveland Indians in 1913, was a capable player and the closest thing the Yankees had to a star in 1914. He suffered through a .223 season at the plate but led the team in RBI with 51. The 24-year-old third baseman Fritz "Flash" Maisel, in his second year with the Yankees, batted .239 but earned his nickname by swiping 74 bases to lead the team. He was second in RBI behind Peckinpaugh, with 47. Ray Fisher (10-12, 2.28 ERA) and Ray Caldwell (17-9, 1.94 ERA) were outstanding pitchers toiling for an underachieving club. That Caldwell could accumulate such a great pitching record playing for this team is a true testament to the right-handed Caldwell's talent on the mound.

Amidst the disappointing showing of the New York club Chance continued to establish less than amicable relations with his team. Ray Fisher recalled Chance "roaring": "I know

Tuesday, April 14, 1914, was Opening Day at the Polo Grounds. The photograph says Roy Hartzell, who played second base this game, has just scored the first run of the season as the Yankees face the Athletics. However, upon further examination (see detail at left) the base runner appears to be center fielder Bill Holden. Holden had a walk in the first inning and scored the third run of the game on shortstop Roger Peckinpaugh's single. Holden had 3 hits in 4 at-bats, helping the Yankees beat the A's, 8–2. Right-hander "Bullet Joe" Bush pitched for the visiting A's against Yankee right-hander Marty McHale. This was one of McHale's 7 victories in 1914. He lost 16 games that season but had an ERA of 2.97 (Library of Congress, Prints & Photographs Division, LC-DIG-ggbain-15776).

there are lunkheads in baseball, but I didn't know they were all on one ball club!" Another incident with Chance involved Fisher's road trip roommate Birdie Cree. Cree, a fine fielder, had failed to throw out an opposing team's baserunner at home plate. Chance said: "I'd like to know where in the hell you got your reputation?" Cree replied: "That's funny, I'm thinking the same thing about you for manager!"

Overall, the 1914 Yankees were a drab entity that paled in fan interest compared to the other inhabitants, and real "home" team, of the Polo Grounds, the National League's New York Giants. Frank Chance was not present to see the final awful results. He resigned on September 12th, after a 2–1 loss to the Athletics at the Polo Grounds, with the Yankees mired in 7th place, 26 games out of first. Chance complained that owners Farrell and Devery had not spent enough money to build a winning team. Big Bill Devery was not thrilled with that summation of events and punches between Devery and Chance were almost exchanged.

Third baseman Fritz "Flash" Maisel in 1914. Maisel led the Yankees and the American League in stolen bases in 1914 with 74. He was an effective leadoff batter, hitting 9 triples and also leading the team in bases on balls with 76. Maisel also scored 78 runs (the entire team scored 587 runs overall). "Flash" played for the Yankees from 1913 to 1917, leading the team in stolen bases 3 times and 2 times in runs scored (Library of Congress, Prints & Photographs Division, LC-DIG-ggbain-13908).

The *Washington Post* reported on September 13th: "After Chance had explained his position to newspaper men in the Yankees' clubhouse after the game with the Athletics, Farrell and Devery came upon the scene. Harsh words were exchanged and Devery made a move as if to strike Chance. The newspaper men interfered." Chance commented: "I see no reason for my remaining here. I cannot hope to finish any higher than sixth or seventh with the material at hand, and for a team that cannot finish any higher than that, Farrell need pay no manager a high salary. He can get a $5,000 man to do that." The comment on the makeup of the team was a direct swipe at Yankee head scout Arthur Irwin. Chance was paid for the remainder of the season and returned home to Glendora, California. Shortstop Roger Peckinpaugh, a confident player, was selected to lead the team. At 23 he became the youngest manager ever in major-league baseball history. The Yankees won 9 and lost 8 games under his guidance ending up in 6th place with a 70-84 overall record. In a puzzling disclaimer given their won-lost record, the Yankees drew 359,477 fans to the Polo Grounds in 1914, above the AL average attendance of 343,449.

So where would Farrell, Devery, and the Yankees go from here? From reports in the newspapers, to the same source that had assisted them in the past and then bowed out only to see his prize New York franchise fall on hard times and become tarnished with age—AL president Ban Johnson. On December 2, 1914, a headline in the *Washington Post* screamed: "Johnson plans to help lowly New York Yankees." The article stated: "After rattling around aimlessly in the

PECKINPAUGH + DOYLE 10/8/14

This photograph was taken during the 1914 "City Series," a five-game exhibition contest played between the Yankees and the New York Giants after the regular season. The first such series was played in 1910, when the Yankees finished in second place behind the Athletics and the Giants finished in second (while the Chicago Cubs won the National League pennant). The Yankees made a friendly challenge to the Giants to play a postseason series and wound up losing the 1910 contest 4 games to 2. Here player/manager Roger Peckinpaugh is shaking hands with Giants second baseman Larry Doyle. The Giants finished in 2nd place in 1914 also (to former Yankee manager George Stallings' Boston Braves). The Giants won the 1914 City Series, 4 games to 1. Jack Warhop pitched well in the final game of the series but two errors by catcher Leslie Nunamaker and one by Peckinpaugh led to a 4–1 Giants victory. In the fourth inning of the final game, Doyle scored the first run as Peckinpaugh mishandled a hard-hit ground ball (Library of Congress, Prints & Photographs Division, LC-USZ62-28952).

second division for years like an echo in a tabernacle the Yankees are finally going to get some attention from the American League."

The exact nature of the help to come from Johnson was not totally clear but it was obvious his intention was to put the Yankees on a firm foundation by importing talent from other clubs. The *Washington Post* article added: "Though long deferred, this assistance will be both timely and welcome, and President Frank Farrell has interposed no objections as far as can be learned. The Yankees have been struggling along for years with poor material, and for the most part with incompetent managers.... In spite of this they have gained a fair share of prestige here, but the club has never lived up to the original expectations held out for it. Though the importance of having a winner in the greatest baseball town in the country was realized, no help was ever given to the local club, and the explanation for this was that any assistance from the outside would give the appearance of syndicate ball. However, with the upheaval in baseball caused by the Federal League, Johnson has seized this as a good opportunity to put the Yankees on a firm basis.... If the Yankees ever win a pennant or make a good fight for one the fans will turn out for them just as they have done for the Giants in the past."

As the Yankees ended another tortuous season and looked with hope to the future, the rest of the world found itself in the throes of an international crisis. World War I had begun in August of 1914, grinding a host of countries into some of the deadliest land battles ever seen in recorded time. While the troubles of one American League baseball team paled in comparison to world events, the United States would not enter the hostilities until April 6, 1917, and the search for a new pilot for the Yankees was foremost on the minds of Ban Johnson as well as Yankee owners Farrell and Devery. Roger Peckinpaugh possessed adequate leadership skills but was far too valuable as a player on the field. The name William "Wild Bill" Donovan was mentioned. Donovan was admired for being a successful major-league pitcher with Brooklyn in the NL and the Detroit Tigers in the AL. Donovan went 25-15 in 1901 and 25-4 in 1907 (while earning the nickname "Wild Bill" for often being unable to find the plate). Donovan managed Providence of the International League from 1913 to 1914

AL president Ban Johnson enjoying a game with Reds owner and major league baseball "National Commission" member Garry Herrmann, possibly during the 1913 World Series (the Giants lost in 5 games to the Athletics). Thomas J. Lynch, National League president from 1910 to 1914, is also present. Lynch had previously been a National League umpire and was well known for his honesty. Lynch was forthright in league dealings, pulling no punches and annoying NL team owners, the reason behind his short tenure at the position (Library of Congress, Prints & Photographs Division, LC-DIG-ggbain-09873).

where he helped a young pitcher by the name of Babe Ruth develop as a player. Donovan denied he was being considered for the role of Yankee manager, using a reference to the ongoing overseas war: "Gather all the men who are going to be mentioned as probabilities for this job and you'll have an army big enough to lick the allies and the Germans put together." In fact, Donovan was hired to manage the Yankees for the 1915 season. However, neither Farrell or Devery would be doing the hiring. Before the year 1914 ended they no longer owned the New York Yankees.

17

THE NEW BREED, 1915

Tired of mediocre showings in the field, widely fluctuating ticket sales, and pressure from other AL owners to field a successful team, Frank Farrell and Bill Devery parted with the Yankees, selling the team just prior to Christmas day of 1914 (the official announcement came on January 11, 1915). The reported sum paid for the team was $460,000. Despite planning for a new ballpark, Farrell and Devery were more than happy to rid themselves of what had become a headache on the field and off. Farrell and Devery sold the Yankees to Colonel Jacob Ruppert and Colonel Tillinghast L'Hommedieu Huston—both these men held the title of "Colonel" for entirely different reasons. Ruppert, whose family emigrated to New York from Bavaria, inherited wealth from his family's beer brewery and was given the title of colonel as an honorary gesture. Til Huston—commonly called "Cap" by his friends since he was actually an Army captain at the time he purchased the Yankees—earned the title of colonel during World War I while he served overseas with the U.S. Army Corp of Engineers. Huston had acquired his wealth via construction and improvement of harbors/ports in Cuba. In an ironic twist, Ruppert and Huston were recommended to Farrell and Devery by Giants manager John McGraw. McGraw was familiar with the resources of Ruppert and Huston and knew they would not tolerate a cellar-dwelling team, but McGraw must have thought the Yankees would always be the "other" team in Manhattan

New York Yankees co-owner Captain (later Colonel) Tillinghast L'Hommedieu Huston (Transcendental Graphics/ruckerarchive.com).

compared to his pennant-contending Giants club. In easing the way for Ruppert and Huston, McGraw badly miscalculated.

The two new Yankee owners could not have been more different in personality and pursuits. Ruppert was a refined city dweller. Huston was a man of simple tastes who enjoyed hunting and guzzling beer for hours while conversing with his many baseball friends and associates—players, owners, newspapermen. Ed Barrow, the Hall of Fame general manager/president of the Yankees from 1920 to 1945, stated in his book *My Fifty Years in Baseball*: "When Ruppert and Huston agreed to buy the Yankees, then a sorry excuse for a major league ball club and a chronic tenant of the second division, it must have been the only time they ever did agree, because they never agreed on anything in my presence, but on the contrary, were continually, and violently, opposed. It is no wonder that they were, because they were two self-willed personalities who, by background, manner, and outlook, were worlds apart." The two men did have two things in common: a vision of what they wanted from

New York Yankees co-owner Jacob Ruppert (Transcendental Graphics/ruckerarchive.com).

Left: New Yankees owner Til Huston in repose (Library of Congress, Prints & Photographs Division, LC-DIG-ggbain-18257). *Right*: A new era: Jake Ruppert signs contractual papers to purchase the New York Yankees in 1915, from *Baseball Magazine*, March 1915, No. 5, page 8 (courtesy LA84 Foundation, 2141 West Adams Boulevard., Los Angeles, California 90018).

17. The New Breed, 1915

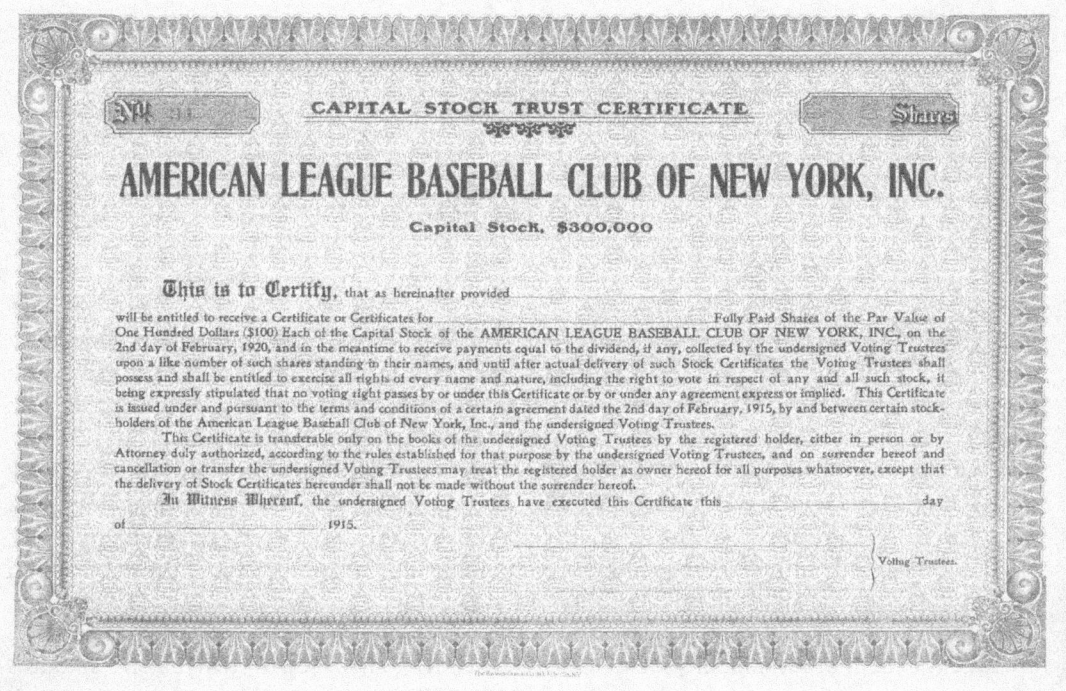

A stock certificate from 1915 was issued to help raise money for the purchase of the New York Yankees by Jacob Ruppert and Til Huston.

their new investment and the business/baseball acumen (plus cash) to put their plan into action. Ruppert later commented on the state of the Yankee team that he and Huston had inherited: "For $450,000 we got an orphan ball club, without a home of its own, without players of outstanding ability, without prestige." Under the guidance of the new owners from 1915 to 1919 the Yankees transformed from a mediocre assemblage of just a few capable players to a well-honed machine just on the periphery of championship-caliber baseball.

18

BIG BILL

Original Yankee owners Frank Farrell and "Big Bill" Devery were introduced and briefly discussed in the introduction. Farrell was the primary business contact for the team and Devery introduced the "NY" logo to the Yankee uniform, but to properly describe their life stories—and Devery's infamous dealings—could easily take up another book.

To understand Devery is to understand Tammany Hall, the corrupt New York City political machine which was founded in 1789. It began as a social club and reportedly took its name from Tamanend, an Indian chief from Delaware. The various buildings, or halls, that housed the Tammany society were referred to as "wigwams," but Tammany Hall morphed into something drastically different from anything related to Native American affairs. By 1800, the Tammany society had become fully emerged in New York city politics. By 1870 the infamous Tammany "Boss"—William Tweed—managed to steal massive amounts of money from the city (estimated to be about $200 million) via a devious operation in which Tweed's employees/followers billed the city excessive amounts for services that cost much less. The scheme was revealed by a disgruntled Tweed follower who felt his portion of the illegally obtained proceeds was too meager. Tweed went to jail but Tammany continued to thrive and existed at varying strengths into the early 1960s. Given Bill Devery's upbringing it's not surprising he would join in some Tammany dealings of his own. Devery recalled: "I carried my father's dinner pail when he was laying the bricks of Tammany Hall." Devery began his "professional" career as a bartender, and in 1878 he is reported to have paid Tammany $200 to join the police force, rising to the rank of sergeant in 1884, through a payoff of $1,400. There may be a slight variation in dollar amounts but regardless of qualifications or dedication to public service, a fixed scale allegedly existed at this time for "prices" of New York City police jobs.

They were as follows: $300, patrolman; $1,600, sergeant; $10,000–15,000+, captain; $20,000, inspector. Devery was supposedly adept at supplementing his salary through unsavory methods of extortion—applied via "protection" money collected from numerous saloons, dance halls, gambling dens and prostitutes that thrived in New York City at the turn of the century. By 1891, Devery could afford to buy another promotion, this time to captain, for $14,000. Devery's comment regarding his activity, and the "one hand washes the other" attitude that permeated his circle and their enforcement of law at this time, was: "It's the fashion in my set, when you're getting rich, to show it forth and not be hiding your light under no bushels, whatever in the hell they are."

Another favorite from "Big Bill," when facing tough questions by reporters, was: "Touchin' on and appertainin' to that matter, I disremember." Devery was dismissed from

"Big Bill" Devery throws out the first ball on Thursday, April 14, 1910, before the season opener at Hilltop Park. The Yankees played the Red Sox in a game which resulted in a 4–4 tie after 14 innings. Home plate umpire Tom Connolly called a halt to the game because of darkness (Library of Congress, Prints & Photographs Division, LC-DIG-ggbain-07913).

the Police Department for "grafting" in 1894 but acquitted two years later on appeal. In 1897 he was charged by the New York Police Department on these specific counts:

1. Neglect of Duty
2. Conduct Unbecoming a Police Officer
3. Failure to Suppress a Disorderly House (House of Prostitution)
4. Bribery

Devery avoided a trial by going to court and getting a stay preventing the NYPD from prosecuting him. By 1898, Devery was chief of police. He conducted "business" each night at the corner of Eighth Avenue and 28th Street, usually remaining until 2 A.M., leaning on a fire hydrant, collecting the "protection" money from bar owners, gamblers and pimps. Devery also made time for the poor of the neighborhood, persons recently arriving to the United States or those just down on their luck, providing a helping hand and possibly finding employment for a small fee. By 1901, a wave of reforms in the city helped legislate Devery's office out of existence. In 1903, the same year he and Farrell purchased the Yankees, Devery made an unsuccessful bid for mayor—his 2,200 vote total out of one thousand election districts indicating the public had lost tolerance for Devery.

The second Tammany Hall, or "wigwam," built in 1868, on the north side of 14th Street, east of Broadway. The origins of the society, from the Delaware Indian chief Tamanend, are evident in the highlighted architectural detail (Library of Congress, Prints & Photographs Division, LC-USZ62-101734).

"Big Bill" did make one everlasting contribution to the Yankee team: under his supervision the interlocking "NY" became the main logo of the Yankees, first appearing in its original form in the 1905 season. Unfortunately, as with most things surrounding Devery, even the origin of the team logo has some discrepancies. The logo itself, originally taken from an award known as the John

McDowell Medal, has long been reported as being given in honor of the first uniformed New York City policeman shot in the line of duty. The cleaned up version of this story is that on or about January 8, 1877, McDowell was on uniformed patrol and noticed that a burglary was in progress at Bernard Courtney's Saloon, located at 315 7th Avenue in Manhattan. McDowell entered the hallway of the saloon, was ambushed from behind by one of the three men involved in the robbery, and was shot and killed. The actual circumstances of this event, supported by sworn court testimony, are different.

19

ORIGIN OF THE "NY" LOGO

Patrolman McDowell was involved in the same shakedown/extortion schemes as Bill Devery and another infamous member of the department, Captain Alexander Williams (known as "Clubber" due to being charged in about 396 cases of "excessive use of force"). Williams and McDowell worked "The Tenderloin" area in Manhattan—which ran roughly from 14th Street all the way to 42nd, between Fourth and Seventh avenues. The name originated when Williams bought a transfer to that precinct from an area that had offered less opportunity to collect "graft." He was overjoyed at the chance for new extortion opportunities saying: "I've been eating rump steak down in the Fourth precinct and now I'm going to get a little of the tenderloin." In actuality, McDowell was a detective who worked in plain clothes and not as a uniformed police officer.

The interior of one of the Tenderloin area police stations (Library of Congress, Prints & Photographs Division, LC-USZ62-50066).

19. Origin of the "NY" Logo

"Big Bill" Devery, the man responsible for the placement of the interlocking "NY" logo on the Yankee uniform, in another photograph from Thursday, April 14, 1910 (Library of Congress, Prints & Photographs Division, LC-DIG-ggbain-07914).

According to sworn testimony, detective McDowell, along with another detective and Captain "Clubber" Williams, were all present—in civilian clothes and allegedly asleep from a night of drinking—on January 8, 1877, at 2:45 A.M. in Bernard Courtney's Saloon. Three burglars entered the building through a skylight intent on stealing anything of value. McDowell awoke and attempted to stop one of the criminals. He was shot during the scuffle by a flintlock pistol, the ball of which slammed into his left ear. Detective McDowell survived.

In 1894, a court investigation into alleged corruption in the New York City Police Department revealed that one of Detective McDowell's primary responsibilities was to collect money for the captain of the precinct—in this case the aforementioned "Clubber" Williams. The other detective with McDowell that night admitted in sworn testimony to being Williams' "bagman." Since the collection was usually made during the day McDowell's presence at the saloon in which he was shot appears to have less to do with investigative police work and more to do with happenstance. Over 300 after-hours bars existed in his precinct and over 3,000 prostitutes inhabited the precinct during this period. Sleeping off a night of revelry rather than stumbling upon a robbery seems the logical cause of the circumstances. The more palatable version of the story was presented to the public. The Tiffany jewelry company was commissioned to create the original medal and "Big Bill" initiated transferring the "NY" from the medal to be a fixture on the Yankee uniform.

20

FRANKLY SPEAKING

Yankees co-owner Frank Farrell operated the types of establishments from which Devery and "Clubber" Williams' bag men collected their ill-gotten gains. One of Farrell's many successful gambling houses—opened in the year 1891 on West 33rd Street in Manhattan—was lavishly adorned with Persian rugs and a roulette room featuring frescoes on its arched ceiling. From a palace in Venice, Italy, came the signature piece of the casino: a $20,000 bronze door that was installed at a rear entrance. "The House with the Bronze Door" became the epicenter of high-rolling gamblers from New York City and a favorite destination of gamblers that lived far beyond New York and wanted to try their luck. One player supposedly won $210,000 in two nights of playing roulette but lost all those winnings, plus $80,000 more, in one week's time. One of Farrell's other ventures was a poolroom at 54 West 29th Street in Manhattan. Farrell delivered money to Devery at the 28th Street fire hydrant and the two men parlayed their funds into ownership of the Yankees.

As outlined in previous sections, Farrell had more of a passion than did Devery in trying to mold a winning team out of the Yankees. Despite a constant influx of new players each experiment met with failure. Farrell's

Catcher Jim "Deacon" McGuire, pictured in 1905. The first incarnation of the interlocking "NY" logo appears on the left side of this 1905 Yankee road uniform. McGuire played in the major leagues for 26 seasons (for the Yankees from 1904 to 1906 and 1 game in 1907). Early in his career, during the 1880s and 1890s, McGuire used a primitive, fingerless glove that provided him with many broken and crooked digits. His career batting average is .278 (*Chicago Daily News* negatives collection, SDN-003890, courtesy Chicago Historical Society).

20. Frankly Speaking

Yankees co-owner Frank Farrell, top right, with American League heavyweights. Others in the top row, from left: Detroit Tigers president "Lucky Frank" Navin and Washington Senators owner Benjamin S. Minor. Bottom, from left: Chicago White Sox owner Charles Comiskey, AL president Ban Johnson, and Boston Red Sox owner Joseph Lannin. None seem amused by the proceedings, specifically Farrell, and since this photograph is dated 1914 this session could involve the transfer of team ownership to Ruppert and Huston. Navin, Comiskey and Lannin enjoyed success in their league while Farrell labored in frustration. Navin purchased $5,000 stock in the Tigers with money he won in a card game and was elevated to team president. The Tigers won consecutive pennants in 1907, 1908 and 1909 and were World Series champions in 1935. Shortly thereafter Navin died, suffering a heart attack after he fell while riding a horse. Comiskey was a player and manager as well as the tight-fisted owner of the Chicago White Sox for 31 years, during which time they won five AL pennants. Lannin, born in Quebec, owned the Red Sox from 1913 to 1916. In 1914, Lannin purchased the contract of 19-year-old Babe Ruth and sent him to the Providence Grays, a minor league team Lannin also owned. Ruth hit his first home run in professional baseball while in a Grays uniform at a road game in Toronto. Ruth joined the Red Sox and under Lannin's leadership they won consecutive World Series titles in 1915 and 1916. Lannin is a member of the Canadian Baseball Hall of Fame. Minor, a prominent attorney and part of the original Senators ownership group in 1905, became owner in 1912 when the team president died (Library of Congress, Prints & Photographs Division, LC-DIG-ggbain-17210).

increasing gambling debts led to increasing quarrels with Devery, leading them to sell the team to Ruppert and Huston. The parting was far from amicable. They never spoke again. "Big Bill" Devery passed away in 1919 of "apoplexy" (an old medical term generally referring to a stroke). During the years he owned the Yankees Devery resided in a mansion on West End Avenue and maintained another impressive home on Mott Avenue in Bayswater, Far Rockaway, N.Y.—a neighborhood once populated by similarly wealthy residents. However, the accumulated fortunes of both men dwindled steadily during the years after they sold the Yankees. At the time of his death "Big Bill" left debts totaling $1,023.

Just prior to his passing, as he leaned once more against his old fire hydrant, Devery tried to sort out the strange twists of fate that left him on the outside looking in—in terms of political and community power as well as personal wealth. He exclaimed to a reporter: "You, f'rinstance, you been a good friend o' mine, and you ain't my friend at all. I mean—oh, Hell, I don't know what I mean. Do you?" One obituary mentioned Devery as "the best Chief of Police New York ever had."* As news of his death circulated his beloved hydrant was "draped in mourning" with a large floral wreath and a card which read: "From Your Friends." Frank Farrell, more quiet and anonymous than Devery, died in 1926. Gambling had taken its toll and Farrell's total assets at the time of his death were $1,072.

A classic Hal Chase photograph, issued as a premium by *The Sporting News* in 1909. The stylized "NY" logo—now in the more familiar design that exists in slight modification to this day—has been relocated to the left sleeve of the uniform. It would reappear on the left front of the uniform in its familiar place in 1912 (albeit with black pinstripes as opposed to the navy blue coloration that followed).

---

*This comment came from—not surprisingly—Robert Van Wyck, mayor of New York City from 1898 to 1901. Van Wyck was deeply involved in Tammany Hall. He was responsible for the construction of the first subway in Manhattan (the contract was reportedly valued at $35,000,000) but Van Wyck was involved in scandals as well—one being the creative and devious "Ice Trust" scandal of 1900, in which the American Ice Company planned to double the price of ice from 30 to 60 cents per hundred pounds. Since refrigeration devices were not yet available at this time, ice was the only product which could preserve food and medicines. It was revealed American Ice was the only company with rights to land ice at New York City area piers (essentially an ice "monopoly") and that Van Wyck owned—but reportedly had not paid for—$680,000 of American Ice stock.

21

WILD BILL, 1915

With the purchase of the Yankees by Ruppert and Huston, plans for a new stadium in the Bronx fell by the wayside. The Yankees, of course, finally found a home in the Bronx—albeit about a decade later than originally thought—while Ruppert and Huston refocused efforts on building a permanent home for their new team in Manhattan, not far from the Polo Grounds. The cost for this new ballpark was in the $425,000 range. Coupling that with the cost of the team, it meant: "When the Yankees are finally housed in their new quarters, Messrs. Ruppert and Huston will have invested more than a million dollars," AL president Ban Johnson commented to the *New York Times*. Johnson continued: "They have the property on which to build, but I cannot make known its location."

Though the whereabouts of the proposed new field was a mystery the new center of Yankee business operations was not. Ruppert and Huston established an office of sorts for the club at the law office of James, Schell & Elkus, at 170 Broadway, Suite 1409, at the southeast corner of Broadway and Maiden Lane—far downtown from the old Fifth Avenue address used in the Farrell and Devery years.* However, the main power base was actually far uptown, at the Ruppert Brewery on Third Avenue and E. 90th Street. This was indicative of the growing power Ruppert would begin to exert over the team while Huston was reduced to an observer—similar to the Farrell/Devery dynamic—though Ruppert would go on to become a far more successful Yankee patriarch than Farrell could have ever dreamed.

The first order of business for Ruppert and Huston was installing "Wild Bill" Donovan as manager. Ruppert and Huston wanted name recognition as well as capability in handling players and decided Donovan embodied those traits. The new owners were impressed with Donovan's reputation as a player and of his developing young talent—like Babe Ruth—while Donovan managed the Providence Grays of the International League from 1913 to 1914. Providence was the International League champion in 1914, with the pitching of Ruth and Carl Mays (24-8) the major reason for their success. (Mays would be traded to the Yankees from the Red Sox in 1919.) Though he was an excellent pitcher in his day, "Wild Bill" was acutely aware of the need for increased offensive production from his team. He essentially molded the foundation by which most Yankee teams of the future would beat their opponents: bludgeoning the other team's pitchers into submission. "We can get millions of good

---

*By 1916, the first "real" office for the team was located at 30 East 42nd Street, near Madison Avenue. Even in this early period, many businesses were springing up in the area, and Ruppert believed it was important for the Yankees to establish their office in the midst of other dynamic business growth in Manhattan.

fielders, but it is no easy job to get men that can hit. I want to get hold of a hard-hitting infielder, and I want to boost the batting ability of the outfield."

Donovan's wants and the Yankees' needs would soon be met. Many excellent players were provided by the new Yankee owners: first baseman Wally Pipp, pitcher Bob Shawkey, and third baseman Frank "Home Run" Baker in particular. American League president Johnson worked behind the scenes to help broker deals to fortify the Yankee team and firmly establish his league in "The Big Apple." On February 3, 1915, the *New York Times* stated: "President Ban Johnson, although he would make no definite statement about the deal which he had in mind, intimated yesterday that before the [AL] league meeting was over it was very likely that the local American League club would be strengthened by several strong players."

Help from Johnson, and money spent by Ruppert and Huston on new talent, was vital to keep the Yankee organization alive. Prior to the 1915 season, a dire warning about the state of the team—especially when compared to the National League's New York Giants—was issued by writer F.C. Lane in *Baseball Magazine*: "Whereas the National League flourishes largely through the productiveness of its New York Club, the American League, with a much more business-like and efficient organization, has succeeded not because of, but rather in spite of, its New York representative. Why has the New York club proved a failure? Why has a fortune thus been lost through the failure of this most fortunately situated of all its clubs?"

Lane made no direct attempt to answer that question in his article since a myriad of answers existed. One thing he did make clear is that the patience of fans and fellow AL team owners were at a breaking point and Johnson, Ruppert, Huston and manager Donovan needed to quickly steer the team down a winning path: "With the club fluctuating from sixth to last place ... how much longer must the public wait, how much longer shall the American League allow a glaring business blunder to exist?" Contraction of the Yankees? Luckily for Ruppert and Huston, and the American League, things turned out much differently. Despite their present-day vilification by fans of the opposing teams, Lane's words of long ago remind us it was apparent that a strong team in New York was, and is, a positive thing for major-league baseball. The Yankees, by extension, help other teams in their efforts to sell tickets, and it is somewhat amusing to think of Ban Johnson hustling just to help keep the franchise afloat during its infancy.

Yankee spring training for 1915 took place in Savannah, Georgia, the site selected by new business manager Harry Sparrow. The Giants' John McGraw, in another odd move of benevolence towards the Yankees, suggested Sparrow for the position. Sparrow had performed similar duties for the Giants

"Wild Bill" Donovan in 1915 (National Baseball Hall of Fame Library, Cooperstown, N.Y.).

and the cheerful Sparrow served as Yankee business manager from 1915 until his early passing five years later. The February 18th headline "Yanks to Stop at Only Highbrow Hotels" seems indicative of the aristocratic upbringing of owner Jake Ruppert being superimposed on his team, but supposedly the idea came from Sparrow: "Mr. Sparrow ... opines that he will do business with the Pontchartrain in Detroit, with the Copley Plaza in Boston, and with other

Top: "Wild Bill" Donovan in the Yankee dugout, possibly before a road game in 1915 since he is wearing a 1915 road jersey. In baseball's early days only two or three pairs of uniforms were provided. Many teams wore the previous season's uniforms in spring training or exhibition games to keep their uniforms new for the upcoming season (Library of Congress, Prints & Photographs Division, LC-DIG-ggbain-18831). *Bottom*: New York Yankees co-owner Til Huston and "Wild Bill" Donovan (Library of Congress, Prints & Photographs Division, LC-DIG-ggbain-18830).

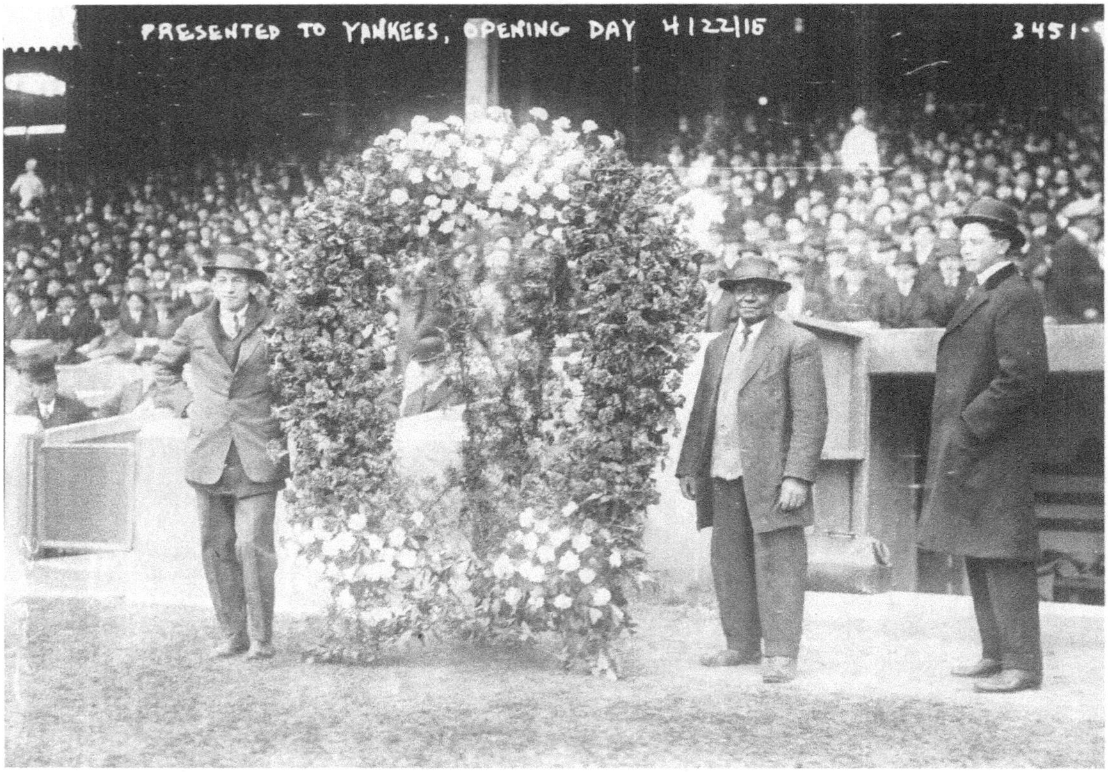
PRESENTED TO YANKEES, OPENING DAY 4|22|15
3451-

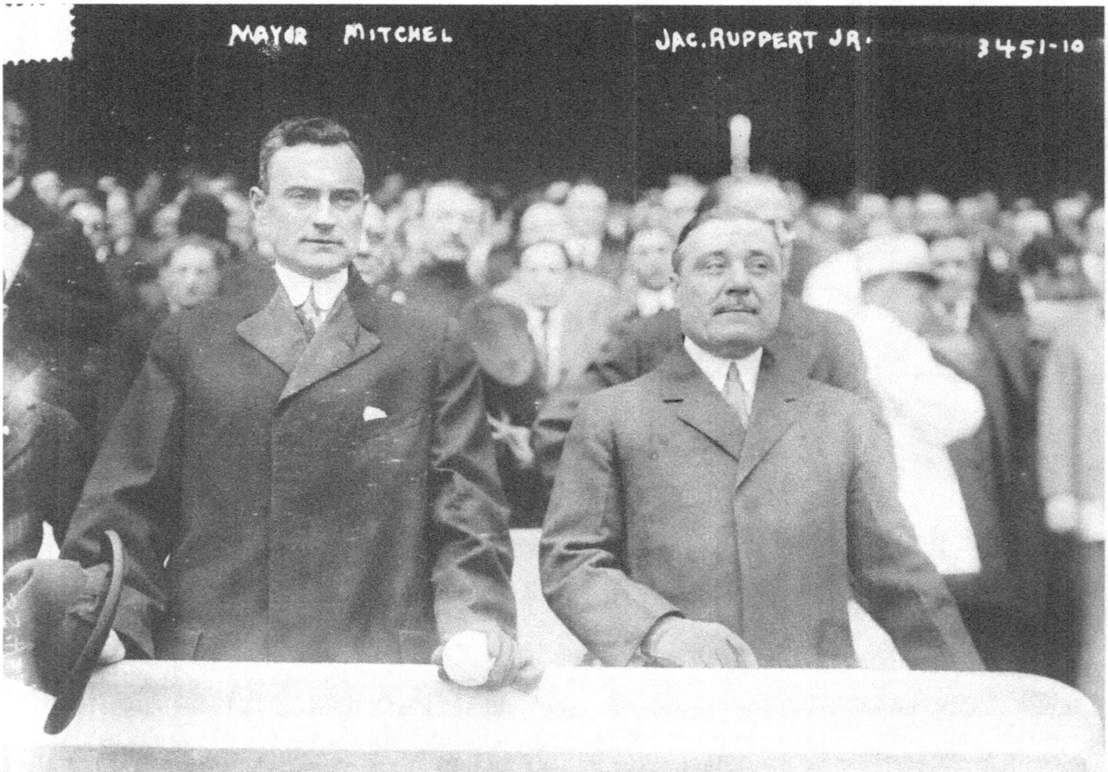
MAYOR MITCHEL
JAC. RUPPERT JR.
3451-10

21. Wild Bill, 1915

Yankee catching staff candidates in 1915: Pius Schwert, Ed Sweeney, Les Nunamaker, and Arthur Pickering. Pickering, a native of Paterson, N.J., signed a probationary contract on his suitcase on the way to 1915 spring training. With three men ahead of him in the Yankee catching plans, Pickering signed with a minor league team in Durham, North Carolina. Nunamaker appeared in 87 games in 1915, batting .225, far below his career average of .268. Sweeney, his career nearing its end, appeared in 53 games with a .190 average (Library of Congress, Prints & Photographs Division, LC-DIG-ggbain-18793).

Opposite top: At the Yankees' 1915 home opener on Thursday, April 22, at the Polo Grounds, a large floral wreath (in a horseshoe pattern) was presented to manager Bill Donovan, wishing him luck for the season. The Yankees lost to the visiting Washington Senators that day, 5–1, in a game started by Marty McHale. This is remarkably similar to the wreath presentation for Frank Chance in 1913 (same day of the week, same opponent, and a Yankee loss). A superstition existed that having the horseshoe upside down meant all the luck had run out the ends. Judging by other photographs, the floral wreath fixation in baseball was not limited to the Yankees. It didn't markedly improve their won-lost records and faded from these celebrations (Library of Congress, Prints & Photographs Division, LC-DIG-ggbain-18928). *Opposite bottom*: New York City mayor John Purroy Mitchel with Yankees co-owner Jacob Ruppert during the home opener on Thursday, April 22, 1915. Mitchel is preparing to throw out the first ball. He was the ninety-fifth elected mayor of New York City, serving from 1914 to 1917, and was the youngest person ever elected mayor of New York City, at the age of thirty-five. Mitchel and his staff devised a zoning plan to govern development, the first such plan to exist in the United States. He also helped standardized salary requirements for city employees. Mitchel enlisted in the Army Air Service in 1918. He died on July 6 of that year, during his final pilot training session in Lake Charles, Louisiana, just a few days before his 39th birthday. Mitchel fell out of the cockpit of his plane, plunging 500 feet. Long Island's Mitchel Field (now the site of Hofstra University) was renamed in honor of Mitchel on July 16, 1918. Mitchel is buried in Woodlawn Cemetery in the Bronx (Library of Congress, Prints & Photographs Division, LC-DIG-ggbain-18929).

1, Cook; 2, Sweeney; 3, Nunamaker; 4, McHale; 5, Warhop; 6, Keating.
Conlon, Photos.
A GROUP OF NEW YORK AMERICANS.

Page from the 1915 *Spalding Baseball Guide* **with previous-season photos. Player 4, Marty McHale, pitched sparingly for the Yankees from 1913 to 1915, losing 16 games in 1914. He fared somewhat better singing and dancing professionally during the off-season, causing Babe Ruth to remark that McHale "was the best goddam singer I ever heard!" (Library of Congress).**

21. Wild Bill, 1915

1, Maisel; 2, Cree; 3, Peckinpaugh; 4, Hartzell; 5, Mullen; 6, Boone.
Conlon, Photos.
A GROUP OF NEW YORK AMERICANS.

Another page from the 1915 *Spalding Baseball Guide* featuring Yankee infielders and outfielders. Jake Ruppert's comment of inheriting a team "without players of outstanding ability" signaled the end of the Yankee careers of Ed Sweeney, Marv McHale and infielder Lute Boone, player 6 on this page. Boone batted .205 in 1915 and .222 the previous season (Library of Congress).

NOTICE.—All agreements, whether for the immediate or prospective release of a player, to which a Major League Club is a party, must be forwarded to the Secretary of the Commission for record and promulgation within five days after execution. (See Article VI., Section 7, National Agreement, on back of this Agreement.)

UNIFORM AGREEMENT
FOR TRANSFER OF A PLAYER
TO OR BY A
Major League Club.

NOTICE.—To establish uniformity in action by clubs when a player, released by a major league club to a minor league club, refuses to report to and contract with the club to which he is transferred, the Commission directs the club securing him to protect both parties to the deal from responsibility for his salary during his insubordination by promptly suspending him. Payment, in part or in whole, of the consideration for the release of such player will not be enforced until he is reinstated and actually enters the service of the purchasing club.

WARNING TO CLUBS.—Many contentions that arise over the transfer of players are directly due to the neglect of one or both parties to promptly execute and file the Agreement. The Commission will no longer countenance dilatory tactics, that result in appeals to it to investigate and enforce claims which, if made a matter of record, as required by the laws of Organized Base Ball, would not require adjustment. In all cases of this character, the complaining club must establish that it is not at fault for delay or neglect to sign and file the Agreement upon which its claim is predicated. (See last sentence of Rule 12.)

This Agreement, made and entered into this 25th day of August 1915 by and between Richmond Exhibition Company (Party of the First Part.) and American League Base Ball Club of New York (Party of the Second Part.)

Witnesseth: The party of the first part does hereby release to the party of the second part the services of Player Charles G. Mullen under the following conditions:

(Here recite fully and clearly every condition of deal, including date of delivery; if for a money consideration, designate time and method of payment; if an exchange of players, name each; if option to recall is retained or privilege of choosing one or more players in lieu of one released is retained, specify all terms. No transfer will be held valid unless the consideration, receipt of which is acknowledged therein, passes at time of execution of Agreement.)

For and in consideration of the sum of Three Hundred ($300.) Dollars, receipt of which is hereby acknowledged, the party of the first part hereby releases to the party of the second part the services of the said player, for delivery September 19th, 1915.

It is further understood and agreed that the said player Mullen shall continue in the service of the said Richmond Exhibition Company until the close of its 1915 playing season.

The parties to this Agreement further covenant to abide by all provisions of the National Agreement and of all Rules of the Commission, regulating the transfer of the services of a player, particularly those printed on the reverse side of this Agreement.

In Testimony Whereof, we have subscribed hereto, through our respective presidents or authorized agents, on the date above written:

(SEAL) Witness: _____ Richmond Exhibition Company
_____ _____
                         (Party of the First Part.)
                         American League Base Ball Club of New York
Corporate name of Company, Club or Association of each party should
be written in first paragraph and subscribed hereto. (See Rule 12.) _____
                         (Party of the Second Part.)

Club officials are cautioned to carefully read the provisions of the National Agreement and the rules of the National Commission, printed on the back of this Agreement, for their information and guidance.

Agreement of a player transfer dated August 25, 1915, signed by New York Yankees owner/president Jacob Ruppert. The agreement is for the player Charlie Mullen and represents a contract between the American League Base Ball Club of New York (Yankees) and the Richmond Exhibition Company (baseball club). The contract also represents the up and down nature of many a player's career during this period. Mullen played first base in 93 games for the Yankees in 1914, batting .260, before being returned to the minor leagues. He was back with the Yankees from 1915 to 1916, batting .267 each season in limited duty at first base, second base and the outfield.

Charlie Mullin during infield drills at the Polo Grounds (Library of Congress, Prints & Photographs Division, LC-DIG-ggbain-16632).

hotels whose guests will shudder if they find themselves compelled to rub shoulders with the red-necked athlete.... As a usual thing, a ball club makes arrangements for a rate of $4 per day per man. Mr. Sparrow, according to a friend, says that money is no object to him, and that everything is ad lib as far as Donovan's [team] are concerned."

The men staying in those hotels did not change significantly from the 1914 roster. Money spoke for the Yankees in the case of one significant pre-season addition—first baseman Wally Pipp. Pipp became the second great Yankee first baseman after Hal Chase. He was originally with the Detroit Tigers in 1913 and in spring training of 1914, but was optioned to the Rochester Hustlers of the International League (a team that still exists today as the Rochester Red Wings). Pipp batted .312 in 154 games at first base with the Hustlers in 1914, with 28 doubles, 27 triples and an International League–leading 15 home runs. That performance led the Tigers to recall Pipp in August 1914, but he never appeared in another game with them. The Yankees acquired the 22-year-old Pipp prior to spring training along with 27-year-old Tiger outfielder Hugh High.

According to a newspaper report: "It is stated that President [Frank] Navin, of Detroit, received about $5,000 for each player." High would contribute little to the Yankees but Pipp played for them for 11 seasons. He led the AL in home runs in 1916 and 1917 (with totals of 12 and 9), far below today's outrageous HR totals but quite good for the era in which Pipp played. The starting players for the 1915 Yankees were Les Nunamaker, C, Pipp, 1B, Lute

Boone, 2B, Fritz Maisel, 3B, Roger Peckinpaugh, SS, Doc Cook, RF, Hugh High, CF, Roy Hartzell, LF. Their combined efforts helped the Yankees lead the AL in home runs for the first time with 31. Peckinpaugh and Boone, two unlikely candidates, led the team with 5 each. On the mound, Ray Caldwell (19-16, 2.89 ERA) and Ray Fisher (18-11, 2.10 ERA) were outstanding. The rest of the pitching staff (Jack Warhop, 7-9, Ray Keating, 3-6, Marty McHale, 3-7, "Boardwalk" Brown, 2-6 and Cy Pieh, 4-5) were not. Despite increased firepower and great seasons from Caldwell and Fisher, the 1915 Yankees finished in 5th place, with a 69-83 record.

22

Mr. Ed (Sweeney)

The careers of a number of notable Yankee players (Ed Sweeney, Jack Warhop, Birdie Cree) and some not as notable (Leonard "King" Cole, Marty McHale, Edwin "Cy" Pieh) came to an end in 1915. Scout Arthur Irwin also left the scene during this time, as many Yankee employees associated with older managerial regimes departed at the beginning of the Ruppert/Huston era.

Ed Sweeney takes his cuts in an intrasquad game during spring training, 1915. Pi Schwert is behind the plate. Sweeney's tenure with the Yankees ended at the age of 26. He returned to the major leagues in 1919 and played sparingly, appearing in 17 games with the Pittsburgh Pirates (Library of Congress, Prints & Photographs Division, LC-DIG-ggbain-18762).

Third baseman Fritz Maisel at the plate during the 1915 preseason, wearing some cool headgear—definitely not team-supplied. Pi Schwert is catching; he was originally viewed as a possible replacement for Ed Sweeney. Schwert received more playing time in spring training than he ever did during the season. Schwert spent 2 years in the major leagues, with the Yankees in 1914 and 1915, playing in 12 games and batting .208 (Library of Congress, Prints & Photographs Division, LC-DIG-ggbain-18760).

Just as catcher Jake Gibbs is associated with the marginal Yankee teams of the late 1960s, catcher Ed Sweeney is saddled as the poster-boy for Yankee ineptitude during the mid-teens. What these two men share in career batting average (Sweeney batted .232, Gibbs .233) they also share as being the primary backstops for some of the poorest teams in Yankee history. Sweeney arrived on the Yankee doorstep in 1908 and found playing time as a reserve catcher through 1910. He combined mediocre batting and fielding skills—his overall fielding percentage at catcher is .964—but raised his batting average after becoming the full-time backstop in 1912, hitting .268 that year and .265 in 1913. Prior to the start of the 1914 season, Yankee scout Arthur Irwin bet Sweeney that he would not be able to steal 15 bases (Sweeney's previous high being 12 in 1910). Sweeney won the bet by swiping 19 bases, which remains the most stolen bases in a season for a Yankee catcher. Sweeney was also a member of the Baseball Players' Fraternity, an early version of a players' union, headed by attorney and former Yankee player Dave Fultz. Sweeney's Yankee teammates Bert Daniels and Roger Peckinpaugh were also part of this organization. This group was not looked upon favorably by team owners. Apparently, some sportswriters also had mixed feelings regarding the Baseball Players' Fraternity and, by extension, had little regard for players associated with the organization. This is apparent in the tone of a story in the *New York Times* published in 1914 which mentioned catcher Leslie Nunamaker being thrown out of a game during August and Pius Schwert, a rookie in 1914, being put in to finish the game as opposed to Sweeney: "It was after 6 o'clock then and, as Walking Delegate Ed Sweeney of the Players' Fraternity objects to working other than union hours, Chance gave a young catcher named Pius Schwert a chance to catch." By 1915, his last season with the Yankees, Sweeney returned to part-time catching duty and bowed out with his .190 average. He was released on August 14th. The epitaph for Sweeney's Yankee career was written by New York humorist and columnist Irvin S. Cobb: "any team missing Sweeney had to be better."

Ed Sweeney early in his career, sitting near the Yankee bench in Chicago in 1909 (*Chicago Daily News* negatives collection, SDN-055478, courtesy Chicago Historical Society).

23

THE UNLUCKIEST PITCHER IN THE LEAGUE

Pitcher Jack Warhop had a nasty disposition and was a great competitor ("Serious When on the Slab" to quote the *Washington Post* from August 29, 1909). Warhop, tagged with the nickname "Crab" during his playing days, was born in Hinton, West Virginia, in 1884. He made a living in his early years working on railroad trains, shoveling coal for the engine furnaces. Warhop joined the Yankees at the age of 23 in 1908. He appeared in only 5 games but became a mainstay on the pitching staff beginning in 1909. Warhop, a right-handed pitcher, utilized an underhanded delivery. He could also throw overhand while mixing a curveball, fastball, and change-up with equal effectiveness. Warhop stood 5'9" and weighed 168 lbs. As noted in the periodical *Baseball Magazine*: "Warhop has not the size or strength to strike a ball down the groove with [Walter] Johnsonian speed. His fast ball and curve, though fair, are not extraordinary, but the way he mixes them with his slow ball—combined with his extraordinary control—would make him a valuable asset to any club."

Warhop's Yankee career win totals of 13, 14, 12, 10, 4, 8 and 7—from 1909 to 1915 respectively—do not look impressive but one has to examine and look inside the numbers that Warhop posted, and remember the wretched teams he was pitching for, to truly assess his career. The "Crab" went 13-15 in 1909 with a 2.40 ERA for the 5th place Yankees (the AL average ERA that year was 2.52). A 2-1 loss to the St. Louis Browns on May 21, a 2-0 loss to Washington on June 1st, a 2-1 loss to the Tigers on August 28th, and a 2-1 loss to the Indians on September 2nd were typical of games in which Warhop pitched well and had nothing to show for his effort. On June 3, 1910, Warhop just missed pitching a no-hitter, holding the White Sox to one "scratch" hit, and losing 3-1. *Baseball Magazine* referred to Warhop as "The Unluckiest Pitcher in the American League." Warhop often yelled to his teammates: "Give me a run and I'll grab this game!" usually with no effect.

The Yankee teams on which Warhop played never finished higher than 4th in total team batting average in the 8-team American League, and typically were far worse, falling to 5th in overall batting in 1911 and 1912, 6th in 1913, and 8th place (dead last) in 1914 and 1915.

In 1914, Warhop posted an 8-15 record with an excellent 2.37 ERA, the league ERA

Opposite top: Jack Warhop stands among his teammates during batting practice in 1909. Why he is wearing what appears to be a Washington Senators sweater from the same period is a mystery (*Chicago Daily News* negatives collection, SDN-055092, courtesy Chicago Historical Society). *Opposite bottom*: Jack Warhop warms up while teammate Ray Caldwell observes from the Yankee dugout (Library of Congress, Prints & Photographs Division, LC-DIG-ggbain-13480).

WARHOP
N.Y. AM.

that year was 2.76. Five of Warhop's fifteen defeats were by a margin of one run (those five one-run losses are a dubious distinction that 6 other major league pitchers currently share with Warhop). Errors accounted for Yankee defeats in four of his other decisions. In 1915, Warhop's record sank to 7-9, and his career was coming to an early end at the age of 30. He had ample reason to be annoyed on May 6, 1915, when, in the third inning of a game against the Red Sox, a player named George Herman "Babe" Ruth slammed his first career home run off Warhop, sending the ball into the second deck of the right field stands at the Polo Grounds. Ruth was the starting pitcher for the Red Sox that day, the Yankees winning 4–3 in 13 innings as the Red Sox committed four errors. On June 2, again at the Polo Grounds, Ruth struck again, at the plate and on the mound, blasting another second deck home run, pitching well and beating Warhop and the Yankees by a 7–1 score.

Warhop led the Yankees in games pitched 4 times, in innings pitched 2 times, and led the team in complete games (21) in 1909. His overall career ERA as a Yankee, 3.09, is the 10th lowest ERA in team history for pitchers with at least 800 innings pitched for the team. One can only imagine what statistics Warhop could have produced on a pennant-winning team.

In his later years Warhop worked as a butler/caretaker for a Wall Street banker in Islip, Long Island. Unfortunately, his employer was familiar with the role Warhop had played in the career of "The Babe." Occasionally, while guests and friends were enjoying themselves at parties, Warhop's employer would mention Ruth and say, "Would you like to meet the man off whom Babe hit his first home run?" The puzzled guests all nodded and: "Wait a minute, I'll call him!" was the response. Poor Warhop was then summoned into the room to recreate and be questioned about the momentous event. This could have done nothing to improve his disposition.

24

MEANWHILE, IN BOSTON

While the Yankees were struggling things were much different about 200 miles north of New York City. Babe Ruth was one of the main ingredients in the pitching staff of the Yankees' fiercest rival—a star player for the Boston Red Sox from 1914 to 1919. Ruth won 18 games in 1915, 23 in 1916 (with a league-leading 1.75 ERA), 24 in 1917, and 13 in 1918 as the Red Sox won the World Series in 1915, 1916 and 1918. By 1918 Ruth was spending less time on the pitching mound and more time in the Red Sox outfield and finding limited duty at first base (13 games in 1918). Ruth was a one man offensive force on the 1918 team,

From left, Boston Red Sox pitchers Babe Ruth, Ernie Shore and George "Rube" Foster and first baseman Del Gainer. The Red Sox beat the Philadelphia Phillies in the 1915 World Series 4 games to 1. The Red Sox also won the 1916 World Series 4 games to 1. Gainer hit a single in the 14th inning of Game Two of the 1916 Series, driving in the winning run and giving the Red Sox a 2–1 victory over the Brooklyn Dodgers. Gainer's hit ended the longest game in World Series history and provided Ruth with his first postseason pitching victory (Library of Congress, Prints & Photographs Division, LC-USZ62-23241).

contributing a .300 average with 11 home runs and 66 RBI (no other player on the team hit more than one home run in 1918 and Ruth's 66 RBI led all players).

Born in Baltimore, Maryland, on February 6, 1895, Ruth said he had a "rotten start" in life. His parents worked long hours in the family business, a tavern on the waterfront. As a result, Ruth was mostly on his own, skipping school, spending many childhood days on the streets and piers, chewing tobacco and tasting whiskey. He was placed in St. Mary's Industrial School, a reformatory and orphanage, at the age of seven, learning practical skills and a love for baseball under the guidance of Brother Matthias. Ruth gained notoriety as a left-handed pitcher for the school team. Jack Dunn, player/manager and owner of the Baltimore Orioles of the International League, was impressed with Ruth. He obtained papers to become Ruth's guardian and signed him to play for the Orioles. Ruth was tagged with his nickname when other players saw the powerfully-built youngster, referring to him as "Dunn's newest babe." In 1914, for the sum of $3,000-$4,000, Ruth's contract was sold to owner Joseph Lannin of the Red Sox. The 19-year-old Ruth honed his skills with the Providence Grays of the International League and appeared in 4 games as a pitcher for the Red Sox in 1914. Ruth went 18-8 with a 2.44 ERA in his first full major league season in 1915.

Overall, with Ruth's help, the Red Sox were a huge success during a period in which the Yankee franchise was searching for light at the end of a seemingly endless tunnel. All that changed upon Ruth's eventual acquisition by the Yankees on January 5, 1920. "Sometimes I still can't believe what I saw," said Hall of Fame outfielder Harry Hooper, Ruth's teammate in Boston. "This 19-year-old kid, crude, poorly educated, only lightly brushed by the social veneer we call civilization, gradually transformed into the idol of American youth ... the symbol of baseball the world over ... loved by more people ... with an intensity of feeling that perhaps has never been equaled before or since." Hooper added: "I saw a man transformed into something pretty close to a god."

25

Mystery Man, Arthur Irwin

Like Hal Chase, Yankee scout and business manager Arthur Irwin had a great mind for baseball and how Irwin's mind functioned in other areas of his life caused controversy and is the stuff of mystery novels. Irwin's influence on the game of baseball cannot be overstated. He was the inventor of the first fingered fielder's glove.

Irwin was born on February 14, 1858, in Toronto, Ontario, Canada, moving to Boston with his family at the age of fifteen. He played amateur baseball and found his way to the roster of the 1880 Worcester Ruby Legs of the National League, being noted as a weak-hitting shortstop with excellent defensive skills. In 1883, during his first season with the NL's Providence Grays, a hard hit ball broke two fingers on Irwin's left hand. He purchased a large "driving" glove, applied padding and sewed the third and fourth fingers together. This glove soon became the standard glove used in baseball, replacing the fingerless models used previously. In 1884 Irwin batted .222 in the World Series as the Grays won the championship. He also produced an instructional manual on playing baseball in 1895. After a succession of managerial positions in the National League, Irwin joined the Yankees as a scout late in the 1908 season. He was responsible for signing many talented players, among them outfielder Birdie Cree and pitchers Jack Warhop, Jack Quinn and Ray Fisher. By 1912 Irwin was a vice president and chief of scouts with the team, securing and supervising spring training sites as well as trying to locate young, talented players. He commented: "Digging in the minors and little jerk-water towns for

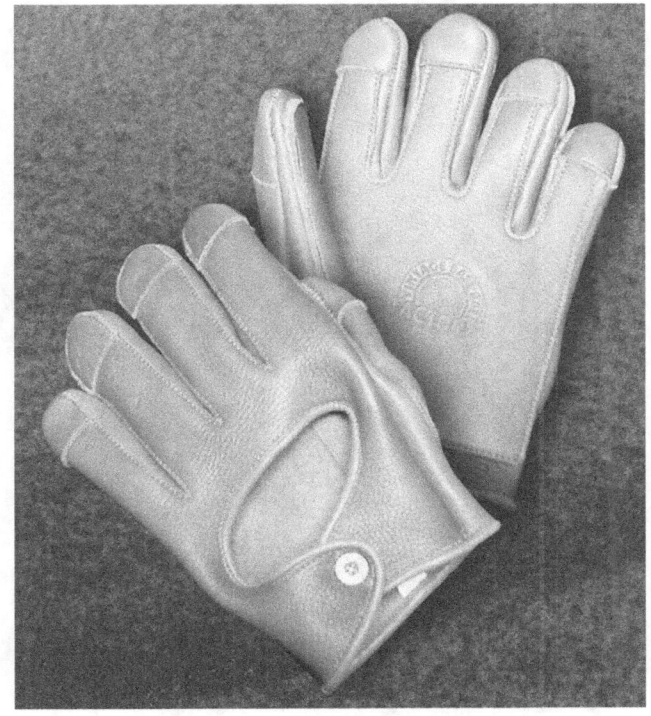

Reproduction of the Irwin model baseball glove, circa 1886–1889 (courtesy www.vintagebaseballfactory.com).

Goodwin & Co. Old Judge brand baseball card issued via cigarette packages in 1890 features Arthur Irwin with the Boston Reds of the Players League. The Reds finished in 1st place that season, winning the Players League championship. Irwin, 32, batted .260 in 96 games in 1890 (Library of Congress, Prints and Photographs Division, LOT 13163–05, no. 6, bbc 0078).

future diamond stars isn't what it is cracked up to be." By 1913, Irwin was promoted to business manager and became the man responsible for the Yankees unfortunate spring training adventure under Frank Chance in Bermuda.

Chance later claimed in December 1914 that Irwin bordered on incompetence, failed to sign good players during Chance's 1913-1914 managerial reign* and that owners Devery and Farrell bordered on apathy towards the situation: "The owners won't get me the players I need in order to win." Chance maintained that he resigned due to the fact that Irwin was retained as business manager/head of scouting. Chance's comments must have registered with new owners Ruppert and Huston since Irwin was dismissed from the Yankees before the 1915 season began.

In regard to Irwin's private life, he was reported to have had two marriages simultaneously, with wives and children in two cities, Boston and New York. They had no idea of each other's existence for thirty years. On July 16, 1921, Irwin set sail on the Calvin Austin, a steamship, going through the Atlantic Ocean from New York to Boston. En route, he either jumped or was pushed off the ship. Whether because of guilt or fear of finally being revealed, Irwin possibly committed suicide. His body was never found. In 1989, Arthur Irwin was inducted into the Canadian Baseball Hall of Fame.

Partial list of players signed by Arthur Irwin as Yankees scout (includes players Yankee career record, years spent with team and overall major-league record):

Birdie Cree	.292 BA, 8 yrs. Major League Totals: same
Ray Fisher	76 Wins, 78 Losses, 8 yrs. Major League Totals: 100 Wins, 94 Losses, 2.82 ERA
Ray Caldwell	95 Wins, 99 Losses, 9 yrs. Major League Totals: 133 Wins, 120 Losses, 3.22 ERA
John Knight	.267 BA, 4 yrs. Major League Totals: .239 BA
Jack Quinn	81 Wins, 65 Losses, 7 yrs. Major League Totals: 247 Wins, 218 Losses, 3.29 ERA
Jack Warhop	69 Wins, 93 Losses 3.12 ERA, 8 yrs. Major League Totals: same

*An honest assessment of the Yankee roster in 1913-1914 indicates Chance was correct. However, Irwin did scout/sign many significant players for the Yankees prior to those seasons.

26

THE ENTERTAINER

Pitcher Marty McHale posted few wins during his 6-season major league pitching career but distinguished himself in many other areas: appearing on the vaudeville circuit,* writing sports columns for newspapers and becoming a highly successful stockbroker. McHale, the living embodiment of the term "happy-go-lucky," was born October 30, 1886, in Stoneham, Massachusetts. He was a star in baseball, football and track at the University of Maine. After throwing 3 straight no-hitters, offers from four teams came in, and McHale signed with the Red Sox, appearing in 2 games during the 1910 season. McHale had a decent fastball and mixed his pitches well, also showcasing a curveball and spitball, and had the ability to change speeds on both those pitches. However, his career in Boston was undistinguished, at least on the field, and he was sent to Jersey City in 1911. Off the field, he formed a singing quartet with other Red Sox players.

McHale was signed by the Yankees for $6,000 during the 1913 season, leading to new career options in addition to his pitching. He joined outfielder Mike Donlin in the vaudeville show entitled "Right off the Bat." While McHale seemed more suited for a career in entertainment, Donlin certainly had the better baseball career—hitting .333 over 12 seasons with the Cardinals, Reds, Giants and other teams. Donlin's baseball career was coming to a close at this time but McHale's was somewhat renewed with the Yankees at the age of 27. McHale pitched the 1914 season opener, at the Polo Grounds on April 14, an interesting selection by then manager Frank Chance considering the presence of Ray Caldwell, Ray Fisher, and Jack Warhop on the staff. McHale pitched well and the Yankees, who batted .229 as a team that year, had an offensive explosion beating the World Champion Philadelphia Athletics 8 to 2.

McHale enjoyed his best season in baseball in 1914, winning 7 games and losing 16, while posting a 2.97 ERA for the 6th place Yankees. One only needs to understand McHale's bright personality to realize he took it all in stride, and the poor record was not so much an indictment of his pitching skills at the time as it was reflective of the poor team on which he played. In addition, McHale was one of few Yankee players to get along with Frank Chance, who admired the pitcher's dedication to his craft. Things changed drastically in 1915, as McHale posted a 3-7 record with a 4.27 ERA. He signed with the Red Sox again in 1916, retiring from major league baseball after the season.

*Vaudeville was a type of theatre that flourished in the United States from the 1880s through the 1920s. A wide variety of "acts" were presented, ranging from comedians, singers/dancers, to opera/dramatic plays, serious lectures and acrobatics or gymnastics presentations.

Top: Pitcher Marty McHale, enjoying life to the fullest in every situation (Library of Congress, Prints & Photographs Division, LC-DIG-ggbain-15259). *Above*: In the early to mid-teens the Yankees acquired pitchers with colorful nicknames—Boardwalk Brown, Cy Pieh and King Cole. Pictured in his Philadelphia A's uniform is Carroll "Boardwalk" Brown of Woodbury, New Jersey. Brown received his nickname since he was discovered playing on a sandlot near the Atlantic City boardwalk by an Athletics scout. He went 17–11 for the A's in 1913, but had no appearances in the A's World Series victory, 4 games to 1 over the Giants. On July 12, 1913, Brown walked 15 Tigers in $7\frac{2}{3}$ innings, still managing to win as the A's plowed over Detroit, 16–9. Brown's contract was sold to the Yankees by Philadelphia after he went 1–6 with a 4.09 ERA to begin the 1914 season. Brown could not recapture his early success of 1913 going 2–6 for New York in 1915 and leaving major league baseball at the age of 26 (Library of Congress, Prints & Photographs Division, LC-DIG-ggbain-14021).

Edwin "Cy" Pieh was with the Yankees from 1913 to 1915, pitching in relief, going 4-4 in 1914 and 4-5 in 1915 with a 2.87 ERA. Pieh was playing with a Dayton, Ohio, minor league team on August 11, 1913, when the Yankees purchased his contract for $1,500. Despite limited opportunities—and some might say limited success ("Lemon Pieh" joked the *Washington Post*)—Pieh could occasionally shine on the mound. On July 2, 1915, Pieh, in a rare start, limited the Senators to 2 hits, winning 1–0 at the Polo Grounds. The *New York Times* reported: "For quite a while he has been leading a hermit sort of existence, seldom coming out of the shadows, and just why such should have been the case is one of the mysteries to which only "Wild Bill" Donovan holds the key. At any rate, he has been on the bench when other Yankees were floundering and losing games, almost his only pastime having been to go in as a relief pitcher." Pieh couldn't carry over his midseason success into convincing Donovan to start him on a regular basis. Pieh was with the Yankees in spring training of 1916, but didn't make the team. By 1917 he had returned to the minors, with San Antonio of the Texas League (National Baseball Hall of Fame Library, Cooperstown, N.Y.).

Pitcher Leonard "King" Cole, standing, and third baseman Fritz Maisel, goofing around. Cole stood 6'1" while Maisel was about 5'7". In 1910, Cole went 20–4 with a 1.80 ERA and a National League–leading .883 winning percentage, helping the Chicago Cubs win the NL pennant. In 1911 he posted an 18–7 record. On February 3, 1914, Cole signed a $3,300 contract to pitch for the Yankees, since Yankee manager Frank Chance admired Cole's talent while Cole pitched for him on the Cubs. On October 2, 1914, in Boston, Cole gave up a double to Babe Ruth as the Red Sox won 11–5. It was Ruth's first hit in major league baseball. According to sportswriter Ring Lardner, Cole was a bad poker player. So bad, in fact, that manager Chance threatened to fine Cole $50 unless Cole improved his playing during team poker games on train trips. Cole went 11-9 in 1914. He appeared in only 10 games in 1915, being sent home to Bay City, Michigan, after a diagnosis of "internal trouble" during a medical examination. On January 6, 1916, Cole died of cancer that began in his lungs and rapidly spread. He was 29 years old (National Baseball Hall of Fame Library, Cooperstown, N.Y.).

From left, Yankee outfielders Luther "Doc" Cook, Hugh High, Birdie Cree, Tom Daley and Roy Hartzell in 1915. This is most likely a spring training photograph since Hugh High is wearing a 1913–1914 home uniform and all of the players' socks are 1913–1914 era team issue. The left-handed hitting Cook, a graduate of Vanderbilt University, was a good player on terrible Yankee teams from 1913 to 1915. He batted .264 in 1913, .283 in 1914 and .271 in 1915. In 1914 and 1915 he was the starting right fielder. Birdie Cree retired after the 1915 season, leaving behind a .292 career batting average in his 8 seasons with the Yankees (Library of Congress, Prints & Photographs Division, LC-DIG-ggbain-18761).

One career came to a close and numerous others began for the multi-talented McHale. During World War I, in 1917, McHale enlisted in the army, serving as lieutenant in the 22nd Regiment of Engineers. Upon his return to the United States McHale became a sports journalist for the *New York Evening Sun*, specializing in baseball. He became a stockbroker on Wall Street in 1920, eventually launching his own brokerage house, M.J. McHale Company Investments and Securities, with an office located on 115 Broadway in Manhattan. McHale retired in Hempstead, Long Island, after 52 years as the head of his very successful firm. He passed away at the age of 90 in 1979.

27

TRANSITIONS, 1916–1917

The Yankees' rise to 5th place in 1915, albeit a modest improvement, coincided with the downfall of one of the strongest teams in the American League—the Philadelphia Athletics. From 1910 to 1914, the Athletics won 4 AL pennants and 3 World Series, with a star-studded cast of players like second baseman Eddie Collins, third baseman Frank Baker and pitchers Eddie Plank, Charles "Chief" Bender and Bob Shawkey (all except Shawkey are in the Hall of Fame). While he couldn't have anticipated it at the time, venerable Athletics manager Connie Mack's plan to disband his great teams of 1910–1914 not only ended the Yankees' early period of mediocrity but put Mack's own team into a 14-year tailspin. Eddie Plank and "Chief" Bender both signed on with the Federal League for 1915 at higher salaries than Mack wanted to pay. "It is more profitable for me to have a team that is in contention for most of the season but finishes about fourth," Mack once said. "A team like that will draw well enough during the first part of the season to show a profit for the year, and you don't have to give the players raises when they don't win."

Mack's business model, or rationalizations, proved profitable for the Yankees. In July of 1915, the Yankees had purchased pitcher Bob Shawkey's contract from the Athletics for the reported sum of $85,000. Third baseman Frank "Home Run" Baker sat out the entire 1915 season in a contract dispute with Mack. The Yankees bought his contract in February 1916 for a reported $37,500. Baker, 30 years of age in 1916, earned his nickname in the 1911 World Series against the Giants, due to hitting game winning home runs two days in a row against future Hall of Fame pitchers Rube Marquard and Christy Mathewson. He also led the AL in home runs from 1911 to 1914, 12 being his highest total during these deadball seasons. Twenty-seven-year-old Lee Magee was also "corralled" from the defunct Federal League. Magee, born Leopold Christopher Hoernschemeyer, played second base for the Brooklyn Tip-Tops in 1915, batting .323. He began his career in 1911, playing in the infield for the St. Louis Cardinals.

Magee became the Yankees starting centerfielder in 1916 as another Federal League refugee, Joe Gedeon, became New York's starting second baseman. Gedeon batted .317 in 1915 while with Los Angeles in the Pacific Coast League. He had signed a two-year contract to join the Newark Peppers, owned by oil baron Harry Sinclair, but the Federal League disbanded and the Yankees stepped in to purchase Gedeon's contract for $7,500. Cash transactions were the name of the game for the Yankees under Ruppert and Huston as the new owners tried to take the quickest route possible to create a winning team.

Mix and match: Infielder/outfielder Charles John "Paddy" Baumann (name misspelled at bottom) in a posed photo circa 1916. The Yankees had two types of home uniforms in 1916—both pinstriped, one with the interlocked "NY" on the left side of the chest and one without. The non-"NY" logo uniform was usually worn with the dark cap shown in this photograph, while the uniform with the logo typically included a similarly styled cap—white with blue pinstripes and a blue bill on the cap. Hitting ability was the main reason the Yankees acquired Baumann. He batted .292 in 76 games in 1915 and .287 in 79 games in 1916, the most games he played in a season during a 7-year major-league career. Baumann finished with a .274 career batting average (Library of Congress, Prints & Photographs Division, LC-DIG-ggbain-19504).

Opposite: In 1916, Frank "Home Run" Baker batted .269 for the Yankees with 10 home runs and 52 RBI. He never posted an average lower than .282 for New York in the next four full seasons in which he played despite swinging one of the heaviest bats—if not the heaviest—ever used in major league baseball history. Baker's bat weighed more than 50 ounces and had almost no taper, the handle of the bat being almost the size of the barrel. Baker's bat was a Louisville Slugger model, manufactured by Hillerich & Bradsby Company of Louisville, Kentucky. A company spokesman once evaluated Baker's bat by saying "It was short ... almost like a piece of lead." Baker's RBI totals from 1917 to 1921 (he sat out the 1920 season) are 71, 62, 83 and 71. Baker never played any position other than third base over the course of his 13-year career. In 1955 he was elected to the National Baseball Hall of Fame by the Veterans Committee (Library of Congress, Prints & Photographs Division, LC-DIG-ggbain-21289).

27. Transitions, 1916–1917

A Love story: In another posed shot, left-handed pitcher Edward "Slim" Love faces the camera. He was aptly named (and nicknamed)—being born on August 1, 1890, in Love, Mississippi. He stood 6'7" and weighed 195 pounds. Love joined the Yankees in 1916 and pitched sparingly in 1916 and 1917. He notched a 13-12, 3.07 ERA record in 1918. Love was second in wins that year on the New York team behind another left-handed starter, George Mogridge, who won 16 games (Library of Congress, Prints & Photographs Division, LC-DIG-ggbain-26806).

Frank Baker, as well as first baseman Wally Pipp, were being counted on to provide power and defense for the Yankees. On February 13, 1916, as his team looked forward to spring training in Macon, Georgia, manager Bill Donovan stated: "Pipp is only a young fellow. He certainly can field his position to perfection, and unless I miss my guess by many yards I think he will begin hitting the ball in approved style." Donovan guessed correctly. Pipp led the Yankees in home runs (12) and RBI (93) in 1916, hitting .262.

On the mound in 1916, 25-year-old right-hander Bob Shawkey emerged as the staff ace, producing a 24-14 record with a 2.21 ERA. Nick Cullop, 13-6, 2.05 ERA and Ray Fisher, 11-8, 3.17 ERA pitched well and the 12 home runs from Wally Pipp and 10 from Frank Baker helped the Yankees led the league in home runs in 1916. Baker sustained broken ribs and missed 50 games after he crashed into one of the Polo Grounds' concrete barriers while chasing a pop fly. Twenty-four-year-old Frank Gilhooley, in his 4th season with the Yankees, was a bright spot in the lineup, batting .278 and playing right field until breaking his right leg near the ankle while sliding into third base on July 3rd. Elsewhere in the Yankee lineup Lee Magee (.257, 3 home runs. 45 RBI) and Joe Gedeon (.211, 0 home runs, 27 RBI) were major disappointments. The overall team batting average of .246 led to a 80-74 record and 4th place finish. The low point of the season came on September 8th in Philadelphia. Twenty-three people showed up at Shibe Park to see the Yanks lose to the Athletics, 8–2. The fact that the A's were on their way to finishing 36-117 in last place explains the sparse crowd, and additional apathy was the result of former A's stars Baker and Shawkey now wearing Yankee pinstripes. Though no one in Philadelphia cared what the Yankees (or Athletics) were doing, there was an air of excitement with the Yankees' new additions and it brought an upswing in attendance at the Polo Grounds.

The Yankees drew 469,211 fans in 1916, above the average league attendance of 431,486. While renewed optimism applied to Baker and the imports from other teams this year, other factors were at work for veteran Yankee spitballer Ray Caldwell, who had been counted on to lead the pitching staff along with Shawkey and Fisher. Caldwell was saddled with a 5-12 record, despite a 2.99 ERA. He became the Jack Warhop of the 1916 Yankee season, suffering poor run support and losing the opening game of the season at the Polo Grounds 3–2 in 11 innings to the Senators. A 2–1 loss to the White Sox in July

Ray "Slim" Caldwell at the Polo Grounds. Despite talk of owners Ruppert and Huston building a new stadium, the Yankees remained at the Polo Grounds as co-tenants with the Giants from 1913 to 1922. Caldwell was a great pitcher on bad Yankee teams. His highest win totals were 14 in 1911, 17 in 1914, 19 in 1915 and 13 in 1917. His overall ERA as a Yankee is 2.99 (Library of Congress, Prints & Photographs Division, LC-DIG-ggbain-12241).

and a 1–0 loss to the Indians the same month were typical of games in which Caldwell was: 1. The losing pitcher 2. Facing the best pitcher on the opposing team—Eddie Cicotte of the White Sox and Jim Bagby of the Indians in the aforementioned examples. Caldwell also had other "issues," so to speak, which adversely affected the Yankees' hopes for finally tracking down their first American League pennant. To say that Caldwell enjoyed New York nightlife to its fullest would be an understatement. His frequent bouts of drinking and some unexplained absences from the team (which dated back to the Harry Wolverton era in 1912) overshadowed his pitching greatness. Caldwell was fined $250 in 1912 after failing to show up in Washington for a road trip and the *Washington Post* commented: "The erring slinger is generally regarded as one of the best men in the league when right." The appointment of the strict Frank Chance as manager did not bring an end to Caldwell's fun-loving ways according to teammate Chet Hoff: "I'll tell you a good one about Ray Caldwell. [During spring training] we were all sitting there on the porch [of the hotel] one night. We had a curfew of 11 o'clock. Ray turns and says 'Well, so long fellas, I'm going up to bed. I'm tired.' There was a window in the room. Ray went out that back window. Down the road they had a dance every Saturday night. Ray went down there—he didn't get back until 4 o'clock in the morning. The nightwatchman of the hotel saw Ray come in. Later that morning Chance was told by the nightwatchman everything that happened. Ray was at breakfast at 9 A.M.— Chance was waiting for him. Then the fireworks started!" Caldwell was fined $50—a large sum back then considering the players didn't receive pay until the season began in April.

Caldwell's partying ways also led to trouble with "Wild Bill" Donovan, a far more easy-going manager and person than Frank Chance. By August 10, 1916, the Yankees plummeted in the standings, falling all the way to 6th place (albeit only 6 games out). Caldwell disappeared. He was immediately fined $100 and received a 15-day suspension. When Caldwell failed to report to the team later in the month he was suspended for the remainder of the season. To his credit, Caldwell was reported to have been undergoing alcohol treatment in St. Louis. He apologized to Yankee owners Ruppert and Huston in person and did return to the pitching mound in 1916—not with the Yankees due to the suspension but in a more exotic location—Panama— pitching under a different name.

Caldwell remained the team's biggest question mark as 1916 turned into 1917. On December 19, 1916, the *Washington Post* reported: "Though nothing has been heard from Ray Caldwell since he visited

While Ray Caldwell was squandering his talent with his hard-partying ways, pitcher Bob Shawkey was quietly consistent. He was a 4-time 20-game winner for the Yankees from 1916 to 1927 (Library of Congress, Prints & Photographs Division, LC-DIG-ggbain-19478).

the Yankee offices late in September, both the owners of the club and Manager Donovan are counting on him as one of the regulars for 1917. They will not talk of any trade or sale involving the big pitcher, who ranks with the stars of the profession when he tends strictly to business.... Caldwell has told friends that he is sorry about his 1916 failure, and is anxious to do his best for the Yanks." Not too anxious apparently. Caldwell was nowhere to be found as the Yankees descended upon Macon, Georgia, for spring training, on February 25th, 1917. The *Washington Post* followed up on the adventures of Caldwell: "Caldwell bobbed up in Panama last winter. He was playing for the Colon team under an assumed name. Manager Donovan was willing to start a clean slate with his pitcher, but Caldwell evidently does not wish to have things that way.... Caldwell is an example of a great pitcher going to ruin by his failure to take care of himself.... Caldwell's presence on the Yankee roster means a chance for the pennant. His failure to report may mean that he will be out of baseball for good."

Caldwell eventually returned for spring training, although one week late. As for the Yankees winning the 1917 AL pennant? That was another matter entirely.

"Wild Bill prophesizes most successful season on record for Captain Huston's Cohorts," read the *New York Times* during the Yankees 1917 spring training preparations in Macon. "If we have better luck than we did last year and none of our players are injured, I think we will

Second baseman Joe Gedeon's good batting numbers in the minor leagues did not translate into success at the major league level—at least with the Yankees. He batted .211 in 1916 and .239 in 1917. Gedeon saved his best years for time spent with the St. Louis Browns, the team he was traded to in 1918. He batted .254 in 1919 and .292 in 1920, his last two years in the major leagues (Library of Congress, Prints & Photographs Division, LC-DIG-ggbain-21196).

be well up in the pennant race.... I look for big improvement at the bat this season with Pipp, Baker, Magee and Gilhooley. I expect that Caldwell will be back in shape by the start of the season, and when he is right, there is no better pitcher in the American League. Shawkey, Mogridge, and Cullop ought to win more games than in 1916, and I look for an improvement in Ray Fisher." Ray Caldwell and Ray Fisher shared the same first name, both threw a mean spitball, and had an amicable relationship as teammates but two players with more divergent personalities could scarcely be imagined. Unlike Caldwell, Fisher never needed to be fined or disciplined because he disciplined himself. (One example being a rainy day in spring training which found Fisher at the local YMCA working out indoors instead of taking the day off.)

Of more significance than hitting, pitching or the Yankee outlook for the 1917 season was the fact that World War I continued to rage overseas as it had since 1914. Yankee co-owner "Cap" Huston oversaw the spring training and early season games before going to Europe as an officer with the 18th Engineers of the United States Army. Huston brought drill sergeants to Macon—where the Yankees carried bats in formation instead of rifles—to inspire his team. Pipp at first base, Peckinpaugh at shortstop and Baker at third base were the core of the New York team. Unfortunately for Donovan, Pipp regressed at the plate in 1917, batting .244, though he was second in RBI on the team with 70 after Baker's 71. Baker notched a .282 average to lead all regulars but Magee imploded at .220 and was traded in mid-season. Frank Gilhooley was lost to injury again—a fractured collar bone in May, and his season ended with a .242 average in 54 games.

The highlight of the Yankees' 1917 season came early in the year—April 24th. Left-hander George Mogridge faced the Red Sox—the reigning 1916 World Series champions—at Fenway Park. Mogridge threw a no-hitter as the Yankees won 2–1. According to the *New York Times*: "The champions scored on the combination of two [bases on balls], an error, and a sacrifice fly, but all afternoon they made nothing that looked the least bit like a safe hit, Mogridge having a great mixture of slow and fast service, which was continually effective." The Yankees also had problems at the plate, being held scoreless through five innings by twenty-five-year-old Red Sox left-hander Hubert "Dutch" Leonard, winner of 16 games in 1917. The Yankees scored in the 6th inning on a double by Angel Aragon (starting at third base due to Frank Baker's illness) and a single by Lee Magee, with Red Sox left-fielder Duffy Lewis making an error on the hit,

Leslie Nunamaker was the Yankees' starting catcher from 1914 to 1917. On May 13, 1914, Frank Farrell paid Red Sox owner Joesph Lannin $5,000 to purchase Nunamaker's contract. Nunamaker batted .262 during his four years with the Yankees. On August 3, 1914, in the second inning of a game in Detroit, he set a major league record by throwing out 3 base runners attempting to steal. As was their tendency that year, the Yankees lost the game, 4–1 (National Baseball Hall of Fame Library, Cooperstown, N.Y.).

Infielders Lute "Danny" Boone, Joe Gedeon, and Charlie Mullen. Boone was a descendant of the explorer Daniel Boone, who was responsible for the exploration and settlement of Kentucky. Lute achieved less notoriety than did Daniel, batting .209 in a 5-season career. Mullen, a right-handed hitter, was used primarily as a first baseman, being relegated to a backup role with the emergence of Wally Pipp. Mullen batted .267 in 1916. During 3 seasons of sporadic playing time in New York, Mullen maintained a .263 average (Library of Congress, Prints & Photographs Division, LC-DIG-ggbain-21197).

allowing it to pass him as Aragon raced home to score. With the game tied in the top of the ninth Peckinpaugh reached first on a sharply hit ball which handcuffed Boston third baseman Mike McNally. Peckinpaugh immediately stole second. He scored the winning run when Yankee catcher Leslie Nunamaker hit the ball to third and McNally threw the ball "into the dirt at [first baseman] Del Gainer's feet" added the *New York Times*.

Mogridge, born February 18, 1889, in Rochester, NY, was a talented pitcher and great competitor. He attended the University of Rochester for two years but solely for athletic reasons. His course of study each year was "penmanship" but a career in baseball was Mogridge's main goal. The *Chicago Daily Tribune* reported: "The fact was that the college team was pretty strong in every department except pitching. So it was fixed up for Mogridge to matriculate and take a course in writing so he would be eligible to pitch." Mogridge gained arm strength and kept in shape by working at his trade as a "slate roofing expert." "Except on extremely cold days, he is on the roofs of Rochester in the offseason. This yields $5 a day," added the *Chicago Daily Tribune*.

The low run scoring in Mogridge's no-hit game continued through the season. A lack of punch in the 1917 Yankee outfield (Elmer Miller, .251, Tim Hendryx, .249 and

Of this group of Yankee outfielders in spring training, only Hugh High was a starting player in 1916. High—like first baseman Wally Pipp and third baseman Frank Baker—was one of a select number of left-handed hitters signed by the Yankees as they began their development into a slugging team, trying to take advantage of the short right field fence (256 feet) at the Polo Grounds. Unlike Pipp and Baker, High showed little power and was used in a different way, usually batting second or lead-off. He was the starting left fielder in 1916, batting .263 with one home run (Library of Congress, Prints & Photographs Division, LC-DIG-ggbain-21288).

Opposite top: Yankee pitching staff candidates in 1916. Right-hander Clarence "Dazzy" Vance, circled, pitched briefly for the Yankees in 1915, didn't make the team in 1916, and appeared in only 2 games in 1918. He was released on December 31, 1919, going to the Sacramento Solons' minor league team. He reappeared on the Brooklyn Dodgers' roster in 1922, getting his first major league win at the age of 31, and became a 3-time 20-game winner. He won 18 games 2 times for pathetic Brooklyn teams. (In 1928, the Dodgers finished in 6th place while Vance won 22 games and had a 2.09 ERA.) Vance was elected to the Baseball Hall of Fame in 1955 (Library of Congress, Prints & Photographs Division, LC-DIG-ggbain-21290). *Opposite bottom*: On the march: Opening Day at the Polo Grounds, April 11, 1917, as the Yankees prepare to face the Red Sox. Attacks by German U-boats (submarines) on American merchant ships were a major reason that President Woodrow Wilson requested that Congress declare war on Germany. This was done on April 6, 1917, and the United States entered World War I. The effects are shown on the baseball field as the Yankees walk in formation with bats on their shoulders. Army Sgt. Gibson leads the group, and Yankee owners Huston and Ruppert are by his side. Huston himself would soon journey to Europe to serve with an army engineer division. The game summary in the *New York Times* read: "With their bats over their shoulders they went through all the manoeuvres of military formations so smartly that the crowd was on its feet cheering the baseball boys for their fine showing as soldiers" (Library of Congress, Prints & Photographs Division, LC-DIG-ggbain-24148).

27. Transitions, 1916–1917

27. Transitions, 1916–1917

The 1917 Yankees. Back row: Nick Cullop, Aaron Ward, Fritz Maisel, Frank Gilhooley, Allen Russell, Roxy Walters, Walt Alexander, Tim Hendryx. Second row: Ray Caldwell, George Mogridge, Ray Fisher, Bob Shawkey, Elmer Miller, Urban Shocker, Joe Gedeon, Roger Peckinpaugh, Coach Duke Farrell (a returnee from the George Stallings era). Third row: Paddy Baumann, Leslie Nunamaker, Slim Love, Manager Bill Donovan, Wally Pipp, Armando Marsans, Angel Aragon. Front row: Hugh High, unknown, Team Trainer James Duggan, unknown, Jim McGovern, Frank Baker (Brown Brothers).

Hugh High, .236), helped doom the team to a collective batting average of .239, lowest in the AL.

A look at the box score of a 4–1 August 19th loss to the Browns in St. Louis shows the following lineup: High (LF), Miller (CF), Peckinpaugh (SS), Pipp (1B), Maisel (2B), Baker (3B), Caldwell (RF), Walters (C), Mogridge (P). The *New York Times* reported: "A grand shakeup of the batting order and lineup was put through by Bill Donovan in the hope that he could get more hitting and tighter fielding, but the club failed in both respects this afternoon." In essence the 1917 Yankee offense was so poor, at least in terms of batting average, that Donovan turned to pitcher Ray Caldwell in a late-season game and had him batting seventh and playing right field. Since Caldwell batted .258 in 1917 you could say he was as good an option as the other Yankee outfielders. (Caldwell also batted .289 in 1913, .291 in 1918 and .296 in 1919—far from an automatic out.)

Opposite: Manager Bill Donovan greets Major General Leonard Wood of the Army before the April 11, 1917, season opener. Attendance was 16,000 fans, far above the average 1917 Polo Grounds game attendance of 4,262 persons per game. Attendance at the Polo Grounds declined from 469,211 in 1916 to 330,294 in 1917 as the Yankees sank to a 71–82 6th place finish in the American League. Pitcher Babe Ruth started for the Red Sox against Ray Caldwell. Boston won easily, 10–3. The Yankee batting order of right fielder Frank Gilhooley, left fielder Hugh High, second baseman Fritz Maisel, first baseman Wally Pipp, third baseman Frank Baker, center fielder Lee Magee, shortstop Roger Peckinpaugh, and catcher Leslie Nunamaker looked strong on the lineup card but did little against the Babe. Yankee batters posted a .239 average for the 1917 season, lowest in the AL, despite leading the league in home runs with 27 (Library of Congress, Prints & Photographs Division, LC-DIG-ggbain-24200).

1, Pipp; 2, Shawkey; 3, Peckinpaugh; 4, Baker; 5, L. Magee; 6, High; 7, Walters; 8, Nunamaker; 9, Fisher; 10, Gilhooley.
Conlon, Photos.

A GROUP OF NEW YORK AMERICANS.

The 1917 New York pitching staff suffered from the lack of run support. Only two starters won more than nine games, and the won-lost records of the staff in general looked poor despite good ERAs. Shawkey was 13-15, 2.44 and Caldwell showed a 13-16, 2.86 mark. Ray Fisher (reportedly earning $6,666 in salary) clocked in with a 8-9, 2.19 ERA showing and George Mogridge was 9-11, 2.98 ERA. The team descended to a 6th place finish (71-82). It proved to be Bill Donovan's last year at the helm of the Yankee ship. He was summoned to the corner of 90th Street and 3rd Avenue in Manhattan, the site of co-owner Jake Rupert's brewery. "I like you Donovan, but we have to make some changes around here," said Ruppert. Donovan responded: "I know it, Colonel." An overall 220-239 record in the three seasons from 1915 to 1917 sealed Donovan's fate. Dono-

Angel Aragon was the first Cuban and Latin American player to wear a New York Yankee uniform. He was a third baseman/outfielder who appeared in 32 games for New York during his career in 1914 and 1916–1917. Aragon played third base for the Long Branch, N.J., Cubans in the Class D Atlantic League in 1913. He made his first appearance with the Yankees as a pinch hitter in the second inning of an 11–8 loss to the Cleveland Indians at the Polo Grounds on August 20, 1914. Aragon hit a single that scored two runs, inspiring the catchy *New York Times* headline: "Angel Pinch Hits, But Yankees Lose." In his later years Aragon scouted for the New York Giants and did maintenance work for the New York IRT (Interborough Rapid Transit Company), the operator of the original subway line that opened in 1904 (Library of Congress, Prints & Photographs Division, LC-DIG-ggbain-17099).

van went on to manage the 1921 Philadelphia Phillies for a partial season (with a 25-62 record) and in 1921 he took over the managerial post for a minor league club in New Haven, Con-

Opposite: This page from the 1917 *Spalding Baseball Guide* shows a group of Yankee players from the 1916 season. Past contributors like Ray Fisher and Roger Peckinpaugh are featured with newer talented acquisitions like first baseman Wally Pipp, pitcher Bob Shawkey, third baseman Frank Baker, outfielder Lee Magee, catchers Roxy Walters and Leslie Nunamaker and outfielder Frank Gilhooley. The catching tandem of Walters and Nunamaker proved more than adequate. Nunamaker batted .296 in 91 games in 1916, and Walters batted .266 in 65 games behind the plate. Walters did buck the evolving Yankee tradition of power baseball. In four seasons with New York—and across an 11-year career with two other teams—he did not hit any home runs. Magee was a controversial player of great ability. Under contract to the St. Louis Cardinals in 1915, he instead became a contract "jumper" by signing with the 1915 Brooklyn Tip-Tops of the Federal League. Magee managed the Tip-Tops and played second base for them in 1915, batting .323. The Federal League disbanded over the winter of 1915-1916 as a "peace treaty" was formed with the AL and NL. Magee was then sold to the Yankees on January 14, 1916, for $25,000. Note the presence of left-handed sluggers Pipp and Baker as well as the switch-hitting Magee. Long before Babe Ruth joined the Yankees, they assembled a lineup that featured left-handed power bats to send home runs flying over the short 256-foot fence in right field of the Polo Grounds. The Yankees led the American League in home runs in 1915 (31), 1916 (35) and 1917 (27) (Library of Congress).

Third baseman Fritz Maisel's last year with the Yankees was 1917. He would soon be part of a multi-player trade with the St. Louis Browns. "Flash" once held the Yankee single-season stolen base record with 74 (now held by Rickey Henderson with 93, set in 1988). Maisel batted .243 in five seasons with the Yankees—only three of those years as a starting player—but his strength was on the base paths. He stole 183 bases in 502 games (National Baseball Hall of Fame Library, Cooperstown, N.Y.).

George Mogridge threw the second no-hitter in Yankee history on April 24, 1917, at Fenway Park. Mogridge's highest win total for the Yankees was 16 in 1918, but he achieved even better totals after leaving them. Mogridge was placed on waivers after the 1920 season, at the age of 31, and was picked up by the Washington Senators. He won 18 games in 1921 and 18 again in 1922. In 1924, Mogridge won 16 games and picked up a win in the 4th game of the World Series as the Senators defeated the New York Giants, 4 games to 3. The Senators of the early 1920s became a Yankee alumni society, as both Mogridge and Roger Peckinpaugh were on the team. Catcher Herold "Muddy" Ruel (signed by the Yankees on August 21, 1917, and with them until 1920) joined the Senators in 1923 as their starting catcher and batted .316. Ruel hit .283 for the 1924 World Series champs.

"Wild Bill" Donovan with New York Giants manager John McGraw before an exhibition game. By the late teens the Yankees were finally gaining a growing fan base in New York. McGraw was not happy with the turn of events, and his look of concern is indicative of the growing uneasy competition between the two Manhattan-based teams (Library of Congress, Prints & Photographs Division, LC-DIG-ggbain-22785).

necticut. It was there that Donovan finally won a pennant—the Eastern League pennant—in 1922. Donovan then guided New Haven to a win the post-season minor league series over Baltimore of the International League. He died under tragic circumstances on December 9, 1923. Donovan was killed in a train wreck in Forsyth, New York, while traveling to Chicago to attend the baseball winter meetings. Donovan exchanged sleeping berths with his business manager, taking a lower berth due to the proximity to the clattering train tracks, allowing the business manager the upper berth for

"Wild Bill" Donovan, October 13, 1876–December 9, 1923. Disappointing seasons with the Yankees left his managerial record at 245-301, for a .449 percentage, but Donovan's baseball talents are unquestioned. His 18-year major league pitching record stands at 186 wins, 139 losses, with a 2.69 ERA (Library of Congress, Prints & Photographs Division, LC-DIG-ggbain-18094).

a better night's sleep. The business manager in the upper berth survived the wreck unhurt. That man was George Weiss, later general manager of the Yankees from 1948 to 1960, a period in which they appeared in 10 World Series and won 7. Weiss was elected to the Hall of Fame in 1971.

Donovan's family and relatives were "prostrated" with grief upon hearing news of the death of "Wild Bill." His father was so overcome that a physician was called. Yankee owner Jake Ruppert, also on his way to the meetings in a different train, said: "This news hits me very hard. It is a great tragedy. I can't express my sorrow at hearing of Bill's untimely end.... When he was with the Yankees Donovan had more hard luck than I have ever seen on a ball field. One player after another was injured, but still Donovan kept plugging ahead, and he never forgot how to smile. 'Smiling Bill' was what they should have called him."

28

MILLER TIME, 1918

Owner Jake Ruppert wasted little time in finding a successor upon Bill Donovan's firing. "Miller Huggins to direct destinies of Yankees in place of Bill Donovan," proclaimed the *New York Times* on October 26, 1917, after Huggins signed a contract the previous afternoon. Though small in stature (standing 5 foot 6 and weighing 140 pounds) Miller Huggins would loom large in influence and success within the Yankee organization. Ban Johnson, the imperious AL president, stepped in again helping steer the destiny of the still floundering Yankee ship, convincing Jake Ruppert to hire Huggins away from the St. Louis Cardinals. Johnson's desire to show up the rival National League rose to the surface once more. Hiring talent away from the NL in trying to improve the Yankees' fortunes presented an irresistible opportunity. Miller Huggins would prove a far more wise selection to pilot the New York team than Frank Chance had been—with far more successful results than could even have been anticipated by Johnson, Ruppert, Huston and the growing legion of Yankee fans.

Making his major league debut in 1904, Huggins was a star second baseman/lead-off man for the Cincinnati Reds and St. Louis Cardinals, earning the nicknames "The Mighty Mite" and "Little Mr. Everywhere" for his habit of getting on base. Prior to his hiring by the Yankees, Huggins was a player/manager for the Cardinals, orchestrating their rise in the standings from 7th place in 1916 to 3rd place in 1917. J.G. Taylor Spink, publisher of St. Louis–based *The Sporting News*, touted as the "Bible of Baseball," counseled Huggins on proper interview attire so the mannered Ruppert would not think Huggins just strolled in off a city sidewalk: "Don't wear that damned street cap. Ruppert doesn't like 'em!" Huggins was hired to the chagrin of Yankee co-owner Huston, who wanted his crony/drinking partner Wilbert Robinson for the job. Robinson was managing the Brooklyn Dodgers at the time. Huston was still away in France participating with the Allied forces in World War I and could only register his objection after Huggins had already been installed as manager. Former Yankee Wid Conroy returned to New York as Huggins' assistant and scout Tom Connery also came to New York with Huggins, joining Joe Kelley and Bob Gilkes, scouts that were retained from Donovan's tenure with the team. "The new Yankee leader is considered one of the smartest managers in the game," said the *New York Times*. However, some New York reporters were disappointed in the selection of Huggins. They found him not as gregarious and talkative as former manager "Wild Bill" Donovan. What Huggins lacked in extroverted behavior he more than made up for in managerial acumen. Upon being appointed manager, Huggins said he intended to "strengthen" the Yankees. The slugging Yankee offense that "Wild Bill" Donovan began to institute would take its final form under the leadership of Miller Huggins. Under the stewardship of Ruppert and Huston the diminutive Huggins assembled a lineup he hoped would demolish Yankee opponents. In most cases, it did. A new era of Yankee baseball began.

Huggins' intention to strengthen the Yankees, at least for the immediate future, was partially achieved on January 22, 1918. The Yankees received second baseman Del Pratt and left-handed pitcher Eddie Plank by sending catcher Les Nunamaker, infielder Fritz Maisel, pitchers Nick Cullop and Urban Shocker, second baseman Joe Gedeon and $15,000 cash to the St. Louis Browns. The 41-year-old Plank, a future Hall of Famer, refused to report to the Yankees and retired, essentially rendering this a 5 for 1 deal. In Pratt, the Yankees acquired a player that provided excellent defensive capabilities with strong hitting. The 30-year-old Pratt led AL second basemen in double plays (82) and putouts (340) in 1918 while batting .275.

Considering that from 1915 to 1917 Yankee starting second basemen hit .204, .211 and .198, Pratt's contribution was most welcome. Unfortunately, the Yankees sacrificed a future star in pitcher Urban Shocker.

Urban Shocker's athletic achievements are not well known today, but one look at the record books indicates his greatness as a pitcher has been overlooked. Shocker posted four consecutive 20-win seasons for St. Louis: 20 in 1920, an AL high 27 in 1921, 24 in 1922 and 20 wins again in 1923. By all accounts Shocker was a quiet, intense competitor. He threw a fastball and curve ball and—like many Yankee pitchers dating back to the days of Chesbro—also threw a spitball.

Born Urbain Jacques Shockcor on August 22, 1890, Shocker began his baseball career not on the mound but behind the plate—as a catcher in semi-pro ball in Michigan and Canada. Shocker then pitched for four years in Canada, most notably for Ottawa of the Canada League, winning 20 games in 1914 and getting the attention of Yankee scout Joe Kelley. Shocker was signed to a contract late in the 1915 season for the sum of $750. Shocker threw his spitball occasionally as a breaking slow ball. He did not have a great fastball, being more of a finesse pitcher, and relied on a variety of curveballs. A bent finger which he sustained from his catching days helped his grip on these pitches. Shocker enjoyed pitching against the Yankees during his time with the Browns. He beat them 20 times while he wore a Browns uniform from 1918 to 1924, while the Yankees won 21 games against Shocker in that time period. Huggins recognized his mistake and reacquired Shocker in 1925. He went 19-11 for the Yankees in 1926 and 18-6 with a 2.84 ERA in 1927, helping vault them into the World Series each year, though he did not appear in the 1927 World Series sweep of the Pittsburgh Pirates. Shocker was only 36 but in very bad health.

Yankee manager Miller Huggins (Transcendental Graphics/ruckerarchive.com).

He suffered from a heart condition known as mitral valve stenosis, in which the mitral valve—responsible for regulating blood flow on the left side of the heart—fails to open as wide as it should. The heart is forced to work harder pumping blood through the narrowed valve and is weakened in the process, eventually leading to heart failure. Shocker appeared in one game for the Yankees in 1928 before being released in July, declaring "that he would retire from baseball and devote his time to the radio business and to aviation." Shocker, who had worked as a radio salesman and intended to get a pilot's license, relocated to Denver, Colorado. He pitched in a semi-pro tournament on August 6th, 1928, but contracted pneumonia shortly after that appearance. He entered St. Luke's Hospital in Denver on August 13th and soon looked to be in recovery. While still under treatment on September 8th Shocker suffered a relapse. He died the following day. Shocker was 38 years old. During the final years of his life he had been unable to sleep in a reclining position due to the threat of blood backing up into his lungs. Shocker tried, somewhat successfully, to keep his illness hidden from friends and teammates. Shocker's funeral was held in St. Louis on September 15th. Yankee manager Huggins and the entire 1928 Yankee team—soon on their way to another World Series sweep (against the St. Louis Cardinals) attended the funeral service to pay last respects to their fallen teammate. Lou Gehrig was one of the pallbearers.

World War I continued through 1918 and the baseball season was shortened accordingly. Thirty-one games were cancelled for the 1918 Yankee season as more important concerns remained in the collective consciousness of the United States as well as the world at large. Baseball did at least serve as a diversion from other grave events. Home Run Baker (.306) led the 1918 Yankee offense while right fielder Frank Gilhooley provided a .276 average. Left fielder Ping Bodie (born Francesco Stephano Pezzolo), acquired from the Philadelphia A's in March, batted .256 (far below his .291 average in 1917) but the overall Yankee team batting average made a dramatic improvement to .257, 3rd in the AL. Wally Pipp, drafted into the Army the past winter, returned but played in only 91 games, batting .304. Bob Shawkey spent virtually the entire 1918 season in the Navy, serving as a yeoman petty officer aboard the U.S. battleship *Arkansas*, leaving a 1-1 record. (Shawkey's military serv-

Urban Shocker: Shocker posted an excellent career pitching record of 187-117, a winning percentage of .615. His career ERA is 3.17 (Library of Congress, Prints & Photographs Division, LC-DIG-ggbain-37985).

ice earned him the nickname "Sailor Bob.") Ray Fisher served in the U.S. Army, missing the entire season. Ray Caldwell, 21-year-old pitcher Hank Thormahlen and Ping Bodie worked in New Jersey building ships for the war effort—as well as playing baseball. George Mogridge was the leading winner on Huggins' staff, going 16-13 with a 2.18 ERA. The 1918 Yankees finished in 4th place, with a 60-63 record, 13½ games behind the Red Sox.

Attendance suffered due to the shortened season and wartime service of many a prospective fan. Only 282,047 persons entered the Polo Grounds turnstiles. For the first time in four years the Yankees did not lead the league in home runs (the Athletics did with 22 round-trippers, just 2 more than New York) but with the shrewd Huggins at the helm the Yankees were undergoing a slow but steady transformation. The *Washington Post* commented: "Small as he is, Huggins has a dominant personality on the baseball diamond ... whatever the fate of the midget manager in New York, he is going to add color to an outfit which has been, perhaps, the most drab in baseball since Clark Griffith left New York."

29

THE VERMONT SCHOOLMASTER

One player that would not get a first-hand look at the changing of the Yankee guard under Huggins was veteran pitcher Ray Fisher, who had endured years of service on underachieving New York teams. Fisher just needed better timing. He made his major-league debut with the Yankees in 1910, but had he joined them just a few years later, Fisher might have been winning pennants instead of laboring for the constantly-in-transition Yankee teams of the early 20th century. As it was, on the strength of his right arm and pitching knowledge Fisher carved out a remarkable career both on and off the baseball diamond.

Ray Lyle Fisher was born in Middlebury, Vermont, in 1887, where his family lived as well as farmed. Fisher excelled in sports (football and basketball as well as baseball) and entered Middlebury College in 1906, after finishing high school in just three years. Fisher pitched for a Hartford, Connecticut, minor league team in 1908 (going 12-1 with a .304 batting average) and 1909 (24-5, including 243 strikeouts). Yankee scout Arthur Irwin came calling and Fisher signed a contract after the 1909 season, thinking: "Here's my opportunity for a career in baseball and a ticket off the farm." A provision in the contract allowed Fisher to finish college first and it underscored a life-long commitment to education that served Fisher well. Like Jack Chesbro before him, Fisher was a spitball pitcher. The key to the use of the spitball in Fisher's case was a substance called "slippery elm." The inner bark of this particular species of elm tree is quite slimy or slippery and was chewed on by players to produce enough saliva/spit to apply to the baseball. Hal Chase, Chesbro's teammate as well as manager, made this comment in 1911: "I look for Ray Fisher to be another Jack Chesbro. Any pitcher who can shove up such a heavy ball as Fisher and has a spit ball such as he can control will make good in the big league."

After his debut in 1910, Fisher taught Latin classes at Newton Academy in New Jersey, earning the nickname "The Vermont Schoolmaster." He was also athletic director at Middlebury College from 1911 to 1915, in addition to coaching football, basketball and teaching girls' gym classes. In eight seasons with the Yankees, from 1910 to 1917, Fisher's overall won-lost record was 76-78, while his ERA was above 3.00 in only four of those seasons. He mostly discontinued the use of his spitball by the 1914–1915 seasons. All things considered, Fisher did well in light of the teams he was a part of as well as the baseball fields on which he played: "We played in a terrible ballpark. Up on a hilltop. They called it Hilltop Park—and it wasn't even a good college field. The foul lines were cockeyed and the outfield was downhill, so when the batter hit one out there, it actually rolled toward the fences!" The move to the Polo Grounds in 1913 brought with it other problems. Fisher commented: "The Polo Grounds had this very short right field fence, maybe 220 feet. A high school kid could hit one over that." Fisher pitched from 1913 to 1917 at the Polo Grounds, the dimensions of which were 277 feet in left field, 455 feet in center, and actually 258 feet in right field. Pop fly balls hit down the left or right field lines easily became home runs. Despite this, Fisher enjoyed his best season at the Polo Grounds in 1915, going 18-11, throwing 20 complete games, with an ERA of 2.11 (the AL average ERA that year being 2.93). One of Fisher's former college classmates had this to say about his friend's 1913–1917 tenure at the Polo Grounds: "His years with the N.Y. Yankees had been heart-breakers. Day after day I saw him at the Polo Grounds pitch games that should have been his with a real team behind him. But he seemed destined to retire from the national pastime with nothing but a record as an average pitcher."

Fisher, like teammate Ray Caldwell, was far

Top: Ray Fisher was an excellent pitcher for a succession of terrible Yankee teams. He compiled an 18-11 record and 2.11 ERA in the 1915 season for a team that finished in 5th place (National Baseball Hall of Fame Library, Cooperstown, N.Y.). *Bottom*: Ray Fisher at the Polo Grounds (courtesy the family of Ray Fisher).

"The Three Rays" of the Yankee pitching staff, from left, Ray Keating, Ray Fisher and Ray Caldwell. Fisher and Caldwell joined the Yankees in 1910 while Keating appeared in 1912. In addition to sharing the same first name, they were all right-handed pitchers and threw a mean spitball. In December 1920, during the winter meetings, the AL and NL voted to ban the spitball except for active major-league pitchers who had used it previously and were registered to do so by their respective teams. All three men were "registered." Keating's last major league season was 1919, with the NL's Boston Braves. He posted a 7-11 record for the Braves but he kept throwing the spitter in the Pacific Coast League until he retired in 1932. In 1928, Keating went 27-10, with a 3.14 ERA for Sacramento. Ray Caldwell retired after the 1921 season, after posting a 6-6 record with the Cleveland Indians (courtesy the family of Ray Fisher).

from average on teams that were often well below average. Four times he led Yankee pitchers in shutouts and twice led the Yankees in ERA and games started. In the top ten list of earned run averages for all Yankee starting pitchers since 1903, Fisher ranks seventh, with an ERA of 2.91.

After he served in the U.S. Army in 1918 and missed the entire baseball season, Fisher's contract was sold to the Cincinnati Reds in March of 1919. Fisher played two seasons for the Reds, going 14-5 with a 2.17 ERA in 1919 and 10-11 in 1920. Mrs. Fisher was urging Ray to "settle down" and he applied for a coaching position at Cornell University in Ithaca, N.Y. Cornell informed Fisher they were not interested in hiring a former major leaguer as coach. They had done so once before and that player "turned out to be drunk." Luckily, another baseball coaching position was available at the University of Michigan. It was there that Ray Fisher's second career began—it would bring him more success and respect than he ever dreamed of earning as a major-league pitcher.

Ray Fisher was the baseball coach at the University of Michigan from 1921 to 1958, also coaching freshman football early in his collegiate coaching career. His lifetime coaching record is 636-295 (8 ties) for a winning percentage of .686. His teams won or tied for fourteen Big Ten Championships and won an NCAA (or College World Series) championship in 1953. Fisher's record makes him the coach with the most wins

Ray Fisher, center, on May 23, 1970, flanked by the two men who coached after him at the University of Michigan, Don Lund, left, and "Moby" Benedict. In front is a painting depicting the relief sculpture of Ray Fisher that is mounted on the front of Ray Fisher Stadium. Both men played for Fisher at the university. Don Lund also played in the major leagues for seven seasons, with the Brooklyn Dodgers and Detroit Tigers, appearing in 4 games for the Dodgers in 1945 and then being called up again in 1947 with Jackie Robinson (courtesy the family of Ray Fisher).

ever in Michigan baseball history—a mark that might well stand for all time. Fisher took his teams on tours of Japan in 1929 and 1932 and was named college baseball Coach of the Year in 1953.

His teams at Michigan sent a host of players into the minor leagues and at least 19 signed with major league teams. Upon retirement as coach, Fisher was inducted into the State of Michigan Sports Hall of Fame as well as the American Association of College Baseball Coaches Hall of Fame. In 1970, the University of Michigan named its baseball stadium Ray Fisher Stadium. One of the players Fisher coached in football at Michigan was Gerald R. Ford, the thirty-eighth president of the United States. This would be of great importance in Fisher's later years. Prior to his acceptance of the coaching job at Michigan, Fisher had signed a contract to play for the Reds in 1921 but Reds manager Pat Moran allowed Fisher to interview at Michigan. Fisher was "declared ineligible for life" by then baseball commissioner Kenesaw Mountain Landis for violating the signed contract and taking the Michigan job. In 1980, through the efforts of history professor Donald Proctor, former president Ford and then baseball commissioner Bowie Kuhn, Fisher was declared a "retired player in good standing." Ray Fisher passed away on November 3, 1982, at the age of 95. In July 2003, a historic site marker reading "Birthplace of Ray Fisher" was erected in Middlebury, Vermont.

30

The Original "Murderer's Row," 1918–1919

Despite their 4th place finish in 1918, Huggins' crew was a good group on the verge of greatness. The Yankee team continued to emphasize power hitting, and while this process was in its infancy during the reign of "Wild Bill" Donovan, it was furthered during Huggins' tenure and also immortalized in print in 1918. The indelible impression made in the minds of fans as well as the general public cannot be overstated. The term "Murderer's Row" has long been associated with the Yankees, mainly as applied to the hitting prowess of the 1927 team featuring Babe Ruth, Lou Gehrig, Bob Meusel, Tony Lazzeri and Earle Combs—generally considered the greatest baseball team of all time. In fact, the "Murderer's Row" nickname was coined by sports cartoonist Robert Ripley in 1918, two seasons prior to Ruth even joining the team.

Robert Ripley, a unique person of great creativity, inquisitiveness, and vision, would achieve success as the creator of the "Ripley's Believe It or Not" empire. Ripley, born in Santa Rosa, California, relocated to New York in 1912, being hired by the *New York Globe* to sketch sports. The slugging Yankee team at the time inspired him to create the cartoon that appears on the following page. Ripley dubbed them "Murderer's Row." This term would be used for years afterward to describe the home-run hitting heroics of the Yankees, long after the players to which it was originally ascribed had been traded or retired.

The public perception of the Yankee offensive onslaught was also helped by some rather hyperbolic newspaper reports. One such story appeared in the *Washington Post* on July 5, 1918. It described a 4–3 loss the previous day, in the second game of a 4th of July holiday double-header split with the Senators. The Yankees blasted Washington in the first game by a score of 7–0, with Bob Shawkey taking the mound for the Yanks and shutting down the Senators' lineup.

In the second game Ray Caldwell faced ace Senator pitcher Walter Johnson. Johnson won 23 games in 1918, posting a 1.27 ERA. The *Washington Post* story ran as follows: "...Murderer's Row showed before the crowd was able to make for the exits. The pitcher-annihilating New Yorkers did some dynamite blasting at Walter Johnson in the eighth and with Peckinpaugh, Baker, Pipp and Bodie all hitting, the visitors came within a run of tying the score. Then with the sluggers out of the way Johnson weathered what little remained of the gale."

The war-shortened year of 1918 brought severe financial losses to major league baseball. World War I has been called "the war to end all wars." In the figurative sense it certainly fits that description with so many countries involved and millions dead. A ceasefire was declared on November 11, 1918, but a state of war still existed between the Allied Powers (British, French, Russian, Canadian, U.S.) and Central Powers (German Empire, Austro-Hungarian Empire, Ottoman Empire) until June 28, 1919. On that day an official peace treaty, the Treaty of Versailles, was signed with Germany. Treaties with the other Central Powers soon followed.

Due to the severe financial deficits the 1919 baseball season would consist of just 140 games (as opposed to the 154-game standard of the time period). Yankee owner Jake Ruppert thought he had witnessed a relation between the performance of the United States forces in the war and the athletic preparedness and awareness needed for sporting competition. In a quote meant as a compliment for the service of some of his own players in World War I—and one not meant to offend British, French, Canadian and Russian troops—Ruppert commented: "There is no question that the physical and mental condition of the American troops was the deciding factor in the war, and that our boys were able to throw into the balance the fighting power which broke the deadlock, sent the Huns reeling back, and ultimately brought about their complete defeat. And the reason that the Americans, many of them but hastily trained troops, were able to make such a splendid

Robert Ripley's classic cartoon appeared on April 24, 1918, with the first reference of the Yankees as "Murderer's Row." Walter Johnson, a future Hall of Fame pitcher with the Washington Senators, depicted as "keeper," had lost to the Yankees, 6–3, on Monday, April 15, at Griffith Stadium in Washington, D.C. This cartoon was part of a series titled "Champs and Champs," featuring athletic facts and achievements. It would turn into Ripley's "Believe It or Not," which featured odd and unusual stories and objects. Ripley was an artist, reporter, author, radio broadcaster, explorer and an eventual star of television. He traveled the world (198 countries in his career), seeking out the odd and unusual objects and people he featured within his cartoon (© 2004 Ripley Entertainment Inc.).

Frank "Home Run" Baker, coaxed out of retirement in 1916, provided fine defense at third base and was part of a middle-of-the-order slugging combination with first baseman Wally Pipp. In February 1920, Baker's wife, Ottalee, died at the age of 31, leaving Baker with two daughters to care for. He sat out the entire 1920 season raising his children at their farm in Trappe, Maryland. Baker returned to the Yankees in 1921, batting .294 with 9 home runs and 71 RBI in 94 games as the Yankees won their first pennant (Transcendental Graphics/ruckerarchive.com).

Wally Pipp, circa 1919, Lou Gehrig's predecessor at first base and a slugging first baseman in his own right. Pipp received the nickname "Pipp the Pickler" thanks to his ability to place a base hit in a tough situation, or—to quote an old expression—to get out of a "pickle." Pipp batted .281 with 90 home runs in 15 seasons, including a .304 average, 6 HR, 108 RBI season in 1923 as the Yankees won their first World Series (in six games over the New York Giants) (National Baseball Hall of Fame Library, Cooperstown, N.Y.).

showing was because of their athletic bringing up—their physical fitness, their ability to think quickly, and to act individually in emergencies. And these qualities they acquired on the ball lots, the gridiron, and other fields upon which brain, muscle, and brawn were put to the test."

The Yankees were now eager to begin the fight for the 1919 AL pennant, letting the American public turn their attention to less destructive and less tragic matters as the world began the slow recovery from the devastation caused by "The Great War." An off-season trade brought 31-year-old outfielder Duffy Lewis from the Red Sox (a career .284 hitter) to complement the rest of "Murderer's Row." Ray Caldwell was one of four players sent north to Boston to obtain Lewis. One concern for the New York team was that third baseman Frank Baker, at 33 years of age, was contemplating retirement and a return to his farm. Miller Huggins visited Baker's home in Trappe, Maryland, convincing Baker to return for the 1919 season. Baker explained: "Because of the world war the business of professional baseball has not been normal since I joined the Yankees, and last year was particularly trying to the promoters. I feel I owe the game of baseball a great deal, for it has done me a great deal of good physically, morally and financially.... In helping bring baseball back to its old-time popularity I feel I am likewise doing my duty to my country, because that will have a strong tendency towards normalizing conditions."

For the first time in their history, the Yankees journeyed to Florida for spring training. The destination chosen was Jacksonville. The Brooklyn Dodgers (or the "Robins" as they were known from 1914 to 1931) shared Jacksonville as a training site and played exhibition games against the Yankees. Yankee manager Miller Huggins, as did manager Bill Donovan before him, held out great expectations for first baseman Wally Pipp. He commented to the *Washington Post* on February 25th: "Pipp can do everything around first base any of the [other first baseman] can do, and his great reach gives him a decided advantage over most of them. And I know of no other first baseman who carries more kick at the bat. He hit .304 for me last year but a batting average does not begin to tell Pipp's usefulness to a team. His ability to make those long hits at critical times makes him one of the most valuable men in baseball.

"He led his league in home runs in 1916 and 1917, and has led his league in driving in runs. Pipp still is a young fellow and I think was just about reaching the top of his game last season. He is improving and I pin a lot of faith on him for next season."

Outfielder Ping Bodie, not a soft-spoken personality and always ready with humorous commentary, was expecting big things from the Yankees—and from himself—as he entered his second season with the club: "But just you wait and watch us this season ... this is going to be my year...," said Bodie. "Ball players used to take it easy in the Winter, but during this last Winter all the players were working, and they are in better shape right now than they used to be in the past seasons after three weeks' training. Say, if we don't just about grab that pennant this season, it will be because we were hit by a cyclone. We've got the pitching, the batting, and the infielding, while modesty forbids me saying anything about the outfield...."

In regard to the pitching, a balance between right and left handed starters (begun during Bill Donovan's second year) continued this season. The 1919 Yankee staff was anchored by returning right-hander Bob Shawkey and left-hander George Mogridge. They were supplemented by right-handed veteran Jack Quinn, who played for the White Sox in 1918. Quinn was re-joining the New York team at 35 years of age (he had previously played for the Yankees from 1909 to 1912). Twenty-two-year-old left-hander Hank Thormahlen, in his

Left: Pictured in 1918 at the Polo Grounds, Armando Marsans was born in Cuba and played sparingly in the Yankee outfield during 1917 and 1918. World War I was ongoing, and he wears a red, white and blue patriotic arm band on his left sleeve. This arm band appeared on home and road Yankee uniforms during the 1918 season. Marsans was acquired from the St. Louis Browns in midseason 1917 in exchange for Lee Magee, a star outfielder of the time, but Magee's 1917 batting average of .220 as a Yankee was a huge disappointment. While his time in pinstripes was brief, Marsans is significant as one of the first Latin American players to appear in the major leagues. Unfortunately, Marsans fared not much better for the Yankees than the man he was traded for, batting .227 in 1917 in 25 games, suffering a broken leg in the process. He hit .236 in 37 games in 1918, playing his last major league season at the age of 30. Marsans, who reached the major leagues with the Cincinnati Reds, led by former Yankee manager Clark Griffith, in 1911, hit .269 overall in his 8-season major-league career (Library of Congress, Prints & Photographs Division, LC-DIG-ggbain-26805). *Right*: Veteran shortstop Roger Peckinpaugh had an off year in 1918, batting .231, but he bounced back to .305 in 1919. He served as Yankee captain in 1921, batting .288 with 8 home runs and 71 RBI, helping the Yankees win the first pennant in team history. Peckinpaugh was traded to the Red Sox on December 20, 1921, but was soon sent to the Washington Senators in a 3-team deal with the Philadelphia A's. He was a hero for the Senators in the 1924 World Series, batting .417 and doubling home the winning run in Game 2 and saving Game 6 with a great fielding play. In 1925, Peckinpaugh was named AL MVP with a .294, 4 HR, 64 RBI season as the Senators again reached the World Series. The 1925 World Series was a disaster for Peckinpaugh. He made a record eight errors, several in important spots, allowing the Pirates to come back from a 3–1 deficit to win the series. That blot on Peckinpaugh's resume does not obscure his whole career and, after retiring, he served as the Cleveland Indians' manager from 1928 to 1933 and part of the 1941 season. Peckinpaugh managed the New Orleans Pelicans of the Southern Association in 1939 and was Cleveland's general manager from 1941 to 1946. He died in Cleveland, at the age of 86, on November 17, 1977. His career tends to be overlooked in recent times—a shame since he continued the line of outstanding Yankee shortstops that began with Kid Elberfeld (and extended through the years to this very day with players such as Frank Crosetti, Phil Rizzuto and Derek Jeter). Note the old-style water cooler with glass container in the dugout (Library of Congress, Prints & Photographs Division, LC-DIG-ggbain-26803).

30. The Original "Murderer's Row," 1918–1919

Forkball specialist Alex Ferguson displays his pitching motion. Ferguson, born February 16, 1897, in Montclair, New Jersey, made his major league debut with the Yankees in 1918 at the age of 21. He was signed after logging a strong 16-3 record in the minors for Bridgeport, Connecticut, of the Eastern League. "One of the most promising lads in the [Yankee] batch of talent ... is Alex Ferguson," proclaimed the *New York Times* in 1919. However, Ferguson did not make the team in spring training and would not return to New York's 25-man roster until 1921, posting a 3-1 record with a 5.91 ERA. Ferguson's contract was sold to the Red Sox on February 24, 1922. In 1924 he won 14 games for a Red Sox team that finished in 7th place. The Yankees re-acquired him on May 5, 1925. He posted a 4-2, 7.79 ERA record in pinstripes and was soon on the move again. His contract was sold to the Washington Senators on August 17 as he joined former teammates Muddy Ruel, Roger Peckinpaugh, George Mogridge and Allen Russell on the Washington roster. Ferguson was acquired just in time for the Senators' run to win the 1925 AL pennant, their second AL championship in a row. Ferguson was the winning pitcher in Game 3 of the 1925 World Series, a 4–3 victory over the Pittsburgh Pirates, but he was the losing pitcher in Game 6 as the Pirates won the series in 7 games. Occasional successes and high ERAs (4.89 overall in 10 seasons) are the hallmarks of Ferguson's career, but he is notable as one of the early throwers of the forkball (Library of Congress, Prints & Photographs Division, LC-DIG-ggbain-28598).

second year with the Yankees, was also counted on to provide quality innings in a starting role. Right-hander Allen "Rubberarm" Russell, with the Yankees since 1915, soldiered on as a relief pitcher, before being traded to the Red Sox along with right-hander Bob McGraw and about $40,000 cash on July 29, 1919, in a deal that delivered star Red Sox right-hander Carl Mays to the Yankees. That deal delivered howls of protest from other AL clubs—and from AL president Ban Johnson himself—as Mays had deserted the Red Sox in mid–July, complaining of poor fielding and offensive support.

Johnson found it impossible to support the New York team in this situation but a court ruling allowed the trade. Despite the optimistic outlook, Ping Bodie's AL pennant assessment for 1919 fell short, though the Yankees were not hit by a cyclone. Bodie batted .278. Wally Pipp did not necessarily live up to manager Miller Huggins' standard with a .275, 7 HR, 50 RBI season. However, the rest of "Murderer's Row" picked up the slack. Red Sox import Duffy Lewis, the starting left-fielder, led the team with 89 RBI, batting .272. The Yankees also led the AL in home runs—for the fourth time in the last five years—blasting 45, 10 more than the Philadelphia Athletics. For that matter, they led all of major league baseball in home runs. Roger Peckinpaugh was tops in hitting for New York in 1919 with a .305 batting average while Frank Baker produced the best offensive numbers of his Yankee career: .293 average, 10 home runs and 83 RBI. Bob Shawkey led the team in wins with a 20-11 record, and a 2.72 ERA. The other starters, Jack Quinn (15-14, 2.61 ERA), Hank Thormahlen (12-10, 2.62), George Mogridge (10-7, 2.77) and mid-season acquisition Carl Mays (9-3, 1.65) pitched well and—for the first time in team history—helped the Yankees lead the AL in earned run average (2.82).

The offensive contributions of Peckinpaugh and Baker, as well as the entire team, were heralded in print during the 1919 season (usually in very dramatic terms). On July 8, 1919, the following report, describing a 3–2 victory over the Senators, appeared in the *New York Times*: "Miller Huggins' famous Murderer's Row, extremely passive for eight innings, came into evidence yesterday in all its fury in the ninth, when the Yankees and Senators clashed in the closing game of their series at the Polo Grounds. In this final frame the members of this famous death-dealing combination vented their pent-up wrath ... and turned what looked like a [loss] into a Yankee victory, by a score of 3 to 2. J. Franklin Baker, Maryland agriculturist and run producer, was the big noise in the Yankees' victorious outbreak. Baker tickled a home run into the far reaches of the upper right field grandstand, scoring Roger Peckinpaugh ahead of him, with the two runs which pulled Miller Huggins' tribe even with

Opposite: Infielder/outfielder Wilson "Chick" Fewster, a valuable utility player, joined the Yankees in 1917 at the age of 21. Not a great fielder, Fewster excelled at the plate despite limited playing time. He batted .283 in 81 games in 1919 and .286 in 1920—a year in which he played in only 21 games because of a life-threatening injury. On March 25, during a spring training game against the Dodgers in Jacksonville, Florida, Fewster was struck behind the ear by a sweeping inside "curveball" thrown by Dodger pitcher Jeff Pfeffer, a pitcher known for brushback pitches. "The impact sounded like a coconut shell cracking, and Fewster went down like an ox felled by an axe," reported the *New York Times*. Fewster was unconscious for 10 minutes before being revived by the team trainer and assistants. He was escorted to the Yankee clubhouse but lost the ability to speak and was taken to a Jacksonville hospital. The *New York Times* further commented: "While the first examination of Fewster's head showed there was no fracture, the bruise extends much deeper than the early examination showed, and some blood vessels right close to the brain have been crushed." Fewster was later sent to a hospital in the Baltimore area, where he was born and where he resided. He made a miraculous recovery and returned to New York at midseason. In 1921, he batted .280 in 66 games as the Yankees won their first pennant (Library of Congress, Prints & Photographs Division, LC-DIG-ggbain-33991).

the opposition. Duffy Lewis, Wally Pipp and Derrill Pratt, other capable members of the famous Row, followed with a bevy of singles which put the finishing touches on Baker's terrific thump."

Owing to the improved record as well as the return of many persons from service in World War I, attendance at the Polo Grounds improved dramatically. On Wednesday, July 30th, the Yankees split a double-header with the first place White Sox, winning the opening game 6–5 behind Bob Shawkey while dropping the second by a 5–3 score with Jack Quinn on the mound. At the end of the day the Yankees were in 4th place, 6½ games behind the White Sox. In a drastic change from the losing era of Harry Wolverton and Frank Chance, the following comment ran in the July 31st edition of the *New York Times*: "The gathering was the biggest weekday crowd the Yanks have ever played to. Wild excitement was rampant from the first,

Left: Catcher Herold "Muddy" Ruel joined the Yankees in 1917 and became starting catcher in 1919. He was one of the notable talents during the early Ruppert/Huston years traded to the Red Sox in a series of deals to gain veteran players from Boston. The deal Reul was included in put future Hall of Fame pitcher Waite Hoyt and catcher Wally Schang in Yankee pinstripes. Ruel was a good player, batting .275 and fielding well during a 19-year career (National Baseball Hall of Fame Library, Cooperstown, N.Y.). *Right*: Infielder Aaron Ward, born in Booneville, Arkansas, joined the Yankees as a rookie in 1917 along with Chick Fewster. Unlike Fewster, "Wardie," as he was called by teammates, remained with the team long enough to win a World Series. Primarily a second baseman, Ward batted .306 in 1921 with 75 RBI and hit .267 in 1922, the Yankees reaching the World Series in both seasons but losing to the New York Giants both times. Ward's most productive season was 1923, with .284, 10 HR, and 82 RBI. He continued hitting in the 1923 World Series, posting a .417 average with one home run, helping the Yankees beat the rival Giants. In three World Series played with the Yankees, Ward holds a .286 batting average with 9 RBI (Library of Congress, Prints & Photographs Division, LC-DIG-ggbain-30913).

30. The Original "Murderer's Row," 1918–1919

and the Yankees' popularity seems to be firmly established." Ping Bodie—not missing an opportunity for more comedic commentary—reportedly looked over the 22,000 person crowd in attendance, saying: "I will take today's gate receipts for my season's salary!" Those 22,000 persons contributed to the mass of 619,164 people who viewed Yankee games at the Polo Grounds in 1919. The American League had finally gained a foothold in "The Big

James Harrison "Truck" Hannah was a Yankee starting catcher from 1918 to 1920, his only 3 major league seasons. Hannah was the primary receiver in 1918 and shared duties with Herold "Muddy" Ruel in 1919 and 1920. "Truck" seems to be nicknamed for his 6'1", 190-pound frame—a tall man in his day—as well as his competitiveness. Hannah, born June 5, 1889, in Larimore, North Dakota, began his career with the Spokane (Washington) Indians of the Northwest League. He was a Northwest League All-Star for Spokane in 1913 and later played in the Pacific Coast League. Hannah was signed by the Yankees from Salt Lake City of the PCL by "semi-official" Yankee scout Fred Snodgrass, a former outfielder with the New York Giants who played for Los Angeles in the PCL in 1917. In the deciding game of the 1912 World Series against the Red Sox, Snodgrass dropped a fly ball hit by former Yankee Clyde Engle. Snodgrass then made a great play on the next batter—catching what looked like a sure base hit—but later in the inning Boston scored the go-ahead run, winning the World Series. Snodgrass was referred to as the "goat" of the 1912 series. This was not lost on Hannah. When Snodgrass first stepped up to bat with Hannah behind the plate, Hannah said: "So you're a Big Leaguer? I guess you're going to come out here and show us how the Giants used to do it, eh? See if you can hit this one." Snodgrass's scouting report to the Yankees read: "I don't like him personally, but I must say he is the best all around catcher in this league." From an offensive standpoint Hannah didn't offer much to the "Murderer's Row" lineups, batting .235 in his 3 year career, but he handled pitchers well and posted above average fielding percentages for AL catchers in 1918 and 1919. The close-up of his face reveals that Truck's nose lost a battle with a pitched ball or an opposing base runner's shoulder (Library of Congress, Prints & Photographs Division, LC-DIG-ggbain-30932).

Sailor Bob. Bob Shawkey, the pitcher who helped usher in the transition to pennant-winning Yankee teams. He went 24-14 with a 2.21 ERA in 1916 and won 20 games four times during his 1915 to 1927 Yankee career. He also won 18 games (1921) and 16 games twice (1923, 1924). Shawkey was known for wearing his "lucky" red sweatshirt under his uniform. That sweatshirt is evident here under his 1919 home jersey, replacing the typical off-white utility shirt worn under the uniforms of this period. He began his career with the Philadelphia Athletics in 1913. As of this writing, Shawkey ranks 6th on the Yankees' career games pitched list (415), 4th on the Yankees' career ERA list (3.10), and 7th on the Yankees' career strikeout list (1,163). Shawkey also managed the Yankees (to an 86-68, 3rd place finish in 1930). He later served as baseball coach at Dartmouth College from 1953 to 1958 (Library of Congress, Prints & Photographs Division, LC-DIG-ggbain-34000).

Left: Del Pratt provided solid defense at second base and powerful hitting in New York, compiling a .295 average in three years as a Yankee (National Baseball Hall of Fame Library, Cooperstown, N.Y.). *Right*: Closely following the trade of Duffy Lewis, Carl "Sub" Mays was another Red Sox star acquired by the Yankees. On July 29, 1919, New York sent pitchers Allen Russell and Bob McGraw and cash to Boston for Mays, who had won 22 games for Boston in 1917 and 21 in 1918. Mays went 26-11 for the Yankees in 1920 and 27-9 in 1921, leading the AL in games, innings pitched, victories and winning percentage (.750), while also batting .343 and helping New York win its first AL pennant. Mays' career record for 15 seasons stands at 207-126, 2.92 ERA, with a .622 winning percentage. He has a lifetime batting average of .268. A moody disposition alienated Mays from teammates, managers and sportswriters. Though his numbers are superior to those of some pitchers enshrined in the Hall of Fame, he was not elected because his career was clouded by two events. First, a tragedy. Mays, who pitched primarily underhand with a "submarine" ball, threw a ball that hit and killed Cleveland shortstop Ray Chapman on August 16, 1920. In this era before the existence of batting helmets, Chapman was known for crowding the plate, and many observers insisted that Mays' pitch was over the plate. Chapman died the following day. Second, rumors surfaced that Mays had "thrown" game 4 or 7 of the 1921 World Series. Anecdotes exist about Mays hanging a curve ball that was hit for a double instead of throwing a fastball as signaled for by manager Miller Huggins. Mays, however, went 1-2 with a 1.73 ERA in 3 starts in the 1921 World Series, allowing only 5 earned runs in 26 innings pitched. Despite the statistics, Huggins later said: "Any ballplayers that played for me on either the Cardinals or Yankees could come to me if he were in need and I would give him a helping hand. I make only two exceptions, Carl Mays and Joe Bush. If they were in the gutter, I'd kick them" (Library of Congress, Prints & Photographs Division, LC-DIG-ggbain-33976).

Left: Outfielder Duffy Lewis joined the Yankees on December 18, 1918, in a big trade which featured pitchers Ray Caldwell and Slim Love, outfielder Frank Gilhooley and catcher Roxy Walters heading to Boston while Lewis and pitchers Ernie Shore and Hubert "Dutch" Leonard were sent to New York. Leonard, a very good left-hander who would turn just 27 at the beginning on the 1919 season, refused to go to the Yankees and was traded to Detroit. Ernie Shore's record in 1919 was 5-8 with a 4.17 ERA, so the deal was essentially 4 for 1. The 31-year-old Lewis did not disappoint the New York fans, batting .272 in 1919, contributing 7 home runs and leading the "Murderer's Row" attack with 89 RBI. The acquisition of Lewis was only the beginning in a series of deals in which talent was taken from the Red Sox roster to fortify the Yankee team. Over the next five years lopsided trades—owing to former Red Sox manager Ed Barrow becoming Yankee general manager in 1921—transformed the Yankee team and provided them with their first World Series victory in 1923. Except for Bob Shawkey, the entire starting pitching staff of the 1923 Yankee World Series team (Joe Bush, Waite Hoyt, Sam Jones and Herb Pennock) were former Red Sox players. Another former Boston player, Babe Ruth, batted .368 with 3 home runs for New York in the 1923 World Series (Library of Congress, Prints & Photographs Division, LC-DIG-ggbain-20077). *Right*: Roger Peckinpaugh, the first of many great Yankee shortstops (National Baseball Hall of Fame Library, Cooperstown, N.Y.).

Top left: Hank (Lefty) Thormahlen winds up for the camera (Library of Congress, Prints & Photographs Division, LC-DIG-ggbain-26810). *Top right*: Thormahlen's biggest year in a 6-season major league career was 1919. He posted a 12-10, 2.62 ERA record as the Yankees finished 80-59, 3rd place in the American League (Library of Congress, Prints & Photographs Division, LC-DIG-ggbain-26809). *Bottom*: The mascots of the Yankees and Washington Senators during a pregame meeting (Library of Congress, Prints & Photographs Division, LC-DIG-ggbain-21475).

Yankee pitching ace Bob Shawkey. On Thursday, April 15, 1976, in front of 52,613 fans on Opening Day, Shawkey threw out the first ball at the refurbished Yankee Stadium. The 1923 team, the first New York Yankee World Series winners (including longtime teammate Wally Pipp), were honored that day (the 1976 Yankees defeated the Minnesota Twins in that day's game, 11–4). Shawkey had pitched and won the 1923 inaugural home opener at the original Yankee Stadium, played on Wednesday, April 18, 1923. Shawkey and the Yankees defeated their hated rivals the Boston Red Sox that day, 4–1. Shawkey died at the age of 90 on December 31, 1980, at the Veterans Administration Hospital in Syracuse, New York. Regarding his successful pitching career, Shawkey had expressed gratitude for the only two major league managers he ever played for: "I started under Mack and finished under Huggins, those were two wonderful breaks in my favor" (Transcendental Graphics/ruckerarchive.com).

Apple." The Yankees reached first place by mid-season but the White Sox stayed in first through virtually the entire season. With increased firepower (45 HRs) the Yankees did improve from the previous season to finish 1919 in 3rd place, with 80 wins, only 7½ games behind the pennant-winning White Sox.

From top left: Right fielder Frank Gilhooley; third baseman Frank Baker; left fielder Ping Bodie. *From bottom left*: Shortstop Roger Peckinpaugh; first baseman Wally Pipp; second baseman Del Pratt.

30. The Original "Murderer's Row," 1918–1919

Murderer's Row. The Yankee lineup that inspired cartoons, dramatic newspaper reports and caused trouble for opposing pitchers typically consisted of the following lineups:

1918
1. Frank Gilhooley RF
2. Roger Peckinpaugh SS
3. Frank Baker 3B
4. Del Pratt 2B
5. Wally Pipp 1B
6. Ping Bodie LF
7. Elmer Miller CF
8. James "Truck" Hannah C
9. P

1919
1. Sammy Vick RF
2. Roger Peckinpaugh SS
3. Frank Baker 3B
4. Duffy Lewis LF
5. Wally Pipp 1B
6. Del Pratt 2B
7. Ping Bodie CF
8. Muddy Ruel C
9. P

31

UNDERCURRENTS

The 1919 White Sox team became infamous for their part in a gambling scandal and the participation of some White Sox players in purposely losing the 1919 World Series to the Cincinnati Reds. Former Yankee pitcher Ray Fisher played with the Reds in the 1919 World Series, starting Game 2, pitching 7 innings and losing despite allowing only 2 runs. Other former Yankee players were also involved in the 1919 World Series—not on the playing field, and not in a positive way.

Former Yankee first baseman Hal Chase, who played for the Reds from 1916 to 1918, was with the Giants in 1919, batting .284 as the Giants finished second to the Reds. On September 25, 1919, against the Boston Braves, Hal Chase made his final appearance in a major league baseball game. He pinch hit and his double drove in one run. Chase and third baseman Heinie Zimmerman* were supposedly dropped from the Giants' roster in late September but both were on the team's reserve list submitted to National League president John A. Heydler on October 18, 1919. Chase was long suspected of throwing games. On August 9th, 1918, he was suspended without pay for the remainder of the season. In a game against the Giants at the Polo Grounds, Reds manager Christy Mathewson and Chase engaged in a bitter argument. It ended with Chase being ordered to the clubhouse and thrown off the team. Chase commented: "Let's not beat around the bush. I'm accused of betting on ball games and trying to get a pitcher to throw a game for money."

As explained by author/historian Eliot Asinof, in his book *Eight Men Out: The Black Sox and the 1919 World Series*, pitcher Jimmy Ring was approached by Chase during a game against the Giants. As Ring strode in from the bullpen, Chase said, "I've got money on this game, kid. There's something in it for you if you lose." Chase's words had a disconcerting effect and Ring threw his first pitch over the catcher's head, the Giants scoring the winning run.

The next morning, as Ring and his fiancée sat in the lobby of the Reds' hotel, Chase walked by and slipped him a fifty dollar bill, telling the couple to enjoy a night on the town. Ring reported the incident to Mathewson.

The final undoing of Chase's major league career was revealed by sportswriter Fred Lieb, as told to him by National League president Heydler: "Eventually, I got a photographic copy of Chase's cancelled check for five hundred dollars given him by a gambler as pay for throwing a game in 1918. I took this evidence to [Giants owner] Charles Stoneham saying, 'When I permitted Chase to play early last spring I had no real proof

---

*Zimmerman allegedly tried to bribe teammates to "fix," or lose, games on purpose.

of Hal's throwing a game. Now I have that proof.' I handed him the affidavit and Chase's cancelled check.... 'Please notify your manager that Chase will not play in any future game with the Giants.' Giants owner Charles Stoneham reportedly responded: 'If that's the way it is, that's it.'"

Chase's career appeared to be finished, though he told a different story. "McGraw [offered a contract and] even offered me a raise. But I turned it down. There was nothing wrong with that contract. I was perfectly satisfied with the terms. But I told the New York management that my marital difficulties were growing more and more complicated, that I was sick of the East, that I had good connections in the West, and that I would be doing myself a favor by quitting the major league baseball scene." On February 29, 1920, the *New York Times* reported Chase would not be attending spring training with the Giants.

On March 23, 1920, former Yankee Lee Magee, who played with Chase on the Reds, was dropped from the Cubs' roster before the season. He stated: "On Saturday, I shall make public the charges on which the National League bases its action in barring me from its circuit. I'll show documents both in my favor and against me and let the public judge if I have been fairly treated.... I'm going to burn my bridges behind me and then jump off the ruins. If I'm barred I'll take quite a few noted people with me. I'll show up some people for tricks turned ever since 1906. And there will be merry music in the baseball world." Hal Chase was one of the "noted people."

On April 14, Magee filed suit against the Cubs for his 1920 salary plus $5,000 extra in lost World Series pay if the Cubs won the 1920 pennant. Chase, meanwhile, had signed to play for San Jose in California's Mission League. Magee's trial began on June 7, 1920. It lasted three days. Magee's story was this: On July 23, 1918, as the Reds traveled to Boston for a double-header, Magee sat in the smoking car, watching out the window. and Chase soon joined him. Chase suggested they should make a large bet on the first game. Chase made it sound that the bet would be placed on the Reds to win. The bet was to be placed with Jim Costello, owner of a pool room at the Oxford Hotel in Boston. Magee knew Costello and was going to place the bet himself, but Chase insisted, "No, I'll make the bet." Chase wagered $500 for both Magee and himself and the Reds won 4–2 in thirteen innings. At the end of the game Chase revealed he had bet on

The "Prince" no longer: Hal Chase wears the road uniform of the Federal League's Buffalo Blues in 1915. He batted .291 for the Blues that year, the same as his overall batting average in a 15-season career. Chase would be in the Hall of Fame today—and honored with a plaque in Yankee Stadium's Monument Park—if not for the gambling scandals that scarred his career (Library of Congress, Prints & Photographs Division, LC-DIG-ggbain-17006).

Lee Magee began his career with good batting and fielding averages (hitting .290 for the St. Louis Cardinals in 1912 and .323 for the Brooklyn Tip-Tops in 1915) and ended it being permanently banned for life by Major League Baseball because of gambling on games and actively trying to lose games on which he had placed a bet. Magee was the Yankees' starting center fielder in 1916, batting .257 (Library of Congress, Prints & Photographs Division, LC-DIG-ggbain-21641).

Joe Gedeon, acrobatic second baseman for the Yankees in 1916 and 1917, was also implicated in the Black Sox scandal. Gedeon, from Sacramento, California, knew Hal Chase very well and was friendly with White Sox first baseman Arnold "Chick" Gandil from their brief time as teammates on the Washington Senators from 1913 and 1914. Gedeon was said to be present during a meeting with gamblers as they discussed the plot to "throw" or "fix" the 1919 World Series. He and Chase supposedly bet on the Reds to win the series, and Gedeon was called as a witness in the Black Sox trial. Gedeon was released by the St. Louis Browns before the 1921 season, returning to California trying to catch on with a Pacific Coast League team. On November 3, 1921, Gedeon was officially and permanently disqualified from playing major league baseball for having knowledge of the 1919 World Series "fix," and that ban was later extended to include PCL teams. Gedeon suffered from cirrhosis of the liver in his later years and died of bronchial pneumonia on May 19, 1941, at the age of 47 (Library of Congress, Prints & Photographs Division, LC-DIG-ggbain-21195).

the Reds to lose. Magee then stopped payment on his check. The real intrigue began when Jim Costello was called to the stand. He contradicted Magee's tale. Here is a portion of Costello's colorful testimony reported in newspapers.

> Q: I wish you would describe what was said between you and Lee Magee, if anything was said, on or about July 24, 1918.

Third baseman Albert "Cozy" Dolan played in 37 games for the Yankees across the 1911–1912 seasons, batting .256. He later coached with the New York Giants. On September 27, 1924, supposedly at the request of Dolan, Giants outfielder Jimmy O'Connell allegedly approached Philadelphia Phillies shortstop Heinie Sand and offered him $500 to "throw" the game, helping the Giants win a close pennant race with the Brooklyn Dodgers. Dolan's response of "I don't remember" to the questions of baseball commissioner Kenesaw Mountain Landis did nothing to remove suspicion. On October 1, 1924, Landis announced Dolan and O'Connell were expelled from professional baseball. Jimmy O'Connell, a Sacramento native like Joe Gedeon, went to New Mexico, where he played for Fort Bayard in the Copper League, the same "outlaw" baseball league in which Hal Chase played. The Douglas, Arizona, club of the Copper League became a "Black Sox" alumni society of sorts, with Chase as manager and banned White Sox players third baseman Buck Weaver, first baseman Chick Gandil and pitcher Lefty Williams signing on (Library of Congress, Prints & Photographs Division, LC-DIG-ggbain-11040).

> A: On the evening [in question], about eight o'clock, Magee came in my place looking for me. I says, "What is it?" He says, "On tomorrow's ball game," he says. "We can't talk details just now," he says, "but I will have another man tomorrow with me and we will talk it over together." I says, "What time?" He says, "Ten o'clock." The next morning about ten o'clock Magee and the other party comes in the room and we go down in the far part of my room.

Q: Before you come to the next morning, what was said by Magee, as to what was to be done?
A: He said it was in regard to a ball game the next day; they were going to "fix" a ball game. By "tossing" a game it means your own side loses the game—bet against his own side... The next morning at ten o'clock Magee and the other party came in my room and we go down in the corner and talk things over.
Q: Who was the other party?
A: I says, "What is your proposition?"
Q: [Repeated] Who was the other party?
A: The other party was Hal Chase. He says, "The proposition is this," he says. "How much money can you place on a ball game in Boston?" I says, "I can bet an unlimited amount." "Well, he says, "I think we can do business with you, Jim." I says, "I don't do business on ball games myself, so I will get somebody else." He says, "What will we do?" I says, "I want you to understand this in the first place: if you are going to throw a ball game, you have to bet some of your own money, because the gamblers won't bet unless you do." I says, "I have a gambler that can handle the thing for you." I asked them how much they wanted to bet themselves. "Well," they says, "we haven't got the money with us, will you take our check?" "Yes," I says, "I will take your check," I says, "for any amount. With this agreement—if you lose that ball game according to agreement, I will give you your checks back and the amount equivalent to your check and one third of what the gamblers win." That satisfied them. So then I walked down to my safe, took out my own checkbook on the Old Colony Trust Company of Boston, and gave them each a check. They crossed out the "Old Colony Trust Company" and filled in their own banks in for five hundred dollars apiece. I took them checks and put them in my safe and took out one thousand dollars.
Q: Well, then, you found out the Reds didn't lose the first game.
A: Well, I had a ticker across the street and I sent the boys over to see the ticker, and they came back and reported the Reds had won the game. The next morning Chase comes and sees me. He says, "It was a tough break we had, Jim. We tried awful hard."

The "tough break" Chase referred to was the Reds' 4–2 victory in the first game of a double-header over the Boston Braves on July 25, 1918. It was a bizarre one and ironic in retrospect—the irony not lost on Magee and Chase. The game extended to the thirteenth inning with the score tied 2–2. Two men were out when Magee trotted to the plate. Magee hit a ground ball to Boston shortstop Johnny Rawlings. It hit a stone, jumped up and smashed into Rawling's nose as Magee reached first base. Unfortunately for Magee and Chase, future Hall of Fame outfielder Edd Roush, the next batter, blasted a home run. Magee was then forced to score the winning run in front of Roush. Magee slowly crept around the bases. Roush, sensing something was awry, shouted, "Run, you son of a bitch!" Teammates in the Reds' dugout eyed Magee suspiciously. As for Magee's suit, it was just about thrown out of court, and the jury ruled in favor of the Cubs, deciding they had more than just cause to suspend Magee.* The purpose the trial served—if Costello told the absolute truth under oath—was to reveal the behind-the-scene maneuverings of Chase that were always suspected but not previously proven.

Seven White Sox players were said to have conspired to lose the 1919 World Series to the Reds. In return for "throwing" games, the seven players received $100,000 from gambling interests. Hal Chase was rumored to be the "go-between" for the gamblers and White Sox players.

By 1920, Chase played for the Mission League in California. In August, he was barred from parks in the Pacific Coast League, his old stomping grounds. Chase allegedly tried to bribe Salt Lake pitcher Spider Baum prior to a game. That incident and allegations that Chase

---

*Magee was soon permanently suspended by major league baseball commissioner Kenesaw Mountain Landis, who was elected to office on November 12, 1920, as baseball took steps to restore the faith of the public in the game after the Black Sox scandal.

Benny Kauff in 1916. Kauff, an outfielder, appeared in 5 games for the Yankees in 1912 and batted .273, not being given an opportunity to break into a starting outfield featuring Bert Daniels hitting .274, Guy Zinn batting .262 and utility player Roy Hartzell at .272 (while Birdie Cree, hitting .332, went down with a wrist injury.) Chet Hoff—a teammate of Hal Chase and Kauff on the 1912 Yankees—recalled a story from 1919 in which Chase and Kauff, then on the New York Giants, discovered an unoccupied, and unlocked, car and proceeded to take it for a short drive. This incident was laughed off by teammates but echoes another incident in February 1920 that resulted in Kauff being arrested and arraigned on a grand larceny charge related to automobile theft. He was acquitted on May 13, 1921, but baseball commissioner Landis expelled Kauff from major league baseball stating Kauff was "no longer a fit companion for other ballplayers." Guilt by association was a contributing factor as Giants third baseman Heinie Zimmerman allegedly approached Kauff to help "fix" a game. Kauff appears here in a Giants plaid home uniform, used for only the 1916 season. Kauff batted .311 in an 8-season career (Library of Congress, Prints & Photographs Division, LC-DIG-ggbain-21542).

tried to bribe an umpire also led to his banishment from parks in the Mission League. As he walked out of a movie theater in San Jose, Chase was arrested. He was implicated in the "Black Sox" scandal and a warrant had been issued in Chicago. Chase was released on a $3,000 bond. Many versions of Chase's involvement, or lack of it, in the scandal have been recorded.

Chase underwent a sad decline in his later years. A headline by writer Harry Grayson of the *New York World-Telegram* on January 4, 1934, describes just how far "Prince Hal" descended from his throne: "One-Time Prince Hal in Tatters." Chase drank heavily and was stricken with beriberi—a disease caused by vitamin deficiency—in 1941. His own story regarding the "Black Sox" World Series scandal, later reported in *The Sporting News* as he lay in a hospital bed, was as follows: "The investigators sent for me. I announced that if they wanted me, they'd have to pay $500 for my time and transportation. I said I would be willing to go because I had nothing to fear. Finally, my name was dropped from the discussion. It was felt, apparently, that it wasn't worth $500 to bring me to Chicago. They couldn't have wanted me very badly if they weren't willing to put up that small guarantee. Some of the boys in the plot wanted to back out and did. My name was tossed around and I received much of the blame for plotting the fix. That is a lie. Had I gone to President Heydler or to Manager McGraw, I could have helped baseball and myself. Later, it was too late. My name, because of my past, was implicated, and no one wanted to believe my story. I didn't get a dime out of the fixed Series, and many of those indicted didn't either. They were paid, sure enough, but look at the scrape they got into. Their payoff went into legal fees for lawyers and their bad name broke them ... I'd give anything if I could start in all over again. What a change there would be in the life of Hal Chase. I was all wrong, at least in most things, and my best proof is that I am flat on my back, without a dime." Chase also commented, "...baseball was good to me, but I'm afraid I wasn't very good to baseball." Hal Chase died at California's Colusa Memorial Hospital on May 18, 1947, at the age of 64. His quiet funeral took place in San Jose, California. None of his former teammates or baseball executives were present. Popular baseball players and personalities Casey Stengel and Lefty O'Doul did attend. Chase was laid to rest in his hometown of Los Gatos at Oak Hill Cemetery.

Babe Borton—one of the Chicago White Sox players traded to the Yankees for Hal Chase—awaits his turn for batting practice at the Polo Grounds in 1913. In 1919 Borton played for the Pacific Coast League team of Vernon, a small town in Los Angeles County. Borton was at the center of another game-"fixing" scandal, in which Vernon players raised a pool of money and paid off other teams so they would not play well against Vernon, helping Vernon win the 1919 PCL pennant. Borton was expelled from the PCL after an investigation. As Al Figone states in his work on the PCL game fixing scandal: "The PCL scandal of 1919 further reinforces the institutionalized or pervasive problem of illegal gambling which had been part of professional baseball since its formal inception in 1876. Since owners were in many cases known gamblers and associates of known big-time gamblers their reluctance in ameliorating this problem is understandable." Does this echo the relationship between original Yankee owner Frank Farrell and Hal Chase? A definitive "yes." (Library of Congress, Prints & Photographs Division, LC-DIG-ggbain-13193).

32

THE PING OF THE BAT

Long before gambling scandals rocked the PCL, another Californian-born Yankee was making his mark there and being scouted by the major leagues. Joining New York on March 8, 1918, was Francesco Stephano Pezzolo, though that particular name was not mentioned in newspaper reports: "The New York American League baseball club completed a triangular deal today, which added Ping Bodie to the team as an outfielder...." Pezzolo, who began his career in 1911 with the Chicago White Sox, was known as Ping Bodie, and not just for the reason of using a more manageable name. "Ping" was said to be the sound of a baseball being dented by his 52-ounce bat, and "Bodie" was the name of a California town in which he had once lived.

Bodie was born in San Francisco on October 8, 1887, and began playing baseball in the California League in 1906. He gained notoriety by hitting 30 home runs for the San Francisco Seals of the Pacific Coast League in 1910, and joined the Chicago White Sox in 1911, hitting .289 with 97 RBI that year. Bodie was struggling with a .229 average in 1914 and ensuing arguments with his manager resulted in Bodie's contract being sold back to the Seals. By 1917 Bodie re-emerged with the Philadelphia Athletics. Of his one-year tenure with the 55-98, 8th-place 1917 Athletics, Bodie said: "I and the Liberty Bell are the only attractions in Philadelphia." Bodie's .291 average, second highest of any 1917 A's regular, team-leading 7 home runs and 74 RBI all supported his statement.

Bodie joined the Yankees in 1918 by way of a cash transaction in which they purchased the contract of first baseman George Burns of the Detroit Tigers, then sent Burns to the Athletics in exchange for Bodie. Bodie was a badly needed addition to the Yankee outfield. He was the starting left fielder in 1918 and starting center fielder in 1919-1920. The regular Yankee outfielders of 1917 (Elmer Miller, Tim Hendryx and Hugh High) managed only 9 home runs between them and all batted below .252. After a poor season in 1918 (.256, 3 HR 46 RBI), Bodie hit .278, 6 HR, 59 RBI in 1919 and .295, 7 HR, 79 RBI in 1920. Bodie's boasts regarding his talent were numerous (and one story reports that his seven-year-old son announced to fans: "My daddy can outhit any man in baseball"). However, these were playful statements and endeared the outgoing Bodie to his teammates.

An honest analysis of Bodie's Yankee career (.272 BA with 16 home runs in 3-plus seasons) would indicate that his self-promotion exceeded his actual accomplishments. In fact, George Burns, the man he was traded for, hit .352 for the Athletics in 1918 (and .307 in a 16 season career). Bodie does remain significant as the first of the San Francisco area Italian players that would play for the Yankees (future stars Tony Lazzeri, Frank Crosetti and

Francesco Stephano Pezzolo (Ping Bodie) in 1919 (National Baseball Hall of Fame Library, Cooperstown, N.Y.).

Joe DiMaggio soon followed Bodie). Bodie retired from major-league baseball following the 1921 season. After seven more seasons in the minor leagues, he worked on Hollywood movie sets for 32 years as an electrician and—not surprisingly given his personality—as an occasional actor in small parts. Ping Bodie died in 1961 at the age of 74, leaving a wife, son, daughter, stepson and stepdaughter, two sisters, a brother and three grandchildren.

33

BEFORE THEY WERE FAMOUS

Many well-known names in sports history passed through the Yankee universe from 1903 to 1919 prior to achieving fame elsewhere. In some cases that recognition was found not on the field but in the front office—or in another sport entirely as in the case of outfielder George Halas, later legendary coach of the Chicago Bears. Hippo Vaughn and Dazzy Vance became pitching stars in the National League, for the Cubs and Dodgers respectively, after their release from the Yankees. Lefty O'Doul, who first tried out for the Yankees as a pitcher in 1919, became a National League batting star compiling a lifetime .349 average.

Branch Rickey

One notable former player on the New York roster to achieve prominence in the National League, and in the national consciousness as well, was none other than Branch Rickey.

Branch Rickey passed through the Yankee universe in 1907 on his way to more important accomplishments (Transcendental Graphics/ruckerarchive.com).

Rickey, as Brooklyn Dodgers general manager, helped integrate major-league baseball by signing Jackie Robinson in 1945. Rickey joined the Yankees in 1907 as a utility player, one year after producing a .284 average in 65 games with the St. Louis Browns, with 55 appearances as a catcher. Rickey achieved no such success while playing for the Yanks, batting .182 in 52 games. On Friday, June 28, 1907, against Washington at Hilltop Park, Rickey entered the game as catcher due to an injury to starting catcher Red Kleinow. Rickey himself had a bad throwing shoulder and Washington proceeded to steal an AL record 13 bases off him in a 16–5 win. His first throw attempting to get a Washington runner at second base went into right field. Lew Brockett entered the game in relief of Yankee starter Earl Moore and his rather deliberate wind-up helped the Washington runners. Former Yankee Tom Hughes, Washington's starting pitcher, and second baseman John Perrine were the only Senators players without a stolen base. Rickey did not return to the major leagues until 7 years later.

He was back with the Browns in 1914, ending his 4-season major league career with a .239 batting average with 3 home runs and 39 RBI. As St. Louis Cardinals general manager in the 1920s and 1930s Rickey created the modern baseball "farm system" as a way of developing players. Rickey was also responsible for the concept of creating a full time spring training facility—establishing one for the Dodgers in Vero Beach, Florida. Later, as general manager for the Pittsburgh Pirates in 1951, Rickey worked to develop the protective batting helmet, since he knew of at least five players in the minor leagues killed after being hit by pitched balls. By 1953 the helmets were in use by Pirate batters. Rickey also signed future Hall-of-Famer Roberto Clemente in 1955. Rickey was elected to the Baseball Hall of Fame in 1967.

Three other players that began their careers with or appeared on the Yankees and became prominent names in sport are featured in the next two sections.

The Deacon, Bill McKechnie

Bill McKechnie toiled as a major-league infielder with moderate success, batting .251 over an eleven-season career, but he "knew more baseball than all the rest of my team put together," according to Yankee manager Frank Chance in 1913. McKechnie, born in Wilkinsburg, Pennsylvania, played mostly second base for the Yankees in 1913, his only season with the club. While not a star on the field, McKechnie proved more than capable leading teams from the dugout. He became a manager at the age of 29, piloting the Newark Peps of the Federal League in 1915.

This image of the 1913 New York team produced by Pictorial News Company was issued in card form by the Liggett & Myers Tobacco Company with Fatima brand cigarettes. Bill McKechnie sits sixth from left in the middle row (National Baseball Hall of Fame Library, Cooperstown, N.Y.).

They finished in 5th place but bigger things were in store for McKechnie. In 1925, McKechnie won his first World Series as manager, leading the Pittsburgh Pirates over the Washington Senators, being helped greatly by former teammate Roger Peckinpaugh's 8 errors in the series, allowing Pittsburgh to claw back to victory from a 3 games to 1 deficit. McKechnie was known for his knowledge and emphasis on pitching and defense and is the only manager to win pennants with three different National League teams—Pittsburgh, St. Louis (1928) and Cincinnati (1939 and 1940). His teams were defeated by the Yankees in the 1928 and 1939 World Series, being swept both times. McKechnie added another World Series championship in 1940, as the Reds defeated the Detroit Tigers in seven games. McKechnie was called "Deacon" since he regularly attended church and preferred to spend time with his family as opposed to carousing with teammates. He posted an overall 1896-1723 managerial record for a .524 winning percentage—with 8 seasons spent with an awful Boston Braves franchise. Bill McKechnie was elected to the Hall of Fame in 1962. McKechnie Field—the Pirates' spring training field in Bradenton, Florida—is named after McKechnie.

Before Gridiron Glory, George Halas

The career of George Halas in the sport of football was one of innovation and great accomplishment but his first love was baseball. Baseball did not return the affection. That certainly proved the best for all concerned—not the least of which were millions of followers of the Chicago Bears, the team Halas would later coach for 40 years and guide to numerous National Football League championships.

George "Papa Bear" Halas was born on the West Side of Chicago, to parents who had emigrated from Bohemia, Czechoslovakia. Halas played football at the University of Illinois and, upon graduating in 1918 with a degree in engineering, entered the Navy. His dream, it was said, was to play for the Yankees and Halas accomplished that goal in 1919. He made the team as an outfielder, appearing in 12 games and batting .091. His career with the Yankees—and in baseball altogether—came to an abrupt end when he slid into third base and suffered a knee injury. Halas was released to St. Paul, a minor league club in the American Association. The baseball dream ended and, in 1920, his long association with football began. Halas moved back to Illinois. While working as recreational director for the Staley Starch Works in Decatur,

Choose your sport wisely. This photograph of George Halas appears to have been taken during spring training of 1919 or during a preseason game in 1919 as Halas wears a Yankee uniform from the 1918 season (Transcendental Graphics/ruckerarchive.com).

he formed the Decatur Staleys, playing end for the team as well as coaching them. By 1921, Halas owned the team and moved them to Chicago. In 1922, Halas renamed his team the Chicago Bears. The rest, as they say, is history. Players such as Dick Butkus, Gale Sayers and Mike Ditka played for, and thrived under, the leadership of "Papa Bear." He was elected to the National Football League Hall of Fame in 1963.

Lefty O'Doul

Francis "Lefty" O'Doul had brief trials with the Yankees as a pitcher in 1919, 1920 and 1922, but his career batting average of .349 attests to the fact he found far more success at the plate than on the pitching mound. O'Doul was born on March 4, 1897, in San Francisco, and, as was the logical course for many baseball players in the area, joined the San Francisco Seals of the Pacific Coast League. The batting skills O'Doul would later demonstrate in the major leagues were exhibited in the PCL as well. The following report from the *Los Angeles Times* describes a 3–2 win over Vernon on May 29th, 1918: "Most of the thrills of today's game were crowded into the ninth inning. Two men had fallen, the Seals were on the wrong end of a 2–1 score when Lefty O'Doul was sent up to bat for John Hummel. Lefty made good with a two base poke to left field. That would have tied the score but Pete Daley ... threw the ball away and Lefty galloped all around the circuit. Yep, the Seals won 3–2." John Hummel, the man O'Doul batted for, joined the Yankees in 1918, appearing in 22 games and batting .295. O'Doul hit .243 in his short time with the Yankees posting an 0-0 record as a pitcher in 11 games. His failure to find a permanent spot on the Yankee roster was attributed to "stage fright" by the *Los Angeles Times*: "He is said to have lost his confidence when he landed in the big town, and confidence is the only thing in which he fell short of in big league standards." After 36 games with the Red Sox in 1923, O'Doul was out of the big leagues from 1924 to 1927, seemingly confirming the *Los Angeles Times*' assessment. He hit the "big town" again in 1928, this time with the NL's New York Giants, and no lapse of confidence was evident. O'Doul hit .319—the first of 5 straight seasons he batted above .300. O'Doul slugged the baseball for a .398 average in 1929 (with 32 home runs and 122 RBI) and didn't stop there—hitting .383 in 1930, .336 in 1931 and .368 in 1932 while playing for the Philadelphia Phillies and Brooklyn Dodgers.

Frank "Lefty" O'Doul's statistical achievements as a batter are only part of his overall influence on the game—and business—of baseball (Library of Congress, Prints & Photographs Division, LC-DIG-ggbain-28601).

In Philadelphia the left-handed O'Doul benefited by playing home games in the Baker Bowl, named after then Phillies owner William F. Baker. The right field dimension of 280.5 feet and 300 feet to right-center helped O'Doul's power numbers but he was certainly an above-average hitter no matter what the ballpark. O'Doul later became known for his All-Star Tours of Japan and spreading the popularity of baseball to the Far East. The first such tour in 1931 included future Hall of Fame players Lou Gehrig and Al Simmons as well as 10 other major league players. After a similar trip in 1934, O'Doul became manager of his former PCL home team, the San Francisco Seals. He helped train a young player named Joseph DiMaggio, who was laboring along as a shortstop, experiencing fielding troubles but showing great promise as a hitter. During the same period another young hitter was playing for the San Diego Padres of the PCL. His name was Ted Williams. O'Doul is reported to have told Williams he would find his way to the major leagues if he never allowed anyone to change his swing. Good advice which Williams followed, helping the Padres win the PCL pennant in 1937, his second year with San Diego. DiMaggio, "The Yankee Clipper," and Williams, "The Splendid Splinter," both benefited from O'Doul's tutoring and rightly credited him with helping them become two of the greatest players in the history of the game.

34

WHERE HAVE YOU GONE, FRANK GILHOOLEY?

On the surface Frank Gilhooley posted a .277 average in 250 games played with the Yankees. Beyond that his 1913–1918 tenure with the team bridged the remnants of the unfulfilling early years that plagued the franchise with its eventual metamorphosis into a perennial pennant-winning team. Gilhooley first took the field with names consigned to the more obscure archives of Yankee, and baseball, history—players like Ezra Midkiff and Hugh High. He was also a teammate of the Yankees' earliest stars: Shawkey, Peckinpaugh, Pipp.

Gilhooley, born in Toledo, Ohio, found his way to New York to attend St. John's University. He first joined the Yankees in 1913, his contract being purchased on August 26, 1913, from the Montreal team of the International League (the International League is a minor league organization that has its origins in 1883 and still exists today). Aside from the reported $10,000 cash, the Yankees traded pitcher George McConnell, owner of a 4-15 won-lost record in 1913, to Montreal. Gilhooley, an outfielder, appeared in 24 games in 1913, batting .341 and showing speed on the basepaths. He sprained his ankle prior to the end of the 1913 season but reported to spring training in 1914 and performed well. Gilhooley received great news as the 1914 season began. Yankee manager Frank Chance appointed him the starting right fielder for 1914. "I was in doubt up to today as to who would be the player in right field, but I have decided on Gilhooley," said Chance. Unfortunately for Gilhooley, Chance also decided his team was in greater need of a second baseman in 1914 than it was of Gilhooley in right field. On April 23, 1914, Chance initiated a trade sending Gilhooley to the Buffalo Bisons of the International League for second baseman Frank Truesdale. Truesdale appeared in 77 games for the Yankees in 1914, batting .212 while Gilhooley generated a .300 batting average at Buffalo and showed himself to be a fine base stealer.

In 1915, Gilhooley batted .322 and stole 53 bases for Buffalo, earning another chance with the Yankees in 1916. According to the *Washington Post*, Gilhooley's throwing arm was "not strong" but he certainly excelled on defense on May 6, 1916, in a 5–4 victory against the Red Sox according to the *New York Times*: "Gilhooley robbed [Harry] Hooper of two three-base drives by catches at the right field fence." On May 31, 1916, Gilhooley hit his first home run (the first of only two home runs in his major-league career). That blast was a grand-slam against the Philadelphia Athletics. Gilhooley is one of five Yankee players whose first major-league homerun was a grand slam: Frank LaPorte (10/7/05), Gil McDougald (5/3/51) Horace Clarke (9/21/65) and Hideki Matsui (4/8/2003). Injuries would essentially derail Gilhooley's Yankee career, or at least prevent him from gaining a foothold to contribute on a regular basis. He batted .278 in 1916 but had his leg broken in a game against the Washington Senators and appeared in only 58 games. On May 7, 1917, Gilhooley fractured his collar bone in the second inning of a game against the Athletics played in Philadelphia. He tried to make a diving catch in right field and smashed into the outfield turf. Gilhooley was able to walk to the Yankee clubhouse but a local physician made the diagnosis of a broken collar bone. Gilhooley appeared in just 54 games. In 1918, he played right field for the Yankees and led AL outfielders in double plays with 8, batting .276 that season.

Frank Gilhooley sitting in the grandstand at Chicago's Comiskey Park in 1918 (*Chicago Daily News* negatives collection, SDN-061588, courtesy Chicago Historical Society).

Gilhooley was traded to the Red Sox on December 18, 1918, with pitchers Slim Love, Ray Caldwell, catcher Roxy Walters and $15,000 cash for pitcher Ernie Shore and outfielder Duffy Lewis. He vacated the Yankees one year before the acquisition of Babe Ruth (and eventually many other Boston stars) helped propel the Yankees to three straight World Series appearances from 1921 to 1923 and their first Word Series championship in 1923.

After his playing career ended, Gilhooley managed the Jersey City Giants in 1929. The Toledo, Ohio, native then became a deputy treasurer in Lucas County, Ohio, and, in 1949, Gilhooley became a sheriff's deputy. During the year 1955 he was one of the first four men chosen as members of the Toledo Baseball Hall of Fame. Frank Gilhooley passed away at the age of 66 in 1959.

Frank Gilhooley, knocking the baseball around en route to a .341 average in 24 games played in 1913 (Library of Congress, Prints & Photographs Division, LC-USZ62-133663).

35

NEW BEGINNINGS

While he could not have known it at the time, manager Miller Huggins presided over his last relative season of calm in 1919, during which he piloted the Yankees to a record of 80 wins and 59 losses, finishing in 3rd place. Huggins suffered from a host of health issues—nerve inflammation, sinus headaches and chronic dental problems among them. All of these help account for—though do not excuse—an often cold disposition and occasional temper tantrums while trying to lead his team. Many such tantrums were directed at— and directly attributable to— Babe Ruth. "Babe Ruth took five years off my brother's life," said Huggins' sister Myrtle to the wife of a newspaper reporter.*

Manager Miller Huggins in front of the Yankee bench at Comiskey Park. World Series championships—and more than a few headaches caused by a man named Ruth—are not far away (*Chicago Daily News* negatives collection, SDN-062204, courtesy Chicago Historical Society).

Ruth, with his off-field antics, along with the dour but talented outfielder Bob Meusel—combined with additional hell-raising players†— gave Huggins plenty of reasons for a bad disposition (along with a vastly improved ball club). The severe Yankee growing pains of 1903–1919 gave way to a more glorious future as the club finally captured its first American League pennant in 1921.

---

*The Life That Ruth Built, Marshall Smelser, University of Nebraska Press, 1975, page 403.
†According to General Manager Ed Barrow dugout fights between Yankee players in 1922 featured Babe Ruth against Wally Pipp, Aaron Ward against outfielder Bobby "Braggo" Roth and Carl Mays facing off against third-string catcher Al DeVormer. DeVormer would return to battle with backup catcher Fred Hofmann (possibly a dispute over their playing time). Ward's fight with Roth actually occurred during the 1921 season since Roth was not with New York in 1922. Barrow can be excused for finding it difficult to keep track of all the confrontations. Roth was nicknamed "The Globetrotter" due to his playing for six teams in an eight-season career.

APPENDIX 1: HONOR ROLL

New York Yankee "All Stars" from 1903 to 1919
(If there had been an All Star Game prior to 1933)

1B	Hal Chase, Wally Pipp	C	Leslie Nunamaker
2B	Jimmy Williams, Del Pratt	SP	Jack Chesbro
3B	Frank Baker	SP	Al Orth
SS	Kid Elberfeld, Roger Peckinpaugh	SP	Russ Ford
OF	Patsy Dougherty	SP	Ray Fisher
OF	Birdie Cree	SP	Ray Caldwell
OF	Willie Keeler	SP	Bob Shawkey

Reserve

Roy Hartzell, IF, OF George Mogridge, P Jack Warhop, P
Fritz Maisel, IF, OF Jack Quinn, P

APPENDIX 2:
THE ONES THAT GOT AWAY

Players that began their careers and/or played with the Yankees in the period 1903–1919 but went on to fame (or at least productive careers) elsewhere:

Hippo Vaughn, P	Urban Shocker, P	George Mogridge, P
Dazzy Vance, P	Lefty O'Doul, OF	Herold "Muddy" Ruel, C

BIBLIOGRAPHY

Primary Sources

Allen, Lee. *The American League Story*. New York: American Book-Stratford Press, 1965.

———. *The National League Story*. New York: American Book-Stratford Press, 1965.

Anderson, Dave, Murray Chass, Robert Creamer, and Harold Rosenthal. *The Yankees: The Four Famous Eras of Baseball's Most Famous Team*. New York: Random House, 1981.

Cobb, Ty. *Memoirs of 20 Years in Baseball*. Marietta, GA: William R. Cobb, 2002.

Dewey, Donald, and Nicholas Acocella. *The Black Prince of Baseball: Hal Chase and the Mythology of the Game*. Toronto: Sport Media, 2004.

Forman, Sean L. "New York Yankees Team Index." Baseball-Reference.com.

Gallagher, Mark. *Day by Day in New York Yankees History*. New York: Leisure, 1983.

———. *The Yankee Encyclopedia*. Champaign: Sagamore, 1996.

Honig, Donald. *The New York Yankees, Revised Edition*. New York: Crown, 1987.

James, Bill. *Whatever Happened to the Hall of Fame?* New York: Macmillan, 1995.

Lieb, Fred. *Baseball as I Have Known It*. New York: Coward, McCann, and Geoghegan, 1977.

Macht, Norman. "History Repeats Itself." In *Baseball Digest*, June 2000.

Neft, David, and Richard M. Cohen. *The Sports Encyclopedia: Baseball*. New York: St. Martin's, 1993.

Okkonen, Marc. *Baseball Uniforms of the 20th Century*. New York: Sterling, 1991.

Postal, Bernard, Jesse Silver, and Roy Silver. *Encyclopedia of Jews in Sports*. New York: Bloch, 1965.

Ritter, Lawrence S. *The Glory of Their Times*. New York: Macmillan, 1966.

Shatzkin, Mike. *The Ballplayers*. New York: William Morrow, 1990.

Smelser, Marshall. *The Life That Ruth Built*. New York: Quadrangle/New York Times, 1975.

Spatz, Lyle. *New York Yankee Openers*. Jefferson, NC: McFarland, 1991.

Sporting Life, 1905–1912.

The Sporting News, 1905–1912.

Stark, Benton. *The Year They Called Off the World Series*. New York: Avery, 1991.

Stout, Glenn. *Yankees Century: 100 Years of New York Yankees Baseball*. Boston/New York: Houghton Mifflin, 2002.

Vincent, David W. *Home Runs in the Old Ballparks*. Birmingham: SABR Publications/Ebsco, 1995.

Weinberger, Miro, and Dan Riley. *The Yankees Reader*. Boston: Houghton Mifflin, 1991.

Websites

The websites www.baseball-reference.com, www.baseballlibrary.com, www.baseball-almanac.com and www.americanheritage.com were invaluable in completing this work.

INDEX

Ables, Harry 90
Adkins, Doc 11
Ainsmith, Eddie 102
Alexander, Walt 173
Anderson, John 18, 25, 34
Aragon, Angel 168, 169, 173, 175
Asinoff, Eliot 206
Austin, Jimmy 61, 69, 70, 71, 75, 77, 80, 81, 82, 83

Baker, Frank 108, 136, 152, 161, 163, 165, 168, 170, 173, 175, 182, 189, 190, 191, 193, 197, 204, 205, 225
Baker, William 219
Baker Bowl 219
Ball, Neal 54
Baltimore Orioles 5, 9, 10, 39
Barrow, Ed 40, 43, 124, 202, 223
Baum, Spider 211
Baumann, Paddy 162, 173
Bender, Chief 108, 161
Benedict, Moby 187
Bergen, Eddie 107
Berra, Yogi 18
Beville, Monte 11, 13, 18
Black Sox scandal 209, 210
Blair, Walter 57
Bodie, Ping 182, 183, 189, 190, 193, 197, 199, 204, 205, 214, 215
Boone, Daniel 169
Boone, Lute 117, 141, 144, 169
Borton, Babe 109, 110, 113, 213
Boston Braves 80, 81, 186, 206, 211, 218
Boston Red Sox 13, 14, 19, 20, 21, 23, 24, 26, 27, 32, 34, 45, 46, 54, 67, 70, 72, 73, 79, 87, 93, 135, 150, 151, 152, 156, 168, 173, 194, 195, 197, 198, 199, 201
Bresnahan, Roger 5
Brockett, Lew 47, 48, 53, 62, 71, 216
Brooklyn, Dodgers 72, 104, 105, 121, 151, 170, 180, 187, 193, 197, 210, 217, 219
Brown, Don 170
Brown Boardwalk 144, 157
Brown University 10, 22, 36
Brush, John T. 7, 12
Burke, James 61

Burns, George 214
Bush, Joe 118, 201, 202

Caldwell, Ray 70, 72, 82, 88, 89, 93, 104, 105, 107, 111, 113, 117, 144, 148, 155, 156, 165, 166, 167, 168, 173, 175, 183, 185, 186, 189, 193, 202, 222, 225
Cantillon, Joe 63, 64, 65
Castleton, Roy 53
Chance, Frank 103, 104, 105, 106, 107, 108, 109, 110, 111, 115, 116, 117, 119, 139, 147, 155, 156, 159, 166, 180, 198, 217, 221
Chapman, Ray 201
Chase, Hal 16, 17, 30, 31, 32, 33, 34, 35, 39, 40, 42, 46, 48, 58, 59, 60, 61, 63, 66, 69, 75, 76, 77, 78, 80, 81, 82, 83, 86, 89, 91, 92, 93, 96, 105, 109, 110, 116, 134, 143, 153, 184, 206, 207, 209, 210, 211, 212, 213, 225
Chesbro, Jack 9, 10, 11, 13, 14, 19, 20, 21, 22, 23, 24, 25, 26, 27, 28, 29, 30, 31, 33, 34, 39, 40, 47, 48, 50, 52, 53, 54, 58, 62, 67, 69, 70, 104, 113, 184, 225
Chicago Cubs 72, 92, 103, 116, 120, 159, 207, 211
Chicago White Sox 7, 21, 24, 29, 44, 45, 46, 47, 69, 80, 110, 133, 148, 165, 193, 198, 206, 209, 210, 211, 213, 214, 222, 223
Cicotte, Ed 72, 166
Cincinnati Reds 15, 17, 47, 48, 87, 103, 115, 116, 121, 156, 180, 186, 188, 194, 206, 207, 209, 211, 218
Clarke, Horace 221
Clarkson, Walter 30, 34, 45, 47
Clemente, Roberto 217
Cleveland Indians 44, 46, 47, 48, 49, 80, 88, 90, 117, 175, 194, 201
Cobb, Irwin 147
Cobb, Ty 36, 40, 64, 99, 102
Cole, King 145, 157, 159
Collier, Frank (cartoon) 27
Collins, Eddie 44, 161
Collins, Jimmy 19, 23
Columbia Presbyterian 73
Columbia University 10, 36

Combs, Earle 189
Comiskey, Charles 69, 133
Connery, Tim 180
Conroy, Wid 9, 11, 13, 15, 25, 27, 40, 45, 48, 52, 53, 180
Cook, Doc 144, 160
Corriden, Red 103
Corridon, Frank 29
Costello, Jim 207, 209, 211
Courtney, Ernie 11, 12, 40
Cree, Birdie 61, 75, 76, 77, 78, 82, 86, 93, 104, 105, 111, 119, 145, 153, 155, 160, 212, 225
Criger, Lou 26, 27, 54, 70, 75, 76
Crosetti, Frank 194, 214
Cullop, Nick 165, 168, 173, 181

Daley, Tom 160
Daniels, Bert 75, 93, 98, 99, 102, 104, 105, 110, 146, 212
Dartmouth College 200
Davis, Lefty 9, 10, 11, 13
Deering, John 13, 40
Delahanty, Frank 40
Demmitt, Ray 70
Derrick, Claud 104, 105, 116
Detroit Tigers 12, 15, 17, 40, 43, 46, 47, 48, 60, 63, 64, 65, 96, 121, 143, 144, 148, 157, 168, 187, 202, 214, 218
Devery, Bill 7, 11, 25, 44, 45, 50, 54, 59, 65, 67, 69, 74, 81, 103, 108, 112, 117, 119, 121, 122, 123, 126, 127, 128, 130, 131, 132, 133, 134, 135, 155
Dickey, Bill 18
DiMaggio, Joe 215, 220
Dineen, Bill 19, 21, 25, 26
Dolan, Cozy 210
Donlin, Mike 156
Donovan, Bill 48, 64, 121, 122, 135, 136, 137, 139, 143, 158, 165, 166, 167, 168, 172, 173, 175, 178, 179, 180, 189, 193
Dougherty, Patsy 8, 19, 22, 23, 25, 26, 27, 34, 225
Doyle, Larry 120
Doyle, Slow Joe 47, 48, 53, 57, 63
Duggan, James 173
Dunn, Jack 152

Index

Ebbets Field 105, 107
Elberfeld, Kid 11, 12, 13, 19, 25, 26, 28, 34, 36, 40, 43, 44, 45, 46, 48, 49, 50, 52, 54, 57, 58, 59, 60, 61, 67, 68, 69, 195, 225
Engle, Clyde 63, 67
Evans, Billy 44, 46

Farrell, Charley 60, 70, 173
Farrell, Frank 7, 11, 19, 24, 25, 32, 44, 45, 50, 51, 54, 57, 58, 59, 60, 65, 67, 69, 73, 74, 80, 81, 91, 93, 94, 96, 97, 99, 103, 104, 105, 111, 112, 115, 117, 119, 120, 121, 122, 123, 126, 127, 132, 133, 134, 135, 155, 168, 213
Fenway Park 168, 177
Ferguson, Alex 195
Fewster, Chick 196, 197, 198
Fisher, Ray 69, 70, 72, 82, 89, 104, 109, 111, 113, 117, 144, 153, 155, 156, 165, 168, 173, 175, 183, 184, 185, 186, 187, 188, 206, 225
Ford, Gerald 188
Ford, Russ 70, 72, 73, 74, 75, 76, 78, 82, 89, 93, 104, 109, 111, 115, 116, 225
Ford, Whitey 13
Foster, Eddie 74, 102
Foster, Rube 151
Freedman, Andrew 5, 7
Freeman, Buck 19, 20
Frolich, W.G. 104, 109
Fultz, Dave 10, 11, 13, 18, 22, 27, 34, 36, 37, 38, 40, 75, 146

Gainer, Del 65, 151, 169
Gandil, Arnold "Chick" 209, 210
Ganzel, John 10, 11, 13, 15, 16, 17, 25, 27, 93, 99
Gardner, Earle 74, 86, 92, 93
Garvin, Ned 25
Gedeon, Joe 161, 165, 167, 169, 173, 181, 209, 210
Gehrig, Lou 182, 189, 192, 220
Gibbs, Jake 146
Gilhooley, Frank 165, 168, 173, 175, 182, 202, 204, 205, 221, 222
Gilkes, Bob 180
Glade, Fred 52, 54, 57
Gomez, Lefty 13
Gordon, Joe 7, 12, 13, 51, 91
Grayson, Harry 212
Greene, Paddy 40
Griffith, Clark 7, 10, 11, 13, 14, 15, 17, 18, 19, 21, 23, 26, 27, 28, 30, 32, 33, 34, 39, 40, 44, 45, 47, 48, 49, 50, 51, 52, 53, 54, 57, 58, 60, 70, 104, 183, 194
Guidry, Ron 13

Halas, George 216, 218, 219
Hannah, Truck 199, 205
Hartzell, Roy 82, 86, 87, 92, 93, 105, 109, 110, 111, 118, 144, 160, 212, 225
Hemphill, Charlie 52, 54, 57, 61, 71, 86
Henderson, Rickey 176

Hendryx, Tim 169, 173, 214
Herrmann, Garry 103, 121
Heydler (NL president) 206, 213
High, Hugh 144, 160, 170, 173, 174, 214, 221
Hildebrand, George 29
Hilltop Park 6, 8, 10, 12, 13, 20, 21, 23, 25, 26, 34, 36, 44, 45, 50, 54, 59, 61, 62, 63, 64, 66, 69, 74, 75, 79, 80, 81, 83, 87, 89, 91, 93, 94, 96, 99, 100, 101, 103, 115, 127, 184, 216
Hoff, Chet 99, 102, 104, 107, 108, 109, 166, 212
Hoffman, Danny 36, 40, 52
Hofmann, Fred 223
Hogg, Bill 30, 34, 45, 46, 47, 52, 53, 61
Holden, Bill 114, 115, 118
Hooper, Harry 152, 221
Horner, Carl 12
Howard, Elston 18
Howell, Harry 13, 18
Hoyt, Waite 198, 202
Huggins, Miller 180, 181, 182, 183, 184, 189, 193, 197, 201, 204, 223
Hughes, Tom 14, 19, 21, 24, 216
Hughes, Tom (Salida) 63, 70, 72, 78, 80
Hummel, John 219
Huntington Avenue Baseball Grounds 21, 24, 26
Hurst, Tim 44, 63
Huston, Colonel 123, 124, 125, 133, 135, 136, 137, 145, 155, 161, 167, 168, 170, 180, 198

Irwin, Arthur 61, 81, 103, 104, 106, 107, 119, 145, 146, 153, 154, 155, 184

Jackson, Joe 102
Jackson, Reggie 39
Jennings, Hughie 64
Jeter, Derek 194
Johnson, Ban 5, 7, 9, 10, 11, 18, 22, 23, 24, 25, 44, 45, 49, 59, 64, 65, 76, 81, 103, 110, 111, 115, 119, 120, 121, 133, 135, 136, 180, 193, 197
Johnson, Walter 77, 86, 93, 148, 189, 190
Jones, Sam 202

Kauff, Benny 212
Keating, Ray 104, 107, 109, 111, 113, 144, 186
Keefe, Bobby 48, 50
Keeler, Willie 10, 11, 13, 21, 25, 34, 39, 40, 41, 42, 45, 46, 48, 49, 50, 52, 54, 58, 61, 67, 69, 87, 225
Kelley, Joe 180, 181
Kitson, Frank 49
Kleinow, Red 18, 25, 26, 27, 28, 40, 52, 57, 63, 79, 216
Knight, John 45, 60, 61, 69, 70, 75, 76, 77, 78, 80, 92, 93, 116, 155
Kuhn, Bowie 188

Lajoie, Nap 10, 80, 91
Lake, Joe 52, 62, 70
Landis, Kenesaw 61, 188, 210, 212
Lane, F.C. 136
Lannin, Joseph 133, 152, 168
LaPorte, Frank 40, 44, 63, 69, 75, 77, 82, 83, 221
Lardner, Ring 159
Layden, Gene 170
Lazzeri, Tony 189, 214
Leib, Fred 206
Lelivelt, Jack 101
Leonard, Dutch 168, 202
Lewis, Duffy 168, 193, 197, 198, 201, 202, 205, 222
Long, Dan 32
Long, Herman 11, 12, 40
Love, Slim 164, 173, 202, 222
Lund, Don 187

Mack, Connie 32, 92, 161, 204
Magee, Lee 161, 165, 168, 174, 175, 194, 207, 208, 209, 210, 211
Maisel, Fritz 117, 119, 144, 146, 159, 173, 176, 181, 225
Maloney, Pat 95, 98, 99
Manning, Rube 54, 62, 63
Marble Hill 94
Marquard, Rube 161
Marsans, Armando 173, 194
Martin, Jack 93
Martin, Mike 52
Matsui, Hideki 221
Mathewson, Christy 36, 99, 161, 206
Matthias, Brother 152
Mays, Carl 135, 197, 201, 223
McAleer, Jimmy 18
McCann, Gene 65
McConnell, George 109, 115, 116, 221
McDougald, Gil 221
McDowell, John 129, 130, 131
McFarland, Herm 10, 11, 13, 36
McGinnity, Joe 5
McGovern Jim 173
McGraw, Bob 197, 201
McGraw, John 5, 91, 95, 123, 124, 136, 178, 207, 213
McGreevey, Michael 20, 26
McGuire, Deacon 18, 27, 28, 40, 132
McHale, Marty 118, 139, 140, 141, 144, 145, 156, 157, 160
McKechnie, Bill 217, 218
Meusel, Bob 189, 223
Middlebury College 184
Midkiff, Ezra 114, 115, 221
Miller, Elmer 169, 170, 173, 205, 214
Minnesota Twins 204
Minor, Benjamin 133
Mitchel, Mayor 138, 139
Mitchell, Fred 79
Mogridge, George 164, 168, 169, 173, 175, 177, 183, 193, 195, 197, 225, 226
Moore, Earl 49, 216
Moran, Pat 188
Morley, Jim 32

Mullen, Charlie 142, 143, 169
Mullen, George 48
Munson, Thurman 18
Murderer's Row 189, 190, 197, 205
Murnane, Tim 32

Nahon, Abe 52
Navin, Frank 133, 144
New York Giants 5, 7, 12, 52, 89, 95, 103, 111, 119, 120, 123, 136, 156, 157, 165, 175, 178, 198, 199, 210, 212, 219
New York University 36
Newton, Doc 17, 30, 34, 47, 52, 61
Niles, Harry 44, 52, 57
Nunamaker, Les 120, 139, 140, 144, 146, 168, 169, 173, 175, 181, 225

O'Connell, Jimmy 210
O'Connor, Jack 9, 11, 18
O'Doul, Lefty 213, 216, 219, 220, 226
O'Loughlin, Silk 45, 54
O'Neil, Bill 22, 23
O'Neill, Paul 67
Orth, Al 23, 24, 25, 30, 34, 40, 45, 47, 48, 50, 52, 53, 54, 62, 63, 70, 104, 113, 225

Parent, Fred 19, 20, 26
Peckinpaugh, Roger 101, 111, 117, 118, 119, 120, 121, 144, 146, 168, 169, 173, 175, 177, 189, 190, 194, 195, 197, 202, 204, 205, 218, 221, 225
Pennock, Herb 202
Perrine, John 216
Pettitte, Andy 13
Philadelphia Athletics 10, 12, 13, 36, 45, 54, 74, 87, 88, 92, 104, 119, 120, 156, 157, 161, 165, 194, 197, 200, 214
Philadelphia Phillies 24, 32, 60, 92, 175, 210, 219, 221
Pickering, Arthur 139
Pieh, Cy 144, 145, 157, 158
Pipp, Wally 136, 143, 165, 168, 169, 170, 173, 175, 182, 189, 190, 191, 192, 193, 197, 198, 204, 205, 221, 223, 225
Pittsburgh Pirates 9, 16, 19, 21, 30, 65, 80, 87, 145, 181, 194, 195, 217, 218
Plank, Eddie 53, 108, 161, 181
Plank, Ira 53
Players Fraternity (Baseball) 36, 37, 38, 146
Polo Grounds 102, 103, 107, 108, 111, 112, 113, 115, 118, 119, 135, 139, 156, 158, 165, 170, 173, 175, 183, 184, 185, 197, 213
Posada, Jorge 18
Powell, Jack 18, 19, 23, 24, 25, 26, 28, 30, 34
Power, Vic 102
Pratt, Del 181, 190, 198, 201, 204, 205, 225
Price, Jim 8

Providence Grays 29, 121, 133, 135, 152, 153
Puttmann, Ambrose 30

Quinn, Jack 63, 70, 72, 78, 80, 82, 86, 89, 102, 104, 113, 153, 155, 193, 197, 198, 225

Reach, Al 85
Rickey, Branch 216, 217
Ring, Jimmy 206
Ripley, Robert 189, 190
Rizzuto, Phil 194
Robinson, Jackie 187, 216
Robinson, Wilbert 180
Roth, Mark 109
Roush, Edd 211
Rucker, Nap 105
Ruel, Muddy 177, 195, 198, 199, 205, 226
Ruppert, Jacob 123, 124, 125, 133, 135, 136, 137, 138, 139, 141, 142, 145, 155, 161, 166, 170, 175, 179, 180, 190, 198
Russell, Allen 173, 195, 197, 201
Ruth, Babe 95, 122, 133, 135, 140, 150, 151, 152, 173, 175, 189, 202, 222, 223

St. Louis Browns 18, 21, 24, 44, 52, 57, 70, 82, 90, 107, 148, 167, 173, 176, 181, 194, 209, 216, 217
St. Louis Cardinals 87, 156, 161, 180, 182, 201, 208, 217, 218
Sand, Heinie 210
Schang, Wally 198
Schulz, Al 104, 109
Schwert, Pi 139, 145, 146, 147
Selbach, Kip 23, 26
Shawkey, Bob 136, 161, 165, 166, 168, 173, 175, 182, 189, 193, 197, 198, 200, 202, 204, 221, 225
Sheridan, Jack 44
Shocker, Urban 173, 181, 182, 226
Shore, Ernie 151, 202, 222
Simmons, Al 220
Simmons, Hack 92, 93, 96, 106, 107
Smith, Harry 9
Snodgrass, Fred 199
Spalding, Albert 85
Spalding Guide 42, 71, 84, 85, 140, 141, 175
Sparrow, Harry 136, 137, 143
spring training: Bermuda 104, 107, 109, 155; Florida 193; Georgia 10, 19, 47, 52, 60, 69, 82, 136, 137
Spuyten, Duyvil 94
Stahl, Jake 52
Stallings, George 48, 60, 61, 64, 65, 67, 69, 70, 72, 75, 78, 80, 81, 83, 120
Stanford University 87
Stengel, Casey 68, 107, 213
Stoneham, Charles 206, 207
Stovall, George 80
Street, Gabby 93
Stricklett, Elmer 29

Stumpf, Bill 101
Summers, Ed 65
Sweeney, Ed 57, 73, 74, 75, 76, 79, 87, 93, 104, 105, 109, 110, 111, 139, 141, 145, 146, 147

Tammany Hall 7, 108, 126, 128
Tannehill, Jesse 9, 11, 13, 14, 21, 25
Taylor, John 23
Tenney, Fred 33, 34
Thormahlen, Hank 183, 193, 197, 203
Truesdale, Frank 117, 221
Tuthill, Harry 64, 65
Tweed, Boss 126

Unglaub, Bob 22, 23
University of Georgia 116
University of Michigan 186, 188
University of Santa Clara 31, 32, 48, 87

Vance, Dazzy 170, 171, 216, 226
Vanderbilt, University 160
Van Wyck, Robert 134
Vaughn, Hippo 70, 71, 72, 73, 78, 85, 89, 93, 104, 216, 226
Vick, Sammy 205

Wagner, Honus 80, 102
Wallace, Bobby 89
Walsh, Ed 29, 45
Walsh, Jimmy 117
Walters, Roxy 173, 175, 202, 222
Ward, Aaron 173, 198, 223
Warhop, Jack 61, 62, 70, 72, 78, 82, 89, 93, 104, 111, 120, 144, 145, 148, 149, 150, 153, 155, 156, 165, 225
Washington Senators 10, 15, 23, 24, 25, 32, 44, 52, 58, 63, 64, 77, 86, 93, 96, 102, 104, 107, 108, 139, 148, 158, 165, 177, 189, 190, 194, 195, 197, 203, 209, 216, 218, 222
Weaver, Buck 210
Weiss, George 179
Wheat, Zack 116
Williams, Bob 87
Williams, Clubber 130, 131, 132
Williams, Harry 117
Williams, Jimmy 10, 11, 13, 16, 25, 26, 33, 34, 40, 45, 46, 52, 54, 99, 225
Williams, Ted 220
Wolfe, Barney 24
Wolter, Harry 75, 78, 82, 86, 87, 93, 104, 105, 111
Wolverton, Harry 92, 93, 95, 97, 99, 100, 102 104, 166, 198
Wood, Joe 73, 93
Wood, Major-General 172, 173
World Series 14, 19, 22, 24, 28, 65, 76, 81, 89, 103, 121, 133, 151, 153, 157, 161, 168, 177, 179, 181, 182, 192, 194, 195, 198, 199, 201, 202, 204, 206, 207, 209, 211, 213, 218, 222, 223
World War I 36, 62, 121, 123, 160,

168, 170, 180, 182, 189, 190, 193, 194, 198

Yankee Stadium 5, 25
Yankees: uniform/logo 63, 67, 83, 86, 99, 126, 128, 132, 134, 162, 194, 200, 218
Yeager, Joe 40
Young, Cy 14, 19, 20, 25, 26, 70, 76

Zeider, Rollie 109, 110
Zeller, Rube 53
Zimmerman, Heinie 206, 212
Zinn, Guy 99, 101, 102, 212